TO THE DEATH

Peiper reacted immediately.

"All guns fire forward; fire, fire, fire!"

The tank cannon boomed and simultaneously a yellow flame burst from the muzzle of the Russian gun.

The flame filled Peiper's vision from horizon to horizon and from its height to its depth. His Panzer rocked as the high velocity shell, striking the turret a glancing blow, ricocheted and produced a coruscation of sparks that flickered in the sun.

The SS officer saw to his right front a deep pit excavated in the snow - a command post. He looked with blank eyes at the Russian soldiers scrabbling in the trampled snow at the bottom of the pit. Them or me - the Eastern Front's deadly alternative. The Reds floundering in the snow looked up at the German commander, their eyes pleading to be allowed to live...

Kill them or die yourself - it was the jungle law.

Forthcoming in the Jackboot series:

Death in Normandy   James Lucas
Red Eagle   James Lucas

SS-Kampfgruppe Peiper

An Episode in the War in Russia, February 1943

James Lucas

JACKBOOT SERIES 001

Published by SHELF BOOKS
BRADFORD, WEST YORKSHIRE, UK.

First published in the UK as 'Battle Group Peiper' by Sphere Books Ltd., 1985
Second Edition by Shelf Books, 1997

Revised and edited by Cheryll A Wood and Robert A Ball

Printed and Bound in the UK by Jade Press, Leeds

Introduction

Several years ago I stood in the drawing room of an elegant house in Munich holding a book which had once belonged to the late Jochen Peiper, sometime Lieutenant Colonel in the Waffen-SS. The book was scorched by burning and smelt of smoke. Those who had murdered Peiper had hoped to destroy by fire their victim and his home.

Tucked into the fold of the dust jacket were several sheets of paper. These I noted had been torn from an Army message pad. The pages were covered with small angular and very precise writing in old fashioned script of a type which is no longer taught in German schools.

The first of the torn sheets was headed, 'Supplementary notes on a mission undertaken during February 1943. Object: to rescue the 320th Infantry Division which had been cut off south-east of Kharkov'.

Beneath the heading were listed names which I was later to identify as villages and towns in southern Russia. Below them the War Establishments of a German armoured Kampfgruppe, broken down to platoons. There was a nominal roll containing the names of SS Officers and men. Under a sub- heading entitled 'Other Troops' were the names and units of soldiers other than SS. Intriguing at the time were several Russian names.

Two pages of notes had dates and times underlined and fragments from what turned out to be wireless log entries. Those sheets described in outline an operation of which I had read nothing. At the time there were no published histories of SS formations and the war diaries, upon which such histories are based, had still not been traced.

Intrigued by the story summarised in these yellowing pages, I checked in the Bundesarchiv. Contained in the War Diary of the 320th Division there was a less than an objective account of the rescue operation written by Postel, at that time the General Officer commanding the Division.

My growing knowledge fed my interest. I met men of Peiper's SS Division, but those who had been on the mission with him could add little to my gained knowledge. To those men the rescue had been merely another incident in a long and bloody war. An introduction to Rudi Hennecke was the turning point. Hennecke is now an elderly, bourgeois citizen of West Germany. Then, in 1943, he was a Lieutenant in a panzer battalion of the Waffen SS. In his diaries and in letters which his family had kept were the impressions and experiences gained during the relief of the 320th. Those documents contradicted Postel's account. Hennecke traced other soldiers who filled in the gaps in the narrative. From their collective accounts this book has been written.

This is the book about war; about a particularly bitter war - that between Germany and Russia. This book records not only the horrors of war and man's inhumanity to man, but also the positive virtues of bravery and compassion. The latter is the more important virtue for it illustrates that human spirit can rise above horror and terror.

All the events described here happened over forty years ago. Within another two decades the last of those who experienced them will be dead. Let this book recall an episode of the terrible war which they fought and the times through which the men remembered here lived.

Chapter 1

Those who fell fighting during the winter battles in Russia during the Second World War vanished quickly from sight, covered by snow driven before the freezing east wind. Days and nights of blizzard could so completely hide the dead beneath a cold white blanket that none could even estimate the number of those who lay concealed. Only when short days of thaw occurred, as they did each winter, were the dead seen again. As drowned men rise briefly to the surface of the sea, thus for a very short time did those snow-concealed bodies reappear, to lie as soggy, obscene bundles on the steppe until the next blizzard hid them.

The scale of military operations on the Russian front was vast and enormous were the losses. Soldiers were killed in thousands and in hundreds of thousands. So great was the toll that there could have been few places in all the vast territory called 'The Eastern Front' which did not have its tally of corpses. Those who fell in the winter season were visible for only a short time and then were covered by their vast, temporary, communal shroud. Beneath it bodies abounded. Some were of men overcome, perhaps, with the hopelessness of the situation and filled with despair, who had laid down in the seducing snow to die alone. Then there were the groups of corpses. Men cut off, maybe, from their parent units and from supplies and who had succumbed in that howling, freezing desolation. The presence of rusting, blackened vehicles might indicate where a stand had been made; an attack undertaken or a short-lived defence established.

The dead soldiers were from every part of the Soviet Union, from Germany and from armies allied to her. All of them, whether Russian, German, Italian, Croat, Hungarian or Rumanian- the snow covered them all, keeping close the secret of Death's dreadful harvest. The impartial snow embraced them and held fast the frost-blackened bodies until the false thaws of winter or the later, true warmth of spring removed the temporary shroud and exposed them.

The Russian winter was as bitter as the war itself; the war that had been fought in the Soviet Union since June 1941. It was a war of extremes in battle as bitter as were the differences in the climate. It was a war of heights and depths, of vast dramatic movements by thousands of men in pursuit of a strategic goal and of the bitter struggles of a handful of men to capture a single house.

3

A war in which base cowardice and the most unbelievable acts of courage were common. The campaigns of the Great Soviet Fatherland war brought the soldiers, particularly of the Western nations, to the edge of physical and mental exhaustion. The terrible experiences of that frightful war left their mark on all who fought there and so deep are those memories etched that today those Germans who came back need only to read or to hear the word 'Ostfront' (the Eastern Front), for them to be taken back immediately to the hardships and danger which were once their daily lot in the war against the Soviet Union.

Only weeks after the first anniversary of the German-Russian war, Army Group South drove forwards across the vast steppeland of southern Russia which lies between the rivers Donets and Volga. The summer campaign had opened with high hopes in German hearts for victory in 1942. Only months later the shattered Divisions and Corps of that selfsame Army Group were stumbling back in retreat. The summer campaign had begun so well. Between July and October, Army Group South had driven the Red Army eastwards from the Donets river line. Late in the autumn the Russians had rallied at the command of Stalin and his High Command, the STAVKA. The German drive on Stalingrad was halted and then the Red Army had gone on to launch its own offensive. From Stalingrad, that great city on the Volga, groups of Red Armies, formed into massive 'Fronts', had flung back the Germans and in a bewildering series of blows had tumbled them into chaos.

The Red Army's winter offensive began strongly in November 1942. By February 1943, the month in which the action of this book is set, the élan with which the operations had opened had begun to flag. The survivors of those Russian battalions, which had marched singing into battle in the first days of the offensive, were exhausted and voiceless veterans three months later. Stalin and the STAVKA had demanded that the winter offensive must not halt. Tired out physically and burned out emotionally though the soldiers were, yet still they were driven on by the Communist Party and its commissars to free the soil of the Soviet Union from the fascist invaders.

From the first days of the Red Army's offensive the German Army's High Command, OKH, had ordered its soldiers to stop the Russian advance. Dourly, the Grenadiers had battled to stem the

Red tide. There were now, in winter, no songs sung on the German side. The confident voices of the summer of 1942 had been silenced by the bitter cold.

In pursuit of the orders from their respective superiors, the exhausted warriors of both sides struggled, suffered and died fighting in temperatures that fell to twenty-eight degrees below freezing. In such Arctic conditions to be without shelter at night was to risk death from exposure. Any hut, any house, any hamlet was an oasis of warmth in the freezing desert of the Russian winter and the opposing armies fought each other to gain even vermin-ridden hovels; anything that would shelter them from the death-bringing east wind. Soldiers battled like furies to capture anything that would give them some protection.

Since the opening of the winter fighting there had been no firm line. Then in the first weeks of February the loosely-knit German front had ruptured allowing the Red Army to reach and, in places, to cross the Donets. Both sides fought desperately. The Russians to retain the initiative and the Germans to regain it. The fighting was everywhere bitter but inexplicable paradoxes occurred. The resistance of a handful of Grenadiers might hold off, for example, a Russian tank column at one place, yet only a few kilometres distant German defenders would retreat at the first sight of a Cossack patrol. A position defended heroically for days would, unaccountably, give way so completely that only hours later it would be twenty or more kilometres behind the Russian forward troops. German counter attacks put in against strong Soviet thrusts might find behind the Red spearheads no defence in depth, just a thin screen of dispirited Red infantry who could be induced to surrender willingly. There was no fixed Front; the Front was everywhere.

In such a fluid situation, if there was no Front then neither could there be a rear area with its guarantee of safety. None could be sure of the identity of units on the flanks. None knew whether out of the dark night a panzer battalion might attack or whether a Cossack Sotnia might sweep out of the snow-storm to create havoc in the rear areas. No unit could be certain whether during a march it might not encounter a pocket of enemy infantry; desperate men, cut off but determined to fight their way through to reach their own Army. The Front was everywhere. Death was everywhere and the snow was overall.

By a strange paradox the warmth of spring, which melted the snow and revealed the true scale of human losses, halted all combat operations. Thaw produced mud which held the armies immobile and halted all military activity until summer hardened the ground again. In this time of relative inaction the survivors could assess what had been achieved for so much effort and for such frightful losses. For the fighting soldiers the winter campaign had seemed to last forever and had gained them nothing. The Red Army had regained lost territory- the Germans had lost the territory which they had taken during the summer. That was all.

Only the eaters of carrion can be said to have gained anything from the winter fighting. Ravens which picked out the succulent eyes of the fallen, dogs which tore apart the decaying bodies, or rats which daintily ate the soft tissues of the dead. They grew fat. For the humans, military or civilian, the sacrifices had been in vain. The war was still going on; the killing would continue.

From the history of the Russian winter offensive of 1942/43, a campaign in which millions were engaged for months across hundreds of kilometres, one small incident has been selected. The number of men involved in this story is small. The action covers a very small sector of the southern battle line and the whole operation was both begun and concluded in a matter of days. Yet within this short action are contained all the elements which made the war on the Eastern Front unique.

Chapter 2

Herbert Bauer, Grenadier in the SS Division Adolf Hitler, woke suddenly and with the speedy reactions of the front line soldier reached out and grasped the rifle by his side. He had come from deep sleep to full alertness within a second. An unusual noise had wakened him. It was no close at hand sound that could have alerted him so quickly. There it was again. Heavy engines. Tanks or self-propelled guns. Were they Russian vehicles? Should he wake his comrades?

Bauer, now completely awake, lay flat on his back, adjusting his eyes to the darkness. He was in a small wooden barn on a Ukrainian Kolkhoz - a collective farm. The log walls plugged with mud, kept out much of the bitter wind and the fully-dressed bodies of those who were sleeping in the barn generated a certain animal warmth. Without having to move at all he could locate his comrades by the noises they each made. Should he alert them? Bauer moved his head to catch the dull green glow where the radio lay. It was silent. There was no sound of wireless traffic, of orders coming through. The motor engines he had just heard could have no significance. If there was a flap on or if it was a Red attack them the wireless would be going sixteen to the dozen, issuing streams of instructions and orders. The vehicles must be visitors for the commanding officer, concluded Bauer.

Dismissing from his mind all other thoughts, the Grenadier concentrated upon the present and snuggled contentedly into the thick straw. In the barn he was warm. Outside it was perishing cold. Breakfast couldn't be far off. A pleasing thought. A cooked breakfast, too; eggs, potatoes, sardines. Lovely. It hadn't been so many days ago that a dry crust had been a delicacy and a hot drink, an unbelievable luxury. A sleepy sigh alongside him brought his mind back and he felt the comforting bulk of one of the girls from the Kolkhoz, a Russian devochka, who in exchange for food satisfied the lusty Grenadiers. Communists may have seen the girls as immoral betrayers of the Soviet Union, but a girl has to eat and if a girl was very good in bed she could eat well. There might even be chocolate. The soldiers were happy with the arrangement. The girls were well experienced sexually, but at least they were not worn out like the raddled shag bags in the Army brothels.

Grenadier Bauer reflected that service life could be a lot worse than it was at the moment. He'd got a grind if he wanted it. There was lots to eat and there were no duties. The battalion was out of the Line. 'And so we should be,' he reminded himself. 'We took a real right bashing in the last battle. Not many of us came out of it. Christ, the blokes we lost. That's why we can have a devochka each instead of having to share or queue up for a shag.'

The Russian girl turned towards him. Even though both were fully dressed against the cold Bauer could feel the swell of her breasts as she turned sleepily on her side. She was awake.

'You want?' she asked.

'Yes, me want,' he replied.

It was basic Russian, but they were the words that were needed. He rolled onto her and the girl's hand guided his urgent pride through the layers of clothing. A couple of minutes later, passion temporarily spent, his mind turned again towards food. The cold, the last battle and the war outside the barn were far from his mind as he lay savouring the delights that were his, here and now. His whole world was now, as it had been for the past few days, the girl's body, meal times and bouts of lunatic drinking. This is the life, thought the twenty year old Grenadier. Long may it continue.

The Panzergrenadier Division 'Leibstandarte SS Adolf Hitler' was in the Line. Late in January it had been brought out of France, where it had been recuperating and had been put in east of Kharkov in the Ukraine. There, together with the other Divisions of SS Panzer Corps, and formations of the German Army, it had been battling against the storming waves of Red infantry, cavalry and tanks, fighting their way westwards to gain the objectives which Comrade Stalin had ordered to be taken. Heights of fury had been reached in the fighting; pitched battles, hand to hand struggles such as the combat-hardened Grenadiers had not encountered before. The battlefield on which the Leibstandarte had crushed the Red Army's VII Guards Cavalry Corps was filled with sickening sights. Thousands of Russian infantrymen had been cut down as they trudged through knee-deep snow in slow-moving attacks against German prepared positions. Their frost blacked faces and cramped hands were evidence of the severity of the battle and of the winter; visible evidences until the snows blanketed them. The Germans too, had suffered terribly. The half-tracks of Leibstandarte's No 11 Company had been trapped in a gully and when a counter attack had driven back the Reds the Grenadiers had found the vehicles filled with the burnt bodies of their comrades, shrivelled by fire to half their normal size. There were terrible memories of the shrill screaming of wounded cavalry horses, and all that battle had been fought out in temperatures usually twenty-eight degrees below zero.

The battlefield sights had been frightening but soldiers are not taken out of the Line because of the terrible scenes which they have witnessed. It was the scale of losses that had compelled Obergruppenführer Dietrich, General Officer commanding the Adolf Hitler Division, to pull out the surviving men and machines of Sturmbannführer Peiper's No 3 Battalion for rest and reinforcement. The battalion certainly needed it. Peiper received orders to take his men to the Kolkhoz near Alexeyeva and late in the afternoon of 2nd February, the battered half-tracks had clattered in through the ruined wooden gateway of the collective farm.

The Grenadiers dismounted and formed rank in front of the vehicles. Their commander, Jochen Peiper, saw the divisional commander's pennant outside the door of a low house.

'Stand the men at ease, please. I'll be back in a few minutes,' he called to his adjutant and strode towards the house. Peiper entered one of the low-ceilinged rooms and saw before him the Divisional Commander, Sepp Dietrich. He saluted. Dietrich noted the thin, drawn face and the blue pouches of exhaustion which ballooned under the tired eyes.

The Divisional Commander acknowledged his subordinate's report and as he walked towards him saw, through the dirt encrusted windows, a double file of mud-stained and exhausted Grenadiers standing in front of four badly used personnel carriers. Light snow covered the shoulders and equipment of the men standing in the yard, softening the outlines of the steel helmets, rounding off the edges of the equipment, settling gently upon the soldiers, cementing them, thought the SS General, cementing them and us in this Godforsaken wilderness.

'Who are they?' asked Dietrich, gesturing towards the double file.

'Obergruppenführer, the 3rd Battalion is on parade, as ordered.'

'That's all of them? That is your battalion?' asked Dietrich. 'That's all that are left? Good God. Come with me.' And the SS General strode out of the room closely followed by Peiper.

Unterscharführer Glaschke noted the two figures. 'Battalion.' He shouted the word of command and then, more loudly, barked out the order, 'Attention.'

The forty-two men stood rigid, muscles tight, faces immobile. All tiredness gone now; the 'old man' was here. Sepp Dietrich the Div Commander. What bloody task did this mean?

'Eyes right,' and forty heads swung towards the General. Dietrich paced slowly along the short front rank. As he passed, each man turned his head so that his eyes followed the stocky, beer-barrel figure. In front of the survivors of 3rd Battalion the General cleared his throat and stood facing them in his typical, straddle-legged pose, hands on hips.

'Comrades. It has been a hard battle.' His accent was a Bavarian one of broad vowels, his voice loud as he strove to be heard by them all. 'It is still a hard battle for the remainder of the Division. But you men have earned the right to a rest. New units are coming forward to take their places in the Line. That's why I can give you seven days completely free. No parades, no guard mounting, no pickets. Nothing. Then, today week you'll be back up the Line with the reinforcements who will replace your honoured dead. Together we shall fight to fling the Ivans back. Now. You've got a whole week. Don't waste it thinking about the past; enjoy yourselves!'

And that is why Grenadier Herbert Bauer and the remnants of Sturmbannführer Peiper's 3rd Battalion are to be found out of the Line in a barn on a Ukrainian collective farm. From their first meal they had fed like fighting cocks and had drunk of the best that the SS Quartermaster's Department could supply. How could this be possible in the middle of a war and in the depths of a Russian winter? It must be recalled that the whole of Europe, from the French Atlantic coast to the gates of Moscow, was a German Empire. From the conquered lands tributes flowed to the Fatherland. The countries of Europe fed the German armies on the Eastern Front. There was Danish bacon and butter, cheese from Holland, Norwegian fish, Polish meat and Italian fruit. The SS Panzer Corps had been on occupation duties in France and had organised trains which ran on an almost direct route from Paris, via Berlin and Warsaw to Kiev. The freight those trains carried included the pick of Europe's food and cases of wine, champagne, and cognac. The boxes that were marked for the SS arrived intact and without being looted. The cases were guarded by veterans of the Eastern Front. Those men may not have been any longer fit for front line service but they remembered the times when they had hungered because the light-fingered swine in the Supply Service had stolen their rations. Those invalided Grenadiers who guarded the SS supplies shot looters and thieves, irrespective of rank or nationality. The word soon spread among the civilians and base-wallahs. Don't try to nick the SS stores. Their blokes will kill you if you try.

Bauer, resting after his three minute wobble, lay above the plump Russian girl, still thinking about breakfast. Suddenly she grasped him tightly and held him enwrapped by her arms and legs.

'You good soldier. You go away today. You go war. You leave me'.

'No, no,' he corrected her. 'We here four days more.' He numbered her fingers. 'We here still four days.'

'No, no. You go. Today evening. Me sad. You good soldier.'

Not for the first time was Bauer aware of a sort of telepathy by which the peasants seemed to know moves which the military would make, even before the orders were received. The girl must be wrong. Dietrich himself had said that they would have a week off and so far they had been only three days out of action. The Line! The danger, the death and the excitement of the Line. Sod the Line. Think about the girl, whatever her name was. With her there was warmth, there was food and there was booze. Bugger the world outside. Don't think about the Line, Bauer counselled himself. Think about Olga, or whatever her name was, and Bauer wished that he could shag like Franzerl Dollmayr, a comrade in his Platoon, who seemed to be ready for action every ten minutes. Bauer tried. 'It's no use. I want to grind her again, but I can't raise a hard. And sadly Herbert, no longer thinking of food, drifted into a post-coital reverie, held fast like a fly in amber by the arms and legs of his Russian devochka.

11

Chapter 3

Inside the small room where three days earlier Peiper had reported to Dietrich, a divisional operation group conference was being organised. The Leibstandarte Division's commanders had driven through the dark of the February night to the Alexeyeva Kolkhoz. It was the sound of their vehicles arriving for the conference that had wakened Grenadier Bauer.

Sturmbannführer Peiper watched as orderlies pinned battle maps to the wall. The room began to fill with officers. Loud voices echoed. The smell of schnapps and of Balkan cigars came across to the young commander who stood wondering why he had been ordered to attend the high level briefing. The officers were called to attention as Dietrich entered the room. He greeted his comrades and then turned to Peiper.

'Sturmbannführer,' he began. The name Jochen was reserved for less formal occasions than this conference. 'There is a task which only your battalion of all the Division can carry out. I know that a couple of days ago your men were promised seven days out of the Line. A crisis has come up and we can't wait another four days to resolve it. Briefly put, the Army wants us to pull one of its Divisions out of the shit. One of their Divs - which one, Kehrer?' The General called over his shoulder to one of his aides.

'Infantry Division 320.' Kehrer's reply in a crisp North German accent was in sharp contrast to Dietrich's broad vowelled question.

'Yes, well,' continued Dietrich. 'It's the 320th. Well, it seems that 320th has been all but buggered. It's a good mob. They were on our right at Sheyev. Last week they were smashed by a couple of Red Guards Infantry Corps and now 320th is out there,' the General gestured in the general direction of the Ukraine, 'with fifteen hundred wounded.

'Of course, we can't let the Ivans get them. So you, Sturmbannführer, will be going in to rescue them. Now Lachmann here,' he continued with a gesture towards Sturmbannführer Lachmann, the Division's GSO, 'will put you in the picture. Right, Lachmann.'

Sturmbannführer Lachmann would have been elegant and distinctive even dressed in rags. Unlike the other officers he had removed his fur-lined combat suit and stood, silent, half facing the maps on the wall. The light of a single, unshaded bulb, hanging from a staple in the wooden ceiling, picked out the silver rank badges and medals on the left breast of his tunic. Lachmann was the youngest son of a family of minor, North German nobility and his voice, as he began the appreciation of the situation, held the well-modulated vowels of good schooling.

'Here,' he began, 'is the Alexeyeva Kolkhoz.' The point of his Volkhov staff, an elaborately carved and decorated walking-stick, touched lightly the surface of the maps. 'Militarily, Army Group South is placed in an unsound situation. Consider the SS Panzer Corps for a moment. It is holding ground east of Kharkov. In the north and centre of the Corps battle line are Das Reich and Totenkopf Divisions. Our Div is here in the south-east of the city. The battle line runs, as you can see, from north-west to south-east. The situation is very, very fluid.'

Lachmann turned to Peiper. 'When you left the Line three days ago we were defending Zmiyev - here. That place was lost two days ago. Ternovaya - here - is under pressure and at Rogan,' he indicated the places he had named with his Volkhov staff, 'our men are fighting for their lives. Literally, it is for their lives. If they are forced out of the hamlets and villages which they hold, then they shall have to fight Ivan on the open steppe. Exposure will kill most of them. So the men are fighting like Berserkers to hold the warm houses.

'Days ago we had already passed crisis point. Things are worse now. We are putting the walking wounded back into the Line. No; correction. We are simply not evacuating them. We cannot afford the transport nor can we let them go to hospital. If a man has two arms and can still stand, then we consider that he can still fight. We have absolutely no divisional reserve. Every man - cooks, bakers, the rear echelons, the lot - they're all in the Line. There is not a single unit to spare - except yours. Yours is the only group not in the fight.

'Manstein learned that 320th Division needs help and he asked for us. He knows our reputation. Hausser, our Corps Commander, has been a comrade of his since the Reichswehr days. So Manstein asks Hausser for a favour, as one regimental comrade asks another for a favour. Hausser passes the baby to us.

'It was fortuitous that the Divisional Commander took you out of the Line when he did. Now we can use your battalion. The task will be to cross the Donets river at this point,' the carved point touched Zmiyev, 'and advance to here, where the 320th is making its slow way westwards.' The point indicated an area about twenty kilometres to the east of the river. 'Imagine an island of resistance; a pocket of encircled troops. Well the 320th is just such a pocket. But it is a moving pocket, fighting its way towards our lines. The unwounded and the lightly wounded hold the outside perimeter. The badly wounded are in the centre.

'Your task is to pick up the 320th and to escort it back to the Donets river, here. Now I'll hand over to Hauptsturmführer Maas. The Intelligence Officer will brief you on the enemy situation.'

Lachmann saluted and stepped back into the semi-circle of officers. Hauptsturmführer Maas hefted his own carved stick into a big beefy hand. The Volkhov staff was the symbol of the survivors of the first shocking winter on the Eastern Front. It meant more than all the Iron Crosses, even more than the red ribbon of the East Front medal. The Volkhov stick was a mystic blood bond within the SS.

'The enemy situation,' began Maas, the clicking gutturals of his Berlin accent cutting incisively through the wreaths of cigar smoke, 'is even more fluid than our own. Ivan's speed of reaction is not as fast as ours so his attacks are not followed up quickly. The commanders opposite still tend to claim to have captured places which their troops have not yet taken. The climate of suspicion over there,' he nodded towards the great bulk of the Soviet Union, 'slows them down. On this we capitalise.' He addressed Peiper directly. 'As you know, Sturmbannführer, some of Ivan's forces are at certain places west of the Donets river. As Sturmbannführer Lachmann has said, you have to reach the river and to cross it. You will, therefore, be passing through enemy held territory from the start of your mission. From a point about here, Red territory starts.' The stick pointed to a village some way east of the Kolkhoz. 'You've got a round trip of about ninety kilometres and most of it will be through the Russian rear areas.

'Now, I've just said that their reactions are slow. That will be your shield. Not one of those thick-headed bastards will think of your group as being a German one. Their thinking is simple; this is our side of the Line, so that German column is either not German or it is a column of prisoners. By the time they get round to reporting you - if they do - you will be long gone.

'I should advise you not to use roads. It's a cross-country trek for you. If you need them, the Luftwaffe will drop supplies. Fuel, ammo, hard tack. They will also parachute in some medical officers if the situation requires it. I'll have wireless codes and Verey light signals arranged with your adjutant. Questions?'

Maas stood waiting, one hand poised elegantly on the staff. He looked like a *flâneur* waiting at a rendezvous. Peiper began to talk; quietly, diffidently, almost as if he were speaking to himself.

'If I have understood it, I have to take my battalion across about forty kilometres of enemy-held territory and then slow march it back to our lines - wherever they might be - against opposition that may become more fierce with each kilometre that we move westwards. We'll be burdened with Christ knows how many wounded.

'I can reach the rendezvous point with 320th in one day. Two at the most. Then we start back. If the Division has no transport then the speed of a tired infantryman will determine how quickly we get back. A tired man marching in column through snow cannot do more than a kilometre each hour for a maximum of say six to seven hours. That is a daily total of seven kilometres each day. Ten would be too much to expect. Assuming that the Line stays in its present location, then to get the wounded out of Ivan's territory and into ours will take a minimum of about four days. I have a total of forty-four men in my battalion - What?' he looked up as Lachmann broke into his monologue.

'Some of your battalion who were sick, wounded or convalescent have come back. They're outside,' began Lachmann.

'How many?'

'About eighty or ninety.'

'So,' Peiper went on, 'we are to fight our way through a whole group of Red Army Divisions, in the hope that none of those Reds we meet will have the brains to report what they have seen. And we shall be one hundred and fifty men strong-'

'No, no,' Dietrich broke in hurriedly. 'We shall make up a Kampfgruppe. A Company of Panzer IV, one of SPs, two Companies of Combat Engineers, the Divisional Defence Platoon, most of the Divisional medical officers, columns of trucks and drivers and enough trucks to carry the 320th, wounded and unwounded alike. So they won't have to walk -'

Peiper calculated very quickly. 'About eighteen tanks, eight to ten self-propelled guns, a hundred and fifty assault trained Pioneers, ninety to a hundred men of the Defence Platoon kitted out with a higher than normal establishment of mortars and machine guns the new '42 pattern. Yes, it might succeed.'

Peiper gathered his thoughts together as Dietrich concluded 'And adequate supplies dropped by a crack Luftwaffe squadron. It' s a brand new hush-hush outfit called KG 200'

Peiper felt all eyes on him. The senior officers were waiting. They could order him to undertake the mission but they were waiting for him to volunteer, to go out not because it was an order but because the job needed to be done. He felt the embossed motto on the buckle of his belt.

'*Melde gehorsamst*, Obergruppenführer.' The formal opening words that he was obediently reporting himself rang through the room, quiet now except for the rustling of officers or a creaking as a heel scraped across the floor. 'I accept the mission and see it as a compliment that you have selected my battalion to carry out the task. The battalion is honoured. How soon do we start?'

Dietrich clasped Peiper's hand. 'I tell you, Wisch,' he exulted, turning to the commander of 2nd Regiment and Peiper's immediate superior. 'I tell you, with such men as this we could carve our way to Vladivostock, if only those striped trousered sods at OKW would stop buggering us about.'

The officers stood in embarrassed silence. They all knew Sepp's hatred of the General Staff and it was true that he was their comrade, but, well, there were limits. Dietrich stopped suddenly.

'I know you sods don't want to hear me going on about those fat arses. Let's show the pig Prussians on the General Staff' - a great number of his junior commanders stiffened at the insult, for they were Prussians - 'what we can do without their bullshit complicated battle plans. It's a simple job, "in and out". Let's show the silly sods at OKW that they need the SS. Come on, Jochen.' He was back to the familiar term again. 'Come to divisional headquarters and see the Kampfgruppe we've got for you. Yes,' he said impatiently, 'leave a message where you are for your adjutant, but come quickly. Time's a wasting.'

The column of vehicles carrying the senior commanders of the Leibstandarte Division drove for miles through the dark night. It was pitch black. The skies were heavy with cloud and there was no moon. Sounds indicated whenever the half-tracks passed buildings. A short whishing sound was a single house. Two whishes was a cluster of buildings. A longer whishing or a series of short whishes showed that the convoy was passing through a settlement. The men in the vehicles sat on the cold metal floor of the vehicles, trying desperately to avoid the biting wind that whistled in through every crack and crevice. Peiper felt sorry for the young Grenadiers manning the on-board machine guns. They had to stand alongside the weapons facing into the icy wind. Their bodies swayed from side to side in a sea-sick-making motion as the great carriers bounced in and out of the pot-holes and ruts.

There are no stars, thought Peiper. It will snow before the night's out. Sod it. Ivan loves this miserable climate. I have a feeling that this mission is going to fail...His black reverie ended as the vehicles swung through a gateway and came to a halt. Slowly, stiff with cold, the officers and Grenadiers debussed, stamping their feet in an effort to restore circulation. The officers crowded into a small room. There was the shared experience of pain as frozen noses, fingers and toes began to thaw out in the fetid warmth.

'Right,' Dietrich's voice rang out. 'Lachmann, Maas and Peiper, you stay here. We'll have a working breakfast here in this room.

You others get your heads down. You'll be awakened at,' he looked at his watch, 'Christ, it's half-past-eight already. Right, one hour's kip. Then breakfast. Parade at ten. By that time Peiper will have seen his Kampfgruppe and can go back to his kolkhoz. Off you lot go.'

He turned to his three subordinates as the last of the other officers left the room. 'Now, I don't have to tell you that this operation must succeed. Let's get down to details. The Luftwaffe's best mob is on call to drop supplies if you need them. One of their Johnnies will be along directly to liaise with you, Jochen. You will have specialist signallers seconded to you, operating on ultra short-wave frequencies. Men who've trained together so they know each other's "fist". Some will be with you, some with us, so that messages can be passed at top speed. We don't want Ivan's wireless detectors to locate your position. No need to tell the Reds exactly where you are, eh? The Luftwaffe promises that within an hour of any supply demand being made they'll have aircraft dropping whatever you want. Try to economise in ammo though, but be assured, even twenty sorties a day will be acceptable, so long as you bring out the 320th. Now the routes you should follow...' The four officers sat round the map discussing terrain, cover, roads and routes. The area was not unknown to the Leibstandarte. The Division had once rested east of the Donets river and the discussion between Peiper and his superiors was filled with remarks like, 'You'll remember there's a very dodgy

17

piece of woodland here,' and 'That village was thick with partisans, remember?'

Peiper did not recall eating breakfast, but when he broke concentration for a moment there was a saltiness of sausage and the pleasant sourness of Bauernbrot in his mouth. His cup was empty, so he must have drunk whatever it was. He focused his eyes - there was a dark stain in the bottom of the cup. It must have been coffee. He looked round. Daylight. Grey, dull light showed through the windows. He glanced at his watch.

'Obergruppenführer, it is nearly ten o'clock.'

'Thank you Jochen. Well we seem to have that operation buttoned up-on paper anyway. Let's go and meet the men you'll command, check the vehicles and meet that Luftwaffe Johnnie. Come on.'

The tanks that were now Peiper's were not new but had been well serviced and were in first class order. So were the self-propelled guns and the half-tracks. Most of the men of his Command were known to him, even if only by sight. The medals and badges they wore were evidence of combat experience. Even those fresh faces, replacements newly come to the Division, were keen and resolute. Peiper felt confidence grow within him as he inspected the men and machines carefully and thoroughly.

'By God, it is possible. If the Luftwaffe can keep its promises and air drop if we need it, then, we've got a goer.'

Chapter 4

'Sturmbannführer?' asked a drawling voice. Peiper turned round. Facing him was a scruffy boy - unshaven and with about four days' growth of beard on his chin. The boy was dressed in a battered flying jacket, a Red Army lambswool cap and Russian felt boots.

'Sturmbannführer?' The languid voice was infuriating; insolent.

'Who the hell are you?' Peiper demanded. There was ice in his voice.

'I'm Schlank,' came the reply in the same languid tone.

'Schlank? Schlank who? What Schlank? Report yourself correctly. Now, start again and this time report correctly. Understand?'

'Perfectly, Herr Sturmbannführer.' Schlank emphasised the rank and then, adopting an exaggerated position of attention, flung up an elaborate salute and shouted, *'Melde gehorsamst, Herr* Sturmbannführer. Oberleutnant Otto Schlank, commanding No 2 Staffel, Kampfgruppe 200, reports himself present, as ordered.'

'Don't play the clown with me, Oberleutnant Schlank. I know you stupid sods in the Luftwaffe. All chat; no do. In the SS it's different. You lot made a real right cock up of supplying the 6th Army down in Stalingrad, didn't you? So let's have none of your casual Luftwaffe approach here. Do you know what we've got to do, my men and I? No? Well, we got to go out into Ivan's country and bring back a whole group of wounded. We're going to be out there fighting all the time in these bloody conditions. We are going to have to depend on you and your comrades to drop over us the stuff we need. All you have to do is to find us, drop the supplies and then fly home to cigars and schnapps in a warm billet. We will be stuck out here. Frankly, on the past record of the Luftwaffe, I wouldn't trust you to find your way out of a tunnel.'

As Peiper ranted at him Schlank unbuttoned the battered flying jacket and flung it wide open. The decorations he wore were eloquent; wound badge in silver, the hundred mission clasp, German Cross in gold on his right breast and at his throat the Knight's Cross, its ribbon hidden by the gaudy scarf around his neck.

'Satisfied, Herr Sturmbannführer?'

'We're not playing a game of my one's bigger than your one,' retorted Peiper. 'We've all got decorations here. I just don't like your

19

flippant approach. I resent it. The mission we're going on is too serious to be seen in a flippant light. Anyway enough of this. We have to arrange identifications, recognition signals and the like. My unit is in the Kolkhoz at Alexeyeva. Come back with me and bring your IO. He can liaise with my own Intelligence Officer. I'll be leaving at 14.00 hours to get back to my battalion. You'll have to stay overnight with us before going back to your own unit. Meet me in the admin block just before 14.00 hours.' Schlank saluted and then turned away.

The ride back from divisional headquarters to the Kolkhoz was a silent one. Peiper was not a conversationalist and there were too many details to consider to allow him to pass the time in casual chat. His mind registered the vehicle engine noise and mentally he went over the equipment that was under his control. Dietrich and the headquarters' staff had said their farewells. From the time that the Kampfgruppe swung out of the dilapidated gateway of divisional headquarters until the time that he - or his successor - brought them back again, these men were his. His to lead. His to command.

Shortly before dark the convoy rolled into the Alexeyeva Kolkhoz and the men of 3rd Battalion watched the vehicles halt in line across the courtyard. Peiper dismounted and waited until Sturmführer Thiele, his adjutant, had come forward to report.

'Thiele, this is our new Kampfgruppe. Please get 3rd Battalion on parade in five minutes. Battle order. I shall address the whole Group.'

Whistles blew; NCO voices brought out the SS troopers. As veterans, they needed little time to prepare themselves for battle Within a few minutes the small group which was the 3rd Battalion was drawn up, each man steel-helmeted, armed and ready to move out. On the snowy square beside them were the new boys of Peiper's group; the panzer crews and the SP detachments together with the Engineers, the medical teams and the Grenadiers of the divisional Defence Platoon. Each group eyed the other; weighing them up. The parade was called to attention as Peiper and his senior officers marched onto the Square.

'Stand them at ease, please.' A short pause and then the young commander began to speak. 'Comrades. Can you all hear me? Yes? Good.' He acknowledged their nodding heads. 'Comrades, we have a special task to carry out. We have been selected to undertake a mission to rescue some Army comrades who are trapped behind

Ivan's front. Dietrich himself asked for us and I was proud to accept the mission on your behalf. We cannot leave our wounded comrades of the Army to fall into the hands of the commissars. Just as you would expect to be brought out if you were wounded, so we shall bring out those of 320th Division, who have been wounded and are out there.' Peiper waved in the direction of Moscow. 'There will be an Officers' O Group in ten minutes. Commanders will brief their men on the mission by 18.00 hours this evening. We move out at 20.00 hours.

'I'll inspect the unit now, Thiele,' Peiper said as an aside to his adjutant, and then the Commander turned back to the stalwarts of 3rd Battalion. 'The Divisional Commander regrets that it has not been possible to give you the full leave period which he promised you. In his own words, he's sorry that he had to drag you randy sods off the nest. But he does appreciate your willingness to sacrifice part of your time out of the Line to help your comrades.'

Parades when a leader took over or laid down his commands were very formal occasions. The commander had to be seen by his men. They had to know his face. Peiper marched along the ranks of his Kampfgruppe, his hand at the peak of his cap. At the end of the line he turned and came back to his position on the right flank of the parade.

'Thank you, comrades. It will be no easy mission but it is a vital one. A hot meal will be served at 17.00 hours. All bottles will be filled with water- water, not schnapps. Take plenty of cigarettes - they will still the hunger pains if we run short of food. Drivers make sure you have tanked up and have enough spares. Dismiss the parade, Thiele, please.'

The Sturmbannführer acknowledged the final salute and went into the small room which was his billet. He lay down on the narrow bed and fell immediately into a dreamless, deep sleep.

The Grenadiers of 3rd Battalion were standing in the snow, just before the time to move off and were discussing the new operations.

'My devochka told me this morning that we were leaving,' said Bauer. 'Bloody uncanny I call it. She seemed to know that we would be making the attack.'

'They seem to know everything before we do,' said another soldier.

'Quiet there.' A voice out of the darkness silenced them.

'Drivers- mount,' the voice said, and then when the drivers had climbed into their cabs, 'Grenadiers - mount.'

'Drivers- start engines,' the voice continued and then above the roar of the motors the statement, 'Kampfgruppe ready to march out, Sturmbannführer.'

'Thank you, Senior Sergeant.' Peiper climbed into his panzer, slid through the hatch and settled himself. He picked up the microphone, adjusted the earphones, switched on and looked around him. The Kampfgruppe stood ready. Peiper took a deep breath. It was time for the 'off'.

'Panzer - *marsch*,' and the gently turning engine roared into life as the driver stepped on the gas pedal. The heavy armoured vehicle began to move.

The Quarter Guard at the main gate presented arms as the Kampfgruppe passed them. As each half-track, lorry and tank went through the Kolkhoz gate the Grenadiers in the vehicles were ordered to sit at attention - their backs rigid and with weapons held firm between their knees. The Quarter Guard standing in the snow and the Kampfgruppe driving out to battle saluted each other in the fashion of warriors.

Once through the gateway the panzer took up a flat wedge formation, adapting immediately to the wirelessed orders. The half-tracks, filled with grenadiers, engineers and signallers took position behind the panzer shield. The Kampfgruppe moved eastwards into the darkness.

Back in the admin block a signaller sent the evening SITREP to divisional headquarters and added the words 'Jochen departed'. The Lieutenant at headquarters, who wrote the War Diary, upon receiving that message, entered in the log the sentence 'Kampfgruppe Peiper departed Alexeyeva Kolkhoz to undertake the rescue operation, at 20.00 hours.'

The operation had begun.

Chapter 5

The encircled German Division was under attack again.

The first wave of Red Army infantry struck out of the woods and advanced at a jog trot towards the positions held by the remnants of 1st Battalion, 385th Regiment of 320th Division. Captain Stumke, commanding the battalion, watched with professional interest as the tall figures of his enemies seemed to glide with effortless ease across the open sunlit ground. The light was good; visibility was perfect. It was, thought the Captain, a good killing day.

'They must be Siberians,' he concluded. 'The depth of snow doesn't seem to worry them. They're tall and by God, they are bloody good,' he commented as he noted the smooth way in which the line unfolded and their machine guns were set up behind and to the flanks of the first wave.

'This first lot are the bait, the sacrifice to test our strength. The other waves will be waiting in the trees back there. You sods,' he lamented. 'If I had artillery on call you would be dead now.'

The troops in the moving pocket which was 320th Division had long since used their artillery ammunition and had destroyed the empty guns. The Div artillery was now only three infantry guns, the 81 mm mortars and rifle grenades. There had been no air drops so that even rifle ammunition was running low. No matter how desperate the situation, firing during an enemy attack was not opened indiscriminately but was strictly controlled until the first furious salvoes could blow away whole sections of the enemy's first lines of infantry. These were the tactics of the Eastern Front; wait until point blank range and then kill with every shot.

'Thank God for the Russian mentality,' thought Stumke. 'Their commanders never allow the field officers to change the basic tactic. They always insist on head-on attacks. Always repeat a new attack at precise intervals. Always in the same place. Hullo, it's starting.'

From within the line of Siberians, now only two hundred metres distant and closing fast, a stentorian voice shouted, 'For Stalin, for Stalin,' and the booming response, 'Ooooohrah, ooooohrah ooooooooohrah,' burst from the throats of the running men.

'Watch your front lads. Sights on?' Stumke asked the machine gunners.

'Sights on, Captain.'

'Right lads, open fire.' The bullets from the chattering, tripod mounted Spandaus swept across the widely-spaced line of Red Army men. Some fell immediately, some staggered for several paces before dropping, but the unwounded still moved forward to close with the Germans. Above the high-pitched rattle of the Spandaus came the slower, heavier thumping; the Red Army's Maxim machine guns were firing in support of the Siberian attack.

'Their gunners are good.' The Captain approved of their professionalism as he saw lines of tracer falling around the German machine-gun posts. Stumke assessed the situation and weighed up the threats which were posed.

'Sniper!'

'Captain?'

'See the Maxim there on the left? Do you think you can get the crew quickly? They're trying to enfilade us.'

'Certainly, Captain. An easy target. They're not bothering about taking cover. What about the one they're setting up behind the line, just in front of the trees?'

'Yes. Take that one out as well and then take out the posts on the right. Ivan will keep on putting in fresh crews, so you'll have your work cut out. Another thing. Watch how you go. Once Ivan knows that you're about, he'll try to get you.'

'Right, Captain. I'll shin up a tree and take out the first lot. Then I'll move about a bit so that I won't be too obvious.'

The Russians were now within seventy metres. The white steam of their breath streamed behind them. Their chests heaved with the effort of the charge.

'Just about right,' thought Stumke. 'Grenades!' he shouted, and then watched the wooden-handled bombs circle through the air to burst among the little group of running men who had survived the machine-gun fire. Flurries of snow and black clouds of explosions surrounded the runners. More fell but three Siberians still charged on. They were so close that Stumke could see their despairing eyes. With an easy movement he rested the black MP 40 on his right hip and fired a long burst into them.

Dotted across the snowy field were the crumpled bodies of the Siberian riflemen. 'There must be about a hundred of them,' thought the Captain, and then realised with a sudden chill that the fallen had worn no white camouflage clothing and they had not fired weapons. Through his binoculars he studied the three men he had shot. Not one of them seemed to be carrying a firearm. The nearest of the three had in his hand what looked like an axe. One of the others had a bayonet. The Siberians had been sacrificed.

'They were a Punishment Company,' he thought. 'Poor devils.' But any thoughts about his late enemies stopped when white-coated figures began to flit in and out of the trees on the far side of the field. A new attack was being built up.

'Everybody OK?' he asked.

'Yes, Captain,' came back the reassurance.

'Good. Right lads, Ivan's massing now and this lot are in snow suits so this will be the big one.' There was little point in telling his men that unless they crushed the Siberian assault on the open field the attack would almost surely end in hand to hand fighting. There were so many of the enemy and so few of his own battalion.

'Christ- ' The air was suddenly filled with smoke and flame as hundreds of Katyusha rockets flew towards the unit's positions.

'Heads down lads; incoming shit.' Explosions rocked the area. Flight after flight of Katyushas came over. The detonations merged into a single rolling peal of thunder and the sky was lit with flame as the rockets burst in the tree tops.

Fifteen minutes passed - an eternity of time for men under bombardment - then, as suddenly as it had begun, the rocket bombardment stopped. But only the rocket bombardment; not the machine-gun fire. When a Corporal of No 2 Company stood up to observe he was riddled with bullets. Machine-gun fire was criss-crossing the short German front with a hail of bullets saturating each Spandau position. At least four Maxims were firing at every single German gun. The Siberian commander had organised the attack well.

'Move the Spandaus to alternative positions,' Stumke ordered, 'It will take the Ivans some time to work out that we've switched them. Rifle grenade men! Set the fuses for seven seconds. When they get close I want the bombs to burst above their heads. Right, stand to, lads, here they come again.'

The first line of white-suited Siberians showed clear against the dark green trees, but then they seemed to vanish from sight as they moved into the snowy fields and lay prone. Before they flung themselves down, the German Captain noted that the hand guns were painted white and the soldier's faces were almost completely hidden by parka hoods drawn tight.

The first wave of Riflemen had halted and were down on the snow. Behind them the soldiers of a second wave were closing up and then a third wave, flitting like ghosts, began to emerge from the dark woods. On command, the other waves of Red Army men lay down blending so well with the snow as to be almost invisible to the German Grenadiers who were only six hundred metres distant. Russian tracer still flickered along the line of German positions and poured into the now abandoned Spandau positions.

Out of the trees the black clouds of Katyusha smoke trails climbed into the sky. Detonations, explosions, the crashing as tree branches were snapped off, filled the air. Under cover of the barrage the Siberians stood up and began to march forward. The gunners waited. 'Range, three hundred metres. Sights on? Take out all tracer rounds. There's no point in giving away our positions.'

'Sights on, Captain.'

'Fire.'

Again the MG 34s crackled into action. The men of the front wave of the attack staggered as if a giant fist had struck them. They fell in groups; they fell singly. Over their bodies, whether they were lying still in death or whether they were scrabbling in pain, the second wave carried on the assault. When they fell, across their bodies the third wave trudged forward. The Spandaus began to jam. They were overheating despite the intense cold. The gunners cursed and swore as they struggled to clear the blocked breeches.

Heads bent as if advancing against heavy rain, the Siberian Riflemen struggled forward. Men dropped at every pace but their lines moved forward, inexorably, like some vast human tide. The Germans fired like madmen and at eighty metres the Soviet attack halted. Flesh and blood could do no more. Here and there individual soldiers still tried to carry out their orders to attack but the others, broken by the machine-gun fire, flooded back towards the woods out of which they had so recently poured.

'Change the barrels on the machine guns,' Stumke ordered, 'and then take the guns back to the original positions. Ivan knows that they are here. Now lads. We've got about an hour before the bastards come on again, so rest a while. One man in five keep watch.'

The tired Grenadiers of the 320th Division lay down on the snow-covered forest floor and began to smoke inhaling in quick puffs, seeking to control their shattered nerves.

The 320th, as a formation, had not been long on the Eastern Front, but its men were aware of the ruthlessness which gave the fighting in Russia its own individual stamp. Together with the 298th Division and 'Großdeutschland' Division, the 320th had come into the Line just before the Soviet winter offensive opened. In late January the great mass of Red Army Corps and Divisions burst through the flimsy German lines. In the battles to the east and to the south of Kharkov the 320th had been cut off from the other units of its Corps. The Red Army's main body had bypassed the 320th and now it was encircled many kilometres behind the Russian front. By 1942 encirclement was, to the Germans on the Eastern Front, no longer the frightening phenomenon that it had once been. The able-bodied and unwounded men of the Division were formed into infantry detachments and took up a tight, hedgehog formation.

The warriors were on the outside; meeting, destroying and frustrating the Russian attempts to destroy the pocket which the Division had formed. Inside the pocket were the wounded, the administrative units and what little transport remained. Much of that transport was made up of one-horse carts - panje wagons - pulled by hardy Russian horses. With an armed and aggressive exterior protecting a weak interior the 320th had begun to fight its way westwards, intending to gain the German lines. Along the line of retreat the Division had been harried and weakened, but not destroyed, by Red Army attacks. These lacked the power to crush the German hedgehog completely for they were carried out by recruit battalions being 'blooded' or by tired troops taken from the battle line for rest and reinforcement. And so the 'pocket' wandered on in the direction of the German lines, its infantry 'spikes' holding off attack after attack.

One such attack was that which Captain Stumke's battalion had just driven off. The Captain's forecast to his men was correct. An hour after the first heavy assault had been made and had been driven off. a second attack came in.

Sergeant Barfuss was the first to realise that Red cavalry was moving in to support the Siberians' second attack. His patrol, recceing the route ahead of the main body of the encircled Division, was moving through the deep woods that lie to the west of Starobelsk and came suddenly into open ground; a snow-covered ridge running down to the valley of a small stream. Barfuss halted his men at the edge of the woods.

'The ground's too open,' he told himself. 'We'd stand out against the snow. We'll get back into the woods again and see if we can find a covered route. Hullo, what's that?'

There was movement, about a kilometre away, in the forest which stretched away in the distance. Among the trees he could see horsemen.

'Cossacks!' The thought leaped into his mind. To the ordinary German soldier all Russian cavalry were Cossacks. They appeared from nowhere, killed without mercy and then vanished. Cossacks were one of the frightening phenomena of the fighting on the Eastern Front.

'Cossacks. Christ, that's all we want.' Barfuss forced down the feeling in his stomach - a mixture of apprehension and excitement and concentrated on his duties.

'Right. Let's think clearly. Who are they? Horsemen. How many? A hundred plus. Where? Let's have a look at the map. What are they doing? Looks like a big recce patrol.' Suddenly he swore fear; the woods seemed to be filled with men and horses. Even as he watched, whole sabre squadrons of cavalry mounted on small, light brown horses wheeled out of the dark trees. Again the panic feeling in his stomach. Barfuss fought hard and mastered it.

'Corporal Koenig, send Naumann here. He can take accurate bearings, can't he? And send the wireless operator forward. I've got an urgent report. There are Cossacks down there.' He indicated towards the trees. Koenig and the two men wriggled forward to the edge of the tree line.

'Right, you, Schulte,' Barfuss spoke to the signaller, 'get in touch with HQ. Get the Intelligence Officer on the set. Quickly. You understand? Right, you, Naumann. Here's the map. I think this is where we are. Do you agree? Take your time.'

Naumann looked at the map, settled the compass upon it, moved the map a few degrees, checked the reading and looked up.

'That's it, Sergeant. Spot on.'

'Have you got HQ yet?' This to the signaller.

'Yes, Sergeant. The IO's on the set.'

'Lieutenant? Sergeant Barfuss here. There are several hundred Cossacks on a bearing 284 degrees from our present position. We are in Square E, Point 241 480. Do you see the stream on the map? My patrol is at the corner of the woods about a hundred metres to the left of the stream. Have you found the place, sir? The

Cossacks - there are about three hundred plus now - are forming in line -'

'Are you sure of your position, Sergeant? No battalion groups have reported horsemen on their sectors. There is Red Infantry on the sector held by 1st Battalion. That's all. No one reports Cossacks. Sergeant, check the bearings again. Out.'

Barfuss and Naumann bent over the map. The Sergeant picked up the mouthpiece.

'Cossacks, bearing 284 degrees from our reported position. Hullo they're moving...' Barfuss watched as the squadrons of Red Cavalry walk-marched through the snow. There was a sudden expletive from the Intelligence Officer which nearly deafened the Sergeant.

'Shit.' The officer's voice was trembling with excitement. 'I can see the bastards now. They're coming over the crest of the hill. Jesus, there are a hell of a lot of them.'

'About three hundred plus,' Barfuss interjected. 'You can only see the leading squadrons; the others will be coming over the crest in a minute. They're moving parallel to me - about five hundred metres on my right flank. The line of the woods will take them out of my view pretty soon. Whose sector are they moving against?'

'Against Captain Stumke's 1st Battalion,' the voice from Regiment answered. 'They're probably coming in ahead of the next Siberian attack to soften 1st Battalion up. The shit'll be flying soon. Best of luck, Sergeant. Out.'

Sergeant Barfuss thought hard and decided that he would move his patrol to an ambush position some way down the ridge while the Reds were busy with their attack on Stumke's battalion. The Red Cavalry would have to come back over the ridge and when they did, his machine guns would shatter them. He explained his plan to the rest of the patrol and went on, 'The snow is deep and quite firm. We'll tunnel so that the surface is not too much disturbed, and we'll pack the snow tight in the gun positions. Then we'll set up the guns and wait for the Red sods to come back. Whatever happen we mustn't break the surface of the snow. Those Red buggers have got eyes like shite hawks. They'll spot it if the surface is broken; so watch it when you dig. Right, let's go.'

The patrol worked with a will and half an hour later everything was ready. Three machine-gun positions had been dug out of the snow and the ammunition belts were loaded and ready. The walls of the gun posts were made of hard-packed snow and within the men of the group lay waiting. Barfuss waited and watched from the woods. He hoped it wouldn't be too long before the Red horsemen rode back. His men were sweating now from the exertion of digging and dragging the guns into position, but soon the cold would get to them. He didn't want that. Thank God it was a clear day. Everything that moved stood out in the bright, clear light. Anxiously, Barfuss looked towards the place where the guns were located. He could see no break in the snowy surface. Good lads. The Reds would get a real bloody shake up when they rode back. They wouldn't be expecting his little surprise, so they would not be riding in formation but in groups, in bunches, relaxed and unprepared.

'Easier to kill them that way,' thought Barfuss. 'That'll teach the sods. Ay, ay, Katyushas,' as he saw to his right the smoke and flames of the rockets as they flew through the air to bombard the positions held by Stumke's battalion.

'Regiment was right. First Battalion is copping it again. What couldn't we do with a couple of panzers in support? Christ, we'd crucify the Red bastards.' Barfuss checked that there was no immediate threat to his patrol from the Ivans and then settled down to wait for the Cossacks to come back.

Captain Stumke's men went to ground when the Katyusha bombardment opened. Others moved out of the area in which the rocket would fall. Thank God for the predictable Russians. They always fired their barrages on the same target. The Captain disdained to take cover. His Prussian mind refused to accept the danger. He had to set an example to his men. Not that they should need it, he thought, they are Prussians like me, but still as their superior I must show that the Ivans do not frighten me.

The rocket bombardment ended and through the thinning smoke and powdered snow Stumke saw cavalry walking in at a shallow angle on his left flank. He took a quick glance at the far woods. The Siberians in their white suits were still forming up; no need to worry about those sods yet. He would concentrate on the horsemen.

'Machine gunners,' he shouted, 'don't worry about getting the horses. Kill the men. Ivan can fight on foot without the nags, so aim high. Get the riders. Right? Face the front.'

The Cossack regiments right-wheeled and swung into line to face the Germans. As squadron after squadron of horsemen formed behind the leading files an apprehension grew in the watching

German soldiers. Men began to glance nervously over their shoulders - looking for a way through the trees, already mentally planning an escape route. Death was parading itself only half a kilometre away. The silent, sinister ranks of Russian horsemen dominated the Germans psychologically.

Stumke felt the nervousness of his men. Most had fallen silent and sat despondent on the ground. Others talked in voices higher pitched than usual and much more quickly. The Captain realised that he had to do something- but what? Then he saw the solution. There was a gap in the front rank of the leading regiment and towards it along the first line of the sabre squadrons rode an Ensign with the escort to the Colour. The huge, red banner whipped and flapped in the morning air. Stumke did not need to read the gold-lettered inscription to know that these silent horsemen drawn up in front of his battalion were Guards cavalry; crack soldiers; first class troops. He called to his Company HQ sniper.

'Do you see that group with the flag? In a minute they will be in the gap in the front rank. Shoot the man carrying the flag. If one of the others tries to pick it up, then shoot him too. Then kill the General - he's the one on the grey horse. I know you're good - now show me you're shit hot.' The sniper grinned.

The rider carrying the Colour, and his escort, reached the centre of the line of the waiting horsemen. They took post. The General on his grey pulled on the reins and swung the stallion in a tight circle. He drew his sabre and waved it in the air. The blade glinted and shone in the bright sunlight.

'Now,' cried Stumke, and the crack of shots broke the silence which had fallen over the battlefield. The General fell backwards from the high saddle. The standard bearer slipped sideways and two more shots felled the escorts.

There was sudden and uncontrolled movement in the cavalry as the frightened horses began to pull and to fret. The grey bolted and was followed by the mounts of the Colour Party. Other horse began to rear. There was a brief period of indecision among the Russians.

'That's buggered them,' Stumke exulted. 'Right, lads. Open fire'. The German machine guns began to fire. Men and horses fell. The Cavalry officers knew that to stay immobile was to die. Arms waved, spurs jabbed into horses. The beasts jumped forward and behind the officers streamed the men. Gone was the cohesion of Troop and Squadron. Gone the frightening precision of fixed

31

formation. Instead there was a mob of horsemen whose lack of cohesion would rob the attack of much of its power.

Explosions burst behind Stumke. The blast nearly threw him over. The noise nearly deafened him. He turned and then laughed weakly. The Division's last three infantry guns, mounted on lorries, were firing point-blank into the thundering mob of riders. Shells burst belly high among the horses. Time fuses had been set for only seconds of flight. Percussion fuses were useless in deep snow. Crashing detonations tore apart whole groups of horsemen. A stream of riderless horses galloped across the front of a Spandau position. One light brown horse was galloping, trailing his blue and red guts like pretty ribbons across the white snow. In other parts of the field, beasts were dragging themselves on two or three legs. The sound of gun fire drowned out the sound of the animals screaming in pain and fear.

The Red Cavalry now formed a single huge wedge rushing down towards the German machine-gun line. Despite the punishing fire of cannon and Spandaus the leading horsemen were soon in and then across the German outpost line. The faces of the riders contorted into masks of hatred and violence. Their sabres rose and fell, striking at the German machine gunners. Other riders fired Shpagin machine pistols into the posts as they rode at them and dropped hand grenades as they leaped over the slit trenches cut in the snow. Stumke saw his outpost line being overridden and destroyed. He knew that he had to save the guns.

'Get the lorries and the guns out of here,' he ordered and swung back to face the oncoming riders. Two cavalrymen were already upon him, riding him down. He flung up an arm in an instinctive move to shield himself. The shoulder of one horse pushed him and Stumke fell backwards and off balance and the rider of the second beast rose in his stirrups to gain extra power as he slashed downwards with his sabre. The German Captain turned as he fell so that blow he received was a glancing one. It did not cut him, but for moment or two it paralysed his left shoulder. His left hand, now powerless, unable to hold the magazine of his machine pistol, dropped away. Instinctively he tried to steady the gun by gripping it more firmly with his right hand. The index finger jerked on the trigger and the Schmeisser began to fire. A burst of bullets struck in to the belly and hind quarters of the horse charging past him. The beast reared and flung its rider. As Stumke fell backwards onto the snowy ground he saw the unhorsed cavalryman fly through the air to land, feet first within a few feet of him.

The Russian landed well, looked round and saw the German trying awkwardly to regain his feet. With a single lithe movement the Cossack rose to a crouching position. To Stumke everything seemed suddenly to decelerate and to run in slow motion. His senses became sharper. Adrenaline was pouring into his blood stream as he faced his opponent. To his sharpened senses the Russian's movements had taken on precise and deliberate menace. The Ivan reached his hand to his waist belt to grasp the handle of a short stabbing knife. The swishing sound as the blade came free from the sheath was loud and clear in Stumke's ears. He could hear the sound of the Russian breathing heavily through his mouth. The whole world was now reduced to the enemy soldier and himself. He saw nothing but his opponent; heard nothing but the noises of his adversary.

The Cossack moved from foot to foot, balancing himself, holding the stabbing knife low. Slav eyes watched Stumke and there was a sudden gleam of understanding in them as they noted the awkward way in which the German carried his injured left arm. Stumke, now himself in a low crouching position, sensed rather than felt that his pistol was not in its holster. His machine pistol was God knew where. The terrible realisation came to him that he might have only seconds to live. He had seen the gleam in the eyes of his Cossack opponent and realised that the Russian knew that he was hurt.

'He knows about my left arm and he's got a knife. Well, this is it, but by God I'll take him with me if I can.'

Realising that his life lay in obtaining and retaining the initiative, Stumke attacked first. Flexing his legs he flung himself at the Russian. The stabbing knife in the Cossack's hand swept upwards to catch the German in the belly. The thrust was caught and held in the skirts of the overcoat. The cavalryman pulled the knife free and struck again. Stumke twisted to avoid the thrust, tripped and fell sprawling backwards onto the forest floor. The Russian shouted with pleasure and sprang forward intending to land with both knees on Stumke's stomach. The German scrambled crab-like to the left and the Russian landed heavily on his knees by the German's side. The knife flashed downwards. Stumke's reaction as the blade sliced towards his face were faster than the Cossack's downward stroke. The Captain's right hand grasped the Russian's right wrist and with a strength born of desperation, he held the arm back from striking. Then, judging his time to a split second, he relaxed his hold. The Russian, taken unawares, was unbalanced and fell forward unable to control his movement. As he fell, Stumke jerked two fingers of his left hand into the opponent's eyes. The Russian screamed. He rolled on the ground, hands covering the half-blinded eyes. Stumke felt for the fallen knife, found it, balanced it and then struck the cavalryman in the throat. Once, twice, three times and again and again in a frenzy. Stumke realised that he was crying. Hatred of the enemy; hatred of the bloody awful country he was in. Hatred of the bastard awful climate and the rotten stinking peasants. Hatred of this Cossack lout, whom he suddenly saw as through a red mist, lying at his feet with blood-stained froth bubbling from his torn throat. How dare this piece of shit lay hands on a Prussian officer? Stumke's body shook as tears ran down his dirty cheeks. Bastards, bastards - he'd make them pay for this. Rotten swine. He gasped, panting like a runner at the end of a race, and then coming to his senses realised that fighting was still going on all around him. He forced himself to be calm again. His mind obeyed. Reacting to years of training, the German Captain picked up a machine pistol lying nearby, loaded and cocked it. The main body of the Cossack had gone through, Christ knew where, but individual riders we still hunting his soldiers through the trees. The Captain raised his Schmeisser. To his right he saw the Company sniper running, hands in the air, screaming with fear as just paces behind him galloped a horse and rider. The Red cavalryman swayed back in the saddle, the blade of his sabre lay flat as the drill book laid down and then, with the full force of his body to drive it, he thrust the weapon into the body of the running German. The blade fouled on the sniper's coat. The Cossack could not withdraw it quickly nor could he check his galloping horse. Stumke saw that the dead weight of the dead sniper was pulling the rider down in the saddle. As the horse thundered past him, Stumke, ice cold, controlled and angry, fired a right to left burst. The bullet pattern struck into the neck of the beast and then the bullets stitched across the face and head of the rider. The face disappeared in a flood of red. Swinging the gun from the hip the German fired another burst into a second cavalryman scrabbling on the ground with a gaping wound in the stomach.

Stumke looked around him. It was all over - for the moment. The Cossacks had broken through, had wheeled round and had charged back over the ridge. The silence that descended now that the horsemen had raced away was suddenly broken by the sound of firing coming from the left flank. Spandaus were firing. The machine guns of Patrol Group Barfuss were in action.

The Sergeant had brought his men to action as soon as the Cossack attack went in against Stumke. They did not have long to wait. Singly, then in pairs, groups and finally in squadrons the Red horsemen breasted the slight slope at a gallop, crossed the ridge and reined to a walk; men and beasts exhausted with the strain of the charge. The Cavalry were relaxed and unprepared. They walk-marched into the killing ground.

Barfuss called out the ranges. Sights were set, instructions whispered from gun to gun and then, once the main body of the Cossacks was on the snowy slope, the Sergeant gave the order to open fire. The snow in front of the gun muzzles was suddenly streaked with black from the cordite fumes. The heat of the firing melted the snow around the barrels as the Spandaus fired belt upon belt into the groups of tired and unsuspecting Russians.

Under the sudden hail of fire the Red cavalry swerved, turned and galloped back over the ridge. In their flight they rode down the lines of Siberian riflemen who were tramping stolidly forward in the second of the day's infantry attacks. The Riflemen should have followed close behind the horsemen in order to exploit the situation - the confusion that a cavalry charge must cause. The premature and disorganised charge had begun and ended too quickly. The German survivors of the charge had had time to pull themselves together before the Siberians could be upon them. Stumke saw the Riflemen coming in with a mixture of fury, despair and hate.

'First battalion,' his voice screamed across the short battle line; all that was left of his battalion. 'First Battalion. The Red shit is coming back. We have all lost friends today. No mercy for the Reds. Kill them, kill them all. It's them or us. Right, lads, now, mow the bastards down.'

The dread realisation that death or defeat were imminent animated the soldiers of 1st Battalion. Their firing was slow, but it was certain and deliberate. The Siberians, who, shocked by the fire, turned to run were allowed to go in the belief that their fear would infect the others. Those foolhardy Riflemen who came forward in long, loping strides, aggressive and confident, were killed. Their battle lust was a frightening danger. The white-robed figures fell to lie almost indistinguishable from the snow, joining in the companionship of death those who had been shot down in the first assaults; the Siberians of the punishment squad and the men of the cavalry charge.

At forty metres, German fire tore away whole sections of the Russian lines. The Siberians, sickened by losses, began to fall back.

'Fix bayonets,' Stumke suddenly heard himself screaming the lunatic order. He took up a rifle and bayonet. 'Right, lads, follow me. Charge!' And he led his handful of men into the charge.

The stupidity of his action soon became apparent as he and his men waded through the knee-deep snow. The Germans struggled forward at a slow walk towards the Siberians who began to falter. A huge Rifleman halted to meet Stumke's attack. The Russian brought down his Nagant rifle and long bayonet to the 'on guard' position and stamped his right foot into the snow the better to balance himself to meet the German's attack. Sunlight glistened on the blade making the triangular bayonet a thin line of silver. Stumke jabbed forward with his own rifle. The Russian parried it nervously. In his heart the German rejoiced. His enemy was afraid.

Stumke lunged forward with all his force. 'Prussia, Prussia, Prussia,' he shouted. The Russian parried right. 'Fool,' thought the Captain and swung a butt stroke which took the Rifleman across the jaw and cheekbone. The face of the enemy soldier, crushed by the violent blow, suddenly became that of an injured young man. The Nagant and its bayonet fell to the ground as the Siberian put up his hands to ease the pain in his jaw. His belly was left unguarded. The Captain steadied himself, rocked on the balls of his feet and then lunged forward in textbook fashion. There was a slight resistance and then the bayonet slid in slickly.

'They don't need more than four inches.' The counsel of his bayonet drill instructor at Döberitz came back to him and, in an almost classic movement, he withdrew the blade and adopted a fresh 'on guard' position. A brown-coated figure ran past. Another Rifleman. The running man stumbled and in a couple of strides the German was behind him. A lunge to the kidneys and a scream. As the enemy soldier writhed in pain Stumke struck him through the right side.

Everywhere the Siberians were in retreat. The bayonet charge, although made by so few men, had dominated them. Groups of them stood, hands in the air, and as token of their surrender had planted their rifles, muzzle down, in the snow. Others were running back towards the woods out of which they had advanced to the attack.

'Quick, lads, back into the shelter of the trees before Stalin's organ opens up.' Stumke led his tired but exultant men and the prisoners they had taken back under cover. Once inside the shelter of the pines the whole group, Germans and Russians alike, fell to the ground, emotionally drained. Slowly conversation started. Lewinski, the battalion interpreter, chatted to the prisoners. Not a formal interrogation, rather a talk between comrades. He turned to the officer.

'They've had it really bad, Captain. Their Colonel is in disgrace for not taking some objectives a couple of days ago. They've had such terrible losses that their regiment was being pulled out of the Line. They were on the road back to the rest area when they were told to attack us. The commissars had taken a couple of hundred of them and put them into a Punitive Company. That's the lot that attacked us first. This lot here were told that they either crush us or one in ten will be sent to the NKVD firing squads. And these poor bastards are supposed to be out of the Line. They say there had been no organisation in their attacks. They did not know that the Cossacks were supporting them. They thought the horsemen were our blokes. They've been in the Line since late November. They're sick and tired and have asked if they can stay and fight alongside us.'

'Well, we can't do that,' replied Stumke. 'We've got to send them back to Regiment who'll send them back to Division. I suppose Div could use them as stretcher bearers or something. The thing is that they'll have to be fed and you know we're on short rations at the moment. What we'll be eating if we don't get relief soon, God only knows. Anyway, when they're rested, we'll send them back to Regiment. Tell them they'll be safe and that Div will employ them.'

Stumke looked through tired eyes at the small number of men who now made up the 1st Battalion.

'Why,' he asked himself despairingly, 'why don't the Reds give in? They're defeated. Why won't they see it? They come in like robots. Time after time, never hesitating. Why don't they chuck it in? Why don't they all chuck it in like these men who have just surrendered?

The Captain looked across the sunlit battlefield with the heaps, piles, mounds and groups of Russian and German dead.

'Oh Christ, they are so many and we are so few. Why don't they just let us go back to our own lines. If they won't jack it in why don't they let us just get back to Kharkov? Why do they make it so hard? They know that we've got wounded. Why won't they let us go?' Stumke found himself crying, his shoulders heaving with deep sobs as he thought of the men he had lost; of the men that the Reds had lost. All of them dead and all for a parcel of ground so insignificant that on the map it had no name.

'They died in a nameless ground,' he mourned and sat rocking himself in grief amid the dead, the destruction and the chaos that are the inevitable concomitants of warfare.

Chapter 6

'Do you mean to tell me,' asked Comrade Commissar Major Lipski, 'that a handful of wounded fascists flung back most of a Guards Cavalry Brigade and two battalions of Siberian Riflemen? What's wrong with your bloody brigades, comrades? Do you need NKVD squads to ensure that your attacks are successful? A few officers shot in front of the rank and file might inspire the men to fight a little harder for Comrade Stalin and the Party.'

Major Lipski of the NKVD was presiding over a tribunal of enquiry hastily convened to establish the causes of the failure of the Red Army units to smash the 320th. The Colonels of the guilty regiments- Marenko, the Siberian Regiment's commander and Volki, Colonel of the Guards Cavalry Brigade - together with the senior officers of both formations, were treated not so much as members of the tribunal as the pre-judged accused at a court martial. All the senior officers were lined up in front of a table behind which sat three NKVD officers who constituted the Tribunal of Enquiry. The setting was a large clearing in the woods about ten kilometres to the east of Vodnoyoya. All regimental troops had been ordered out of the area and double cordons of NKVD sentries and party activists had been set up.

Volki could only have been a cavalryman. Dark, squat and bowlegged, he acted as if he were in a saddle, seeming always to be adjusting his balance. He stood impassive as the Commissar ranted. Colonel Marenko was tall and slender. A Siberian by adoption. Together with his Ukrainian father he had been exiled to the East in one of the purges. Marenko's high-cheek-boned face was flushed with anger. His prominent nose, high-bridged and flared at the nostrils, was white with anger. He moved impatiently from foot to foot during the political officer's tirade, waiting his chance to speak. Lipski continued to shout, condemning the Regular Army, the officers in front of him, the lack of spirit shown by the failure of the attacks. His insults gnawed and gnawed until Marenko could stand no more.

'How dare you?' He could contain himself no longer. 'How dare you question the courage of my men? All right, we commanders may have underestimated the resistance that the Nemetski would put up. But whose fault was that? Your Intelligence service had told us that what we were attacking was a remnant of wounded men, a rear-guard - dispirited, weak and defenceless. That's why we went in

39

without proper artillery preparations. My men, I might remind you, have been in the Line for two months now, and they were put in as a result of your Intelligence assessment and the enemy they met was not a shattered remnant. There was nearly a whole Division of Germans.

'God only knows where you got the idea that they're dispirited. They're not. They are fighting their way through to their own lines and we shall not be able to stop them until we put fresh troops in against them; well-equipped troops. Not men like mine who've been fighting without pause since before the New Year.

'No, let me talk.' He shouted, the words drowning out the Commissar's voice. 'As I said, perhaps we commanders may have been at fault. I don't think we were, but let that pass. You will not insult my men.' His voice rose as he began to lose control of his feelings. 'I will not allow you, you front-dodging bastard, to insult my men. When did you last go in with a rifle and bayonet against the Fascists? You've never done that have you, you shitbag? What do you know of war? Butchering defenceless peasants, shooting helpless women, bayoneting babies. That's all you communist scum are fit for. Fit just to persecute the innocent. You don't dare take on real men. You won't go in against fighting soldiers like the Nemetski, up there. No, you ponce about here, a long way back, pontificating about our lack of courage, surrounding yourself with bodyguards of your own despicable NKVD breed. War? - you bitches' droppings you, you don't know what it means.'

Lipski had bowed his head during the Colonel's outburst. When the Siberian finished the Commissar looked up malevolently at the officers in front of him. His eyes moved along the line of faces. Some were shocked at Marenko's words. Other faces showed support for the Siberian's courage.

'You heard that fascist liar speak, didn't you? Well, didn't you?' The Commissar bellowed the question at the line of officers. 'Not one of you made a move to stop his filthy mouth and this leads me to only one conclusion, and that is that you agree with him. If that is so, then you are all guilty; equally guilty with he who accused me and through me the Party of Comrade Stalin.

'Since you are all guilty, you will all be dealt with. You have acted in concert with each other. You are all, collectively, guilty of mutiny. You will all be punished.

'This court today set out to establish the reasons for the lack of victory in the attacks. Now we see why. You are all Fascists, enemy agents, Trotskyites, Capitalists, Tsarists, pogrom butchers. Oh yes, it's easy to see why our brave lads are lying out there dead on the soil of our beloved Soviet Fatherland and why you lot of stinking corruption are still alive.' Lipski wiped his brimming eyes on the sleeve of his overcoat.

'You sent those poor men out while you stayed behind the lines hiding in dugouts, living in luxury, safe with your whores and your bum boys.' The Comrade Major had a rich imagination. He stopped suddenly, turned to Comrade Commissar Major Arseev seated at his right and whispered an order to him. If his judgement was correct then he would have trouble with these Siberians. The Cavalry officers were different. First of all they were Guards Troops, crack regiments. Secondly, they despised the infantry. Volki and his officers stood in a group saying nothing, waiting to see how the situation developed.

Not one of the Army officers moved to stop Arseev as he left the table and entered a headquarters dugout in the trees. There he spoke urgently into a field telephone, ordering forward the Stand By Companies of 2nd Battalion, 14th NKVD Regiment. These, he knew, would be embussed and on the move within minutes, but it would take the lorries about fifteen minutes, at fast pace, to reach the woodland clearing, and during that time those primitive Easterners might turn nasty. 'Safety first,' thought Major Arseev and detailed a Section of the inner line of sentries to accompany him back to the clearing and to bring machine guns with them. He was taking a risk. Lipski might see this act as a criticism, implying that he could not handle the situation. The rank and file NKVD were armed robots. They were not to intervene without orders - whatever happened.

The scene to which Arseev returned had deteriorated. All the Siberian officers were shouting at Lipski, gesticulating; threatening. They formed an angry group in front of the table. The cavalrymen still stood silent and grouped around Volki. Arseev took in the situation immediately. Drawing his pistol he fired a shot into the air. That single explosion restored calm and before it could be broken again Arseev gesticulated with his hand towards the NKVD machine gunners sitting behind their weapons, the machine guns covering the officers. There was a thin smile on Lipski's lips.

'The Party is always right, comrades, because the Party has the machine guns. Now, I shall show you that not only is the Party in the right because it has the power, but that in the exercise of that power it can be magnanimous. You have failed in the executing of an

41

order and you all know what that means. It means that your lives are forfeit. But I shall exercise mercy - to some of you. You lot are guilty of dereliction of duty.' He waved a hand towards the cavalrymen, not deigning to name them or to accord them the dignity of rank.

'You are therefore sentenced.' Lipski rose to his feet to pronounce judgement as Field Service Regulations demanded. 'You lot of so called Guards Cavalry officers will be degraded to the rank of private soldiers and sent to a Punitive battalion. You lot' - the wave embraced the Siberians - 'will be shot. In the presence of your men. Orderly,' he called to one of the line sentries.

'Comrade Major?'

'Present my compliments to the Comrade Commissar of the Siberian regiment and tell him to parade the battalions in hollow square in thirty minutes time. Orderly.' He called a new man. 'Present my compliments to the Political Commissar of the Cavalry Brigade and tell him to report here to me, when I return from the Siberian regiment.'

At a hand wave from Arseev, a double file of NKVD troops advanced to reinforce the single rank whose men had stood silent and watchful twenty paces behind the accused. Lipski walked forward. The pleasure he was about to get from degrading the officers more than compensated for Arseev's insolent actions. The boy was young. He would forgive him - in time. Lipski stood in front of the cavalrymen. With relish he tore off the broad epaulettes from the shoulders of the disgraced officers and the medals from their chests. He addressed the cavalrymen.

'Now you are nothing but shit,' he began. 'To get you accustomed to being shit you will be attached to our headquarters to act as orderlies. I don't reckon you'll last a couple of days of the treatment we shall give you. You'll beg to go back up the Line, to do mine lifting, attacking machine guns, anything to get away from us.

'You lot,' he almost spat in contempt for the Siberians, 'will take your last ride back to the battalions you misled. You have not been condemned for insulting me,' he added sanctimoniously, 'but because you have failed the Soviet people. It is they who condemn you. I am only the mouthpiece of the Soviet people whom you betrayed.'

The prisoners stared stolidly ahead. Their lives were forfeit just as they had been even before their Colonel's outburst. That had merely set the seal upon the inevitable. Under Soviet law an individual counted for nothing. He had a task to do. If he failed in this then he paid with his life or his liberty. The officers expected nothing else. Neither mercy nor pity. It was Soviet justice.

A panje cart drove up and the officers were seized and flung in over its low back. The method of their handling was deliberately humiliating and in like fashion they were flung out of the cart when it arrived in the regimental area. The officers struggled to their feet. The Siberian battalions, dressed in full battle order, were drawn up to form three sides of a hollow square. The fourth side was made up of condemned officers, the NKVD escort and the staff car in which Lipski and Arseev had ridden.

The eyes of the Siberian Riflemen, fixed on Colonel Marenko and the other officers, were without expression. The flat, Slav eyes noted that the overcoats no longer carried the shoulder boards of rank. Nor were the officers carrying small arms. It was obvious to them all what had happened. The CO and the other officers had been tried for something. In some mysterious way they had been judged guilty of failing the Party and had been sentenced. The regimental Commissar saw Lipski's hand movement and flanked by two Party men, he marched in slow, parade steps across the clearing to where Lipski and Arseev stood. In a loud voice he announced that the regiment was on parade.

'Order the men to Present Arms, comrade,' Lipski ordered. 'This is a formal proclamation.'

The ranks stood rigid at the Present. All heads turned towards the small group of Commissars and prisoners.

'Comrades, we have here,' began Lipski, 'proof positive of Fascist treachery in our midst. Even here at the Front the Nazi devils are at work. Look at these animals. They sent you into battle determined to get you all killed. Many of your comrades lie dead because of these traitors. The Party protects you and punishes your oppressors. The Party has unmasked them and has condemned them. You will be able to demonstrate your love of the Soviet Fatherland and show your thanks for the protection it gives you by executing these traitors. From your ranks I want volunteers to shoot these filthy traitors. Don't all clamour. I want only ten men. Right, ten of you step forward - now.'

Not a man moved. The political officer had misjudged the fighting men. They would kill for Russia; they would not be butchers for the Party. Lipski was shocked. To him the guilt of the officers was established. That the rank and file could not see it astonished him. He tried again.

'You all lost comrades today, sacrificed by the incompetence of these brutes. Those who lost dear comrades should cry out for vengeance. The Party is giving you the chance to revenge yourselves on the slayers of your innocent comrades. Step forward those who want revenge.'

The ranks of tall, brown-overcoated men still remained stiffly at the Present. None stepped forward. The Commissar of the Siberian Regiment whispered into Lipski's ear.

'Comrade Major, they won't do it. The Colonel lost a nephew in the fighting today. He's a popular officer with a fine record. May I suggest that you dismiss the parade. You and I can deal with the prisoners somewhere else.'

'What do you mean?' demanded Lipski. 'Back down? Admit that the Party lacks firmness? Certainly not!' Turning to face again the still, immobile ranks he shouted, 'Very well. If you little girls won't administer Soviet justice then we of the Party shall.' He beckoned to several of the NKVD escort who strode forward, briskly, drawing their pistols as they marched.

'The Party swine are going to kill our officers.' A deep bass voice from the rank echoed round the clearing. 'Death to the Party butchers! Kill the Party bastards! Revenge! Death to them!'

A crackle of shots dropped the NKVD soldiers moving towards the Colonel. Lipski realised the danger. Without waiting, he jumped into the staff car and drove off at speed, leaving Arseev, the regimental Commissar of the Siberians and the remaining NKVD soldiers to face the Riflemen. The battalions broke ranks. The Riflemen knew that their act of mutiny had cost them their lives. In for a penny in for a pound. One Red swine more or less made no difference now to the punishment that each would receive for his part in this act. With nothing to lose the tall men from the eastern territories of the Soviet Union killed with despatch and without hesitation, but with absolute pleasure, all the Politicals they could find.

Lipski drove the car at a mad pace along the narrow forest paths. His foot pressed hard down on the accelerator and the Zis bounced and swayed its way towards the area in which 2nd Battalion of the NKVD regiment was encamped. The careering drive did not last long. Sliding round a shallow bend in the forest track, the

Commissar saw the lorries of armed and equipped, blue-capped political soldiers whom Arseev had alerted. Inside the open trucks the men stood silent and vigilant.

The Comrade Commissar skidded the car to a halt. 'Where's your Company Commander?' he screamed. The men nearest to him pointed to a small truck which had begun to slow down as it approached them. When it halted a young captain sprang out.

'Respectfully report, Comrade Major, three Companies en route as ordered.'

'Come with me,' ordered Lipski. 'Get the men out of the trucks first of all'. He was more controlled now that his nerves were beginning to quieten. He was once more among men of his own branch of service.

'I have just escaped with my life. Our other comrades did not. The Siberians have mutinied. Their Fascist officers have perverted them. They're all ignorant peasants, you know that? What I want you to do is to take your men in and to destroy them. You may feel that more artillery and armour is needed. If you do, use our NKVD men to collect it. Don't let the Army in on this mutiny. We'll clear the mess up ourselves.

'You are to commandeer any guns or tanks you feel you need we'll crew them with *our* men. You may need more infantry. Get them and we'll go in. *Our* infantry, of course, not the Army's. When we go in again not a Siberian is to escape. I want them all dead. Those captured alive are to be shot on the spot. I don't have to tell you how the fascist Siberian traitors must have treated our men whom they captured by treachery? You can guess. We either get them or they'll get us. So you know what to do, don't you?'

'Yes, Comrade,' responded the NKVD captain. 'I don't think we'll need extra infantry. I'll order up a squadron of flame-throwing tanks. I'll set up TAC HQ here. Orderly, bring my map. Signaller, bring your set. Officers and senior sergeants to me.'

'Don't tell them too much,' Lipski warned. 'Just enough for them to carry out your orders.'

'Of course; Comrade Major. Ah, here they are,' the Captain said as the members of the Orders Group arrived. 'Comrades,' he began, 'there is a serious situation. A group of Red Army men, Siberians, have turned themselves over to the enemy and are refusing to obey orders. They have also shot and mutilated our comrades. We are going in to get them. Gather round this map. Can everybody see? Right, we're here. The Siberians, a couple of hundred plus, are there.' His stick tapped the map. 'Although they may have moved by now; dispersed and moved eastwards.

'Section patrols will go out at the double to cordon the area. Our main force will go in with armour and under a tank gun barrage. Pavlov and Dimitri, you will find a tank battalion, here.' He pointed to the map again. 'Commandeer a squadron of vehicles, flame throwing vehicles. Bring them here. Use the Army crews. We'll take the tanks over when they arrive in our area and then crew them with our men. I'll send a wireless signal to the armoured regiment commander telling him to prepare his unit for you to take over. The rest of us will move out when the tank support comes up. Cordon troops will leave in about twenty minutes. We want to surprise the Siberians. We'll set up a cordon and then the main attack will either smash the traitors or else will drive the Riflemen onto our guns. What? Prisoners? Don't take prisoners. Shoot them where you take them. Kill the wounded where they lie. Do you have anything to add, Comrade Major?'

Lipski shook his head wearily. The Captain's high tenor voice continued.

'Commanders take post. Explain the situation to your men. Scouts will move out now.'

Vedettes of the political soldiers were soon moving down the forest rides. The remainder of the men of the Companies took up all-round defensive positions. Each man knew his task. With the arrival of the tanks, and they should not be too long in coming, they would comb the area. The rounding-up should be a doddle. An hour or two would see it all over.

Chapter 7

'Driver, stop.'

The drive had lasted a scant forty minutes and now the Commander had halted the Kampfgruppe. He was well aware that almost as soon as his column had left the Kolkhoz an informer among the Russian workers there would have got back to the partisans detailing the strength of his detachment and the direction it had taken.

'We are changing the direction of our advance from east to south-east,' the Sturmbannführer announced over the radio. 'You don't have to be a military genius to realise that a Kampfgruppe as powerful as ours is going out on a special job. Still, the change of direction should baffle Ivan for a short time.'

Below the Commander's feet there was a crackle of sound. Wireless messages were coming through. The Lance Corporal Signaller adjusted his earphones, listened intently, writing quickly on the signal pad. At the end of the transmission he swung in his seat and tapped the Sturmbannführer on the foot. Peiper reached down, took the flimsy paper and read, 'From Divisional Headquarters. Plan changed. Proceed now to Kharkov. Drop off your B Echelon at Red Square. Then RV at Podolkov to pick up soft skin column made up of all available lorries and ambulances. '

Peiper came back up through the turret into the cold air, adjusted his eyes to the darkness of the night and looked around him. The clear air magnified the stars and in their light he could see the vehicles of his group spaced tactically. The brightest stars shone overhead almost as big as saucers in the dark blue sky. Towards the eastern horizon they began to lose their brilliance and those on the horizon had vanished completely, outshone by the flashes of the artillery fire. The Front was unquiet. From horizon to horizon there stretched an arc of light. Heavy artillery bombardment.

'Theirs, of course,' thought Peiper bitterly. 'We haven't enough guns to fire a proper barrage and even if we had there would never be enough shells to maintain it. Those sods over there can shell us for days and we can make no reply. If we had only a quarter of what they have - Ah well.' Dejectedly, he watched the flickering white glow stretching like a sickle round the German armies in southern Russia.

47

Burning wooden hovels in the villages forming the southern outer suburbs of Kharkov lit up the area as Peiper's Kampfgruppe entered the town. The streets of the inner city were jammed with traffic. What is euphemistically termed a withdrawal of non-essential military units was under way. As usual, those who were demanding urgent and escorted passage out of the city were the Party members, in this case the 'golden pheasants'; the Nazi politicals, whose brutality to the Slavs made them feared by the Russian civilians and detested by the German fighting troops. The Mercedes cars of the 'golden pheasants' were piled high with loot and they crawled, but oh so slowly, through Kharkov's ankle-deep mud. The pompous, brown-uniformed Party members, swastika armbands gleaming in the light of the fires, demanded clear passage, determined through frantic horn blowing to secure for themselves and their doxies priority through the press of the traffic. It was a vain hope. Fear of the Red Army had infected all the rear echelon troops. Priority was accorded to none.

Kharkov's Red Square, the principal open place, was held by SS police units who turned back, often by force, anyone hoping to use the square as a short cut out of town. Liaison aircraft, Fieseler Storch, landed and took off from the square and there was a constant stream of DR's and Staff officers arriving and leaving the buildings which surrounded it. The whole place was given over to SS Corps HQ. In its south-eastern corner, a harassed SS Transport Corps officer was at work. Peiper reported to him.

'Right, Sturmbannführer,' said the young lieutenant. 'Park your B Echelon vehicles over there. When do you expect to collect them again? I only ask because as you can see it looks as if we're pulling out of the city. I'd leave them no more than a couple of days if I were you. If you haven't got back before then you may find that they've been commandeered. What, Sturmbannführer? The best route out of town? You mean going in the direction of the Front, of course? Well, I would suggest that you leave by the Moskovska Prospekt. Then drive for a couple of kilometres up the Rogan road and then turn right onto the southern ring route. That way you'll avoid the Party "Bonzen" and their bloody charabancs. Those sods are choking the road and they all want an armed escort. Anyway, good luck, Sturmbannführer.'

The journey out of Kharkov by the eastern road was less difficult than had been the drive into the city from the south. The eastern road ran towards the Front and there was little traffic going up the Line. It was all coming back. Half of the width of the highway - that half that led towards the city - was packed with columns of trucks, guns and tanks. That half of the road which led up the Line was kept empty for the movement of men and weapons to hold back the Ivans. The vigilant patrols of SS military policemen were under orders to keep the eastern half of the road free for front line traffic and their interpretation of the orders was draconian. Only rarely was their authority challenged. At one place half a battalion of Bersaglieri from Italian 8th Army's headquarters defence unit had swung out of the westbound traffic jam and had driven along the empty eastern half of the road, overtaking the slow-moving German columns which were keeping well to their own lane. A request and a direct order for the Bersaglieri to mesh their trucks into the correct lane were ignored.

Traffic Control centre was informed. Orders came back. There is a deep cutting just west of Rogan and in that cutting an SS police detachment set up a Spandau on a tripod fixed to fire up the eastern half of the road. The police waited.

They did not have long to wait. The first Italian truck, its engine roaring in low gear, came into sight around a bend in the road and entered the narrow defile. 'Open fire.' A long burst of tracer poured into the radiator and left the lorry halted in a cloud of steam. Bersaglieri riflemen leaped from the halted truck and ran along the cutting towards the machine gun. A second burst of fire just above their heads brought them, panic stricken, face down in the mud of the road. An SS sergeant looked at them in contempt.

'Corporal, round them up. Take them back to their lorry and then make them tow it away. Then drive all the lorries in their column off the road, and immobilise them. We'll let the macaronis march the rest of the way.'

The second incident of disobedience to traffic police orders also concerned Italian troops. A battalion of Sardinian Engineers was in a damned ugly mood. Its men were cold and hungry. The unit rations had been taken by the officers who had removed what they wanted and had had those provisions cooked. The sergeants ate next and what was left over went to the Italian rank and file. The little fuel that had been available had all been used to cook the officer's rations. The NCOs ate lukewarm food. That of the men was cold stew eaten on a freezing steppe. There, wrapped in blankets, the Sardinian Engineers tried to keep themselves warm

Seeing the men of the Italian unit standing idly at the side of the road, a traffic police lieutenant asked for their help to bring a column of horse-drawn carts forward through the mud. The request was turned down. The police officer explained that the carts held ammunition for guns in the Line. The refusal was repeated. A half-hearted attempt to insist that the Italians help was casually ignored. The German lieutenant had failed. He could not use force. He knew, as everybody in Army Group knew, that the Italian 18th Army was in direct contact with Mussolini and that any pressure upon Italian units resulted in a protest to Hitler. And the Führer, needing the alliances with Italy, would not support his own troops. The police lieutenant was defeated.

The Italians were triumphant. They had gained a moral victory. They had demonstrated their independence and there the incident might have ended. Except that the unit needing help was a Slovak artillery battalion. In the days of the Hapsburg Empire there had been bitter enmity between the Slav and Latin regiments of the Army and old wounds are deep. Advised by the SS that Mussolini's men would render no help, the Slovaks attacked the Italian camp, burned most of the trucks and seized the others. The shiny riding boots were taken from the feet of the Italian officers; the rank and file lost their overcoats. To retrieve them was a simple matter, said the Slovaks. Bring the ammunition carts forward to the guns and the clothing would be restored.

It was, for the Germans, a perfect solution. *They* had not coerced the Latins. The Slavs had done that and, of course, the Slovaks, as allies of the Third Reich, had as much right to claim independence of action as had the Italians.

The military police had orders that half of the width of the road to Rogan was to be kept free for the flow of reinforcements to the Front. They kept it free and along that cleared road Peiper's Kampfgruppe roared eastwards towards the flickering wall of light that was distant gunfire, until, at the Kilo 12 milestone, the column swung off the highway and headed southwards towards Podolkov.

At Podolkov a mass of soft skin trucks and ambulances was waiting. It was long past midnight. Peiper's column was hours late, delayed by the drive into Kharkov. It was not until 02 00 hours on the morning of 12th February that the Sturmbannführer opened the Operations Group in the only stone building in the village. The ugly concrete block had once been Communist Party headquarters in

Podolkov and fragments of the tawdry Soviet interior decoration were still visible, even after more than a year of German occupation. Whitewash covered the Soviet slogans but pieces of flimsy red cloth, the colour faded to a pale pink, hung from picture rails. Lighter patches on the grubby walls showed where the mandatory pictures of Lenin, Marx and Stalin had once hung.

In the main room of the Party house Peiper looked at the faces of those whom he would soon lead in the rescue operation.

'Gentlemen; comrades.' There was a long pause. The Sturmbannführer was not an orator. He hated speaking in public, even to a gathering of his own comrades. His sombre face was flushed with embarrassment as he struggled to find words to explain the mission that was to be undertaken. It's a dodgy operation, he thought, but I must sound confident.

'Gentlemen, er, er, comrades. Please look at your maps and find where we are. It's called Podolkov and you'll find it just to the south of Borovoya. Got it?

'Our task is to strike through the enemy lines, rescue the 320th Infantry Division, which has about two thousand wounded, and bring it and them - our Army comrades - back into our lines. The 320th is still a fighting formation and has been ordered to strike west, via Liman to Zmiyev. We shall head for Zmiyev to link up with 320th.'

In the dim light of the room he saw flash across the faces of the men in front of him the thought that was in all their minds. Another suicide mission. Be confident, he told himself.

'You all know that our Army Group is under pressure, but nowhere is that pressure more intense than here. You all know, as well, that the Front moves backwards and forwards with every attack and counter attack. Where we are now could be miles behind Ivan's front line tomorrow. So how far we have to escort the 320th back to our lines depends upon where our Front is. Do you understand?

'Anyway, the line at the moment is just down the road. When we set out - we're leaving at 04 30 hours this morning - we shall be inside enemy territory from the word go, so from the start line on, everybody will be alert.

'We shall pass through the sector held by Leibstandarte's 1st Battalion and then drive to Krasnaya Polyana. From that place due south to Zmiyev. Order of march; recce group will be No 11 Company. The Pioneer Platoon will follow immediately behind No

11. Then comes No 12 Company, then the SP group and then the Assault Engineers. Following them will come the Panzer Company in double file. In that way, until we get to Krasnaya Polyana, the armour will be protecting the soft skin column. Lastly will come the rearguard. This will be made up of the Divisional Defence Platoon and No 13 Company. The soft skins, together with the remainder of the rearguard, will stay in Krasnaya Polyana while the Kampfgruppe moves on Zmiyev. When we reach Zmiyev I shall bring the soft skins forward to porter the sick and wounded after rescuing the 320th. With the main body we shall have only a skeleton medical team to deal with just the most serious cases. The main medical team will be with the rearguard.

'Each Company will send out flank patrols during the march. No 11 will send out theirs on the left, No 12 on the right. No 13 Company and the Divisional Defence Platoon will guard both flanks and the rear.

'If we need supplies during the operation these will be dropped by the Luftwaffe. We have only direct artillery support - that of our tanks and SPs. We have no back up from Divisional or Corps artillery regiments, but we do have Stukas that we can whistle down if we need them. I'd sooner not. They're not accurate enough and if Ivan sees Stukas operating behind his lines he'll come out to investigate. Speed is our safety.

'Synchronise watches. It is now 02.30 hours. We move out at 04.30. There'll be no time to rest but there will be a hot meal at 03.30. Questions? None? Dismiss gentlemen. Good morning.'

The Orders Group left the building to find that snow was falling. The temperature had dropped and an icy wind was blowing. The soldiers cursed, but not too much. If the weather was bad for them it might make the Ivans less alert, and anyway snow muffled engine noise. It was still snowing at 04.15 when the Kampfgruppe was paraded. Punctually to the minute the lead vehicles moved off. Three quarters of an hour later - the drive was slow because of the blinding snow storm - a guide group from 1st Battalion rose up out of the snow waving blue lanterns. Peiper halted the column.

'Our front line lies about four hundred metres ahead, on the banks of a stream,' the patrol leader told Peiper. 'We made a recce earlier this evening. The bridge will just about bear the weight of the armoured vehicles, but the structure is mined. The Reds on duty seem to be a dozy lot. They don't move about much.'

'Thank you.' Peiper acknowledged the report and then spoke into the microphone. 'No 11 Company, move out in extended line. Cross the river and attack the houses on the outskirts of the village. The bridge is mined, so your task is to seize the firing point before Ivan can blow us all up. Move out.'

Tracks rattled and creaked, throwing powdered snow into the air as the armoured personnel carriers descended the low bank of the river Udy, a narrow tributary of the Donets, crossed its frozen surface and climbed the far bank. The column of machines of No 11 Company deployed into line abreast and from three of them a group of Grenadiers rushed forward into the first houses.

Peiper could imagine, although he could not see, the scene that was being played out in the wooden hovels of Krasnaya Polyana. He could see the grey-coated Grenadiers pouring through doorways, hear in his mind the shots and the explosions of grenades, the screams of the dying, the hissing intake of breath as man fought against man in the dark and fetid rooms. He waited, holding down his impatience, until a red signal flare burst into the air. The firing point had been taken; his Group could cross the bridge.

'Panzer - *marsch*,' and the main body moved forwards. Peiper's tank was the first vehicle to reach and cross the narrow bridge and had covered more than half its short length before the other Russians in the village reacted. Tracer slid lazily through the darkness, red beads which seemed to accelerate in speed as they slipped past the panzer to disappear into the snowy night. From the eastern bank of the river there was a sudden bright light at about man height and Peiper, standing in the turret of his Panzer IV, felt the anti-tank shot fly past his head.

'Gunner. Russian Pak. One hundred metres. Load with HE. Right traverse, right, more right, a bit more,' Peiper called as the huge 7.5 cm cannon traversed, and then more urgently as the Russian gun fired again, 'more, on now, on. Fire.

'Driver, fire the bow gun. It's a hit, a hit,' he cried as the shower of sparks and a dull red glow showed where the German tank shell had struck the enemy Pak and had ignited the ammunition packed around it.

The Panzer IV rolled off the bridge and onto the road followed by the other armoured fighting vehicles. These fired left and right into the fields, the houses and into any suspected enemy position. Dark figures which ran out of the houses were cut down by machine-gun fire before they had covered ten paces. The half-tracks of No 11 Company came forward into line on the right flank of the Panzer Company and, together, in a crescent-shaped wave, the armour of Peiper's Kampfgruppe swept forward. Behind the main force the Assault Engineers searched by flashlight for the little blue packets of explosive, working with frozen fingers, feeling for the wires which bound the bags to the wooden timbers of the bridge. Through the falling snow Peiper could make out a bundle of low buildings, the outlying houses of the village of Krasnaya Polyana. The column halted. There was little to be seen; visibility was down to forty metres. There were no lights. The Commander's voice came up over the radio.

'Watch out for trouble as we pass through this place. Any vehicle knocked out; only one other vehicle will stay with it until the crew is picked up. There will be no, repeat no, hanging about. Here we go.'

The tank roared along the narrow alley between the single-storey houses, emerged on the other side and took up a watching position. High white flashes suddenly tore the black night wide open. That's about the middle of the village, thought Peiper, then farther back, that's about the bridge, he thought. There were other flashes and then a dull red glow. A vehicle was burning. Another fire ball. A second machine was burning.

'Listen out.' Peiper needed information. 'Troop Leaders report.' The commander of No 13 Company, forming the rearguard, came up on the air.

'We are being attacked by what I think is a line of Pak some two hundred metres to my left. I think Ivan's got infantry too.

We've lost two soft skins - Christ, there goes another. Bale out, you fools.'

The young lieutenant had forgotten that he was reporting to his superior officer and was more concerned for the driver and for his mate in the burning three-ton truck.

'Can you cope, Jürgen?'

'Certainly, Sturmbannführer. I'll put in the Assault Engineers and the Defence Platoon. We'll smash the bastards. We'll be all right and will link up with you soon.'

'Hanni, how about you?'

'We're being fired on from Pak in the houses,' Lieutenant Johannsen reported. 'There's one huge bastard sticking through a window. We've got him, but it's bloody unnerving. We're putting m-g fire into the walls but whether it's penetrating and killing the Ivans,

God alone knows. Ivan's got his infantry here, too. One cheeky sod tried to stick a mine under our trucks. I blew him away - Aaah.'
There was a sudden silence.

'What's happened, what's happened?'

'Sturmbannführer! Sergeant Liebhab here. The Lieutenant has been killed. A sniper I think. Probably on the roof of a house. All tanks rake the roofs with machine-gun fire.'

Through the concealing snow curtain Peiper could see the brilliant tracers criss-crossing the darkness behind him. Suddenly there were five fires burning. Could they all be lorries or were some of them panzer? He forced himself to wait until the armoured vehicles of his Command had closed up. Peiper considered his position.

'We're in and nearly through Polyana,' he thought. 'Once we're on the main road, Zmiyev is only fifteen kilometres distant. To hell with Lachmann's advice about going across country. Ivan knows we're here. We'll form one solid wedge and belt down towards Zmiyev. Dietrich said that we'd be mistaken for a Red Army column and so we shall.' The young commander turned to the signaller.

'Give me the set. Are all the vehicles of our Kampfgruppe netted in on our frequency?'

'Yes, Sturmbannführer.'

'Very well,' and then into the throat microphone, 'I am now going to issue orders for the next stage of our advance. This is the stage where opposition will grow- '

A harsh voice broke in.

'SS swine, you will all die. We know you here. We kill you all'.

A Russian voice, speaking ungrammatical German, was on the Kampfgruppe's frequency. The words that the voice was speaking were badly accented but the message was crystal clear. Peiper reacted immediately.

'Radio silence from the end of my message. All commanders to me in five minutes. Remainder all round watch. Out.'

'Too late SS swine. We know where you are ' And the harsh voice laughed gutturally. On the Eastern Front this sort of interruption was common on telephone lines, which could be tapped, but its use on wireless had been less frequent. What was unnerving to the German soldiers was the realisation that the Reds had men to waste on conducting a psychological operation such as listening to conversations. It was frightening to know that somewhere in the

55

God-forsaken, frozen wilderness which was Soviet Russia, there was an enemy soldier listening to the messages passing between German operators. It was a sick-making feeling. It was an invasion of privacy. Dammit, it was downright obscene.

Two SS men doubled across from a troop carrier. 'Reporting as ordered. '

'Right. I want you to put up a light tarpaulin so that I can show a light when I brief O Group.' The two troopers pulled at the heavy waterproof and fixed it onto the vehicle's hull. Peiper and his subordinates huddled together inside it.

'I called you here,' began the battle commander, 'so that the Reds won't be able to overhear us. That sod came on the air just in time. I had forgotten that they can listen on our frequencies! We're not too far from Zmiyev. I intend to drive down the highway in a single force. Div recommended a cross-country, line-abreast approach, but I think a two-column armoured fist will be better. Order of march. Armour; half-tracks. What's our strength, by the by? How many vehicles have we lost? Six? All lorries? Thank you. Lorries will follow the half-tracks and the end of column will be armour. The watchword is "bash on". No halting - for anything. Remember if a panzer has a track blown it is not finished. It may not be an armoured fighting vehicle - a runner - but it is an armoured fighting strong point and will fight to the last or until we get back to pick up the crew on the way back.

'Refuel and re-arm now. While that's being done get a brew on. Get something hot inside the men and in twenty minutes time, that is at 06. 00 hours, we advance on Zmiyev. Thank you comrades.'

The flames given out by the little solid-fuel Esbit stoves produced hot water very quickly and the men of the Kampfgruppe were soon standing about in the freezing night, gaining a little warmth from cups of scalding-hot beef tea. There was little conversation and less movement. The Eastern Front was not a place where one did anything that was not absolutely vital to survival or to comfort. Talking and moving about were neither.

'Mount up.'

At 06.00 hours the tank engines, which had been idling to prevent them freezing solid, suddenly roared into life as the drivers gunned the motors and engaged first gear. Tracks squealed in the snow as they were locked to swing the heavy vehicles round. It was all done so slickly that before the melted snow around the burnt-out spirit stoves had had time to freeze, the double column was on its way southwards. It had stopped snowing.

Peiper, leading the right-hand line, looked across to where, only two or three yards away, Tiejens, senior sergeant, an SS man since 1930, led the other armoured group. Tiejens waved to show that everything was in order. Peiper balled his fist and jerked it several times into the air. It was the hand signal to increase speed. Exhausts glowed red as the powerful Maybach engines, which powered the heavy steel machines, forced the panzer through the clinging, knee-deep snow.

Peiper was exhilarated. The biting icy wind was forgotten in the ecstasy of the drive. Through his mind roared the sounds of Wagner as he led his own Valkyries to the light. It was for this that he lived; for the feel of his armoured vehicle thrusting into the enemy's land. For the smell of oil, cordite and sweat - the unmistakable perfumes of the panzer man. He strained his eyes into the dark and considered how much his feelings paralleled those of the Teutonic Knights who, centuries before, had carried the German banner into Russia. For him the tempo of the advance could not be fast enough; the rush of wind, the swaying, bone-bruising progress, the jolting as the heavy machines bounced in and out of the great potholes in the road. All those things were his excitement, his thrill, his fulfilment.

'Sturmbannführer.' A voice came up on the tank intercom. 'Driver reporting.'

'Yes?' Peiper was annoyed at the interruption to his reverie.

'Sturmbannführer, I cannot keep up this speed. I am almost blind. I do not know where I am driving.'

'Of course,' the commander apologised. 'Stupid of me. Slow down in two minutes when the column has been warned.'

Peiper was angry with himself. He should have appreciated the difficulties under which the drivers laboured. Their only vision was forward through a narrow slit. Their only visible points of reference were the glowing exhausts only a tank length or two away, and the drivers of the two lead tanks did not even have those.

From inside his parka the Commander brought out a hand torch, flicked the blue filter into position and shone it to attract the attention of Tiejens. The answering blue light came back. Peiper switched the celluloid disc to red and shone the light again, switching it on five times, the recognised signal to slow the speed. The red acknowledgement signal came back. Both column leaders turned in their turrets to show their blue lights and received the acknowledgement from the tank behind them. The instruction by red light was then passed and the column leaders faced again into the wind confident that the signal was being passed down the column.

Five minutes later the pace was slower - too slow, thought Peiper. It may be better for the drivers but we must maintain pace. The only solution was to give the drivers light and then to increase speed.

'Driver.'

'Sturmbannführer?'

'Switch on headlights.'

'Sturmbannführer?'

'I said switch on full headlights.'

'Very good.' Twin beams of blinding white light cut through the darkness. Peiper flashed a white light from his hand torch. .The outline of Tiejens' tank disappeared in the darkness, swallowed up in the sudden blinding glare. The torch message was passed back and as each commander acted upon it a new pair of beams lit the night. The bright white light reflecting from the snow was brilliant and dazzling.

'Driver.'

'Sturmbannführer?'

'Can you see now?'

'Yes, Sturmbannführer.'

'Increase speed.' And the throbbing Maybachs thundered as the driver moved through the gear changes. Behind him Peiper saw how the column lengthened in relation to each driver's reactions to the demand for speed and then closed up again as the vehicles responded. The Commander was satisfied - it was a tight, compact pair of columns whose identity was not immediately obvious. Things are getting better, he reflected. The road from Kharkov to Zmiyev passes over a series of low and rolling hills, and as the German columns breasted one rise Peiper saw in the headlights and only a hundred metres distant a marching column of infantry moving down the road away from him. The men in the last ranks were each carrying a warning lamp. Peiper's driver saw the Russian column, twelve files deep and reacted instinctively - he braked.

'What are you stopping for?' Peiper barked into the microphone. 'Run over them.'

The Red Army infantry were unnerved by the double column of bright lights roaring down upon them. Those who turned to look were held by the glare like hypnotised rabbits. The soldiers realised suddenly and with horror that the vehicles, now only metres away, had no intention of stopping. The rear tanks began to waver then the tanks were upon them. The Commander heard above the vehicle noise the screaming of men being crushed to death under the wide metal tracks. He wanted to halt, to slow down, to give the foot soldiers a chance to escape across the snowy fields, but he knew that there could be no compassion. These were the enemy. Either he killed them or they would kill him.

The Red Army men were dying under the tracks, horribly but quickly. If he and his men fell into their hands as prisoners, how many hours of torture might they face before death released them?

'Bow gunner, open fire.' The rapid chattering of the machine gun blotted out the shouting. The lead tanks sprayed the road ahead, the gun muzzles sweeping from side to side. Tracer flashed like the flickering tongues of snakes. Bullets poured into the infantry, fleeing in panic now, across the snow-covered open ground.

A group of panje wagons at the front of the marching column was overrun. Peiper's iron resolve was lost, but only momentarily. As the right track of Tiejens' vehicle ran over the beast pulling one of the wooden carts, Peiper looked down and saw, illuminated by the headlights of the tank behind him, the head and shoulders of the horse, twisted upwards so that the beast seemed to be looking directly at him. In its dying eyes Peiper imagined he could see concentrated the whole agony of the patient Russian people.

'Idiot,' he told himself sharply. At last he reached the head of the Russian column and silently offered thanks to God that the nightmare was over. The panzer raced downhill, crossed the frozen ice of a narrow stream, climbed the hill on its southern bank and rounded the great right-handed bend in the Zmiyev highway. Through his night glasses Peiper looked southwards. That dark mass, can that be the town? No. The columns rushed along a mass of buildings which turned out to be a village, desolate and abandoned. The road dipped again. The tank tracks slid and squealed as the vehicles crossed the frozen ice of the little river Mush. They gained purchase on the bank of the frozen river and brought the heavy machines up the bank, onto the road. Recollecting details of the map which he had consulted earlier, Peiper knew that only three kilometres separated them from the objective, Zmiyev. It was a sizeable town of tactical importance, for it not only guarded the crossing across the northern Donets river, but controlled the main north-western road to Merefa.

The most important question was what would the column find as it turned the last bend and entered the town? Already the first low, wooden houses on the outskirts of the town showed in the blazing headlights. The road climbed steadily for the last kilometre to reach the top of the hill upon which Zmiyev stands. There was no opposition. Not a soul to be seen. No human, no dog or cat. Nothing. It isn't possible, thought Peiper. It may not be a big place but it is important. There must be a garrison; billets for the troops moving up the line. There must be somebody about.

'Driver, slow down.' Peiper flashed the signal to Tiejens column, 'Mesh yourself in and form single file.'

Slowly the file of armoured vehicles, headlights blazing, drove through the deserted streets. The Sturmbannführer raised his hand; the signal to halt. There was nothing. In the rays of the headlights the only movement to be seen were doors slamming open and shut as the wind blew them. It was uncanny. There was no sign of any living thing, until, as the column turned into 'River Udy' street, a flash of steel reflected back from the headlights. The sight of a hand weapon held at the firing angle. Then the weapon was gone. It was enough for Peiper.

'Gunner. House, four hundred metres. Bring the gun round, more right, more. Load one round HE.'

As the Panzer IV turned, a headlight picked out a familiar image; the divisional sign. Peiper frowned in concentration. There were no Leibstandarte units out here and yet the sign was fresh looking. There were a series of images; light reflecting from metal. He prepared to open fire when suddenly a man in an SS winter camouflage jacket came into view.

'There is someone coming out of a house immediately to my front,' reported the Sturmbannführer to his crew. 'He looks genuine, but keep an MG on him. Gunner, you watch the house which he left. It may be a trap.'

The mysterious soldier was close now. The Sturmbannführer watched the man's hands. They held a German MP 40, loose but controlled. If he suddenly points that at me I'll kill him, thought Peiper, then he noticed the way in which the man walked. He rolled like a sailor. It could only be 'Captain' Hennecke, a lieutenant from 1st Battalion, an Obersturmführer.

'Rudi, is that you?' Peiper shouted through cupped hands. 'Hennecke, Rudi Hennecke.'

The figure shouted back but the words were lost in the roar of the tank's engine and it was not until the man had clambered onto the vehicle and was clinging to the commander's cupola that Peiper could make out the face.

'*Gruss di*' Rudi. You look terrible.'

'Jochen, you? What are you doing here? Is our counter-offensive coming in?'

'No, we're still moving back, but I've been given a Kampfgruppe to bring in 320th Division. It's been wounded - .'

'Yes I know,' broke in Hennecke. 'That's why I'm here. I was sent out three days ago. They didn't tell me about you. '

'Nor me about you,' Peiper retorted. 'I saw nobody about, then to see your sentry in the doorway was a bit startling. We nearly shot your HQ up. But the town looks empty. I haven't seen a soul. What's happened?'

'I don't know myself,' rejoined Hennecke. 'The regiment pulled out, as you know. Then we were sent back in to bring out the 320th. We found the place just as you see it now. It's a sort of military limbo. I can guess what's happened. The Red Cavalry Corps knows that Zmiyev has been taken but haven't yet nominated a unit to garrison it. You know what Ivan's like. Won't use his initiative and no commissar will allow a fighting unit to take over and garrison a town. The warriors have all got to be at the Front. So our Div pulled out and left a nice little town deserted but no Ivans have arrived yet and, as I say, when we got here Zmiyev was just as you see it - empty.'

'What were your orders?' Peiper asked.

'To receive 320th and to bring them back into our lines.'

'Same as ours. How many men do you have?'

'Just under sixty. We started out with eighty but met trouble. Since we've been here it's been easy enough, but I wish there was a little more information on the 320th.'

'Right Rudi. Consider yourself and your men as part of Kampfgruppe Peiper. We'll leave you here in your outpost as a back-up force to hold open the road and we'll pick you up on the way back after we've picked up the 320th. Do you have a medical officer with you? How are you off for food and ammunition?'

'We've no shortage of them. We found an Army Quartermaster's store, stacked to the roof with everything. We haven't got an MO but a couple of our stretcher bearers have been carrying out certain surgical operations. No brain surgery or anything like that, but gun-shot wounds and a broken arm. It's not been too bad. Lonely though with no-one about.'

Peiper consulted his watch. 'It's 06.40 now. Sun up will be in about an hour. I'll get my men billeted - get your men to show them where. Then my group will sleep for a couple of hours. We'll have breakfast after that and by midday we'll know what the situation is. We are to link up with 320th here in this town. I've got a Luftwaffe liaison officer with me and some specialist signallers. We'll soon be in the picture.'

Fifteen minutes later the outpost position of Lieutenant Hennecke's kampfgruppe was surrounded by a press of armoured vehicles and trucks, each deployed tactically. The SS officers and sergeants stayed in the tanks. The other ranks, and particularly the drivers, were told to sleep. They were all tired out. They had been on the move for less than eight hours but it had been a nerve-racking time.

Peiper did not sleep. He worked without pause like a robot, but unlike a robot his actions were reasoned and considered. Several times he had ordered trucks to be moved, vehicles that would have blocked the road in the event of a sudden need to deploy, and before his men were allowed to rest each tank crew had refuelled their vehicles and had carried out the daily maintenance task.

Inside Hennecke's dimly-lit command post, Peiper called for Lieutenant Panasch, the Luftwaffe liaison officer, and for a sergeant signaller.

'I want you,' he told the lieutenant, 'to organise a recce to establish exactly - and I do mean exactly - where the 320th is. Any other details, the location of enemy groups which are between the 320th and ourselves, would be welcome. Please write out a signal. The sergeant here will send it.' Then he turned to the NCO. 'Raise Div HQ and get them on standby when the lieutenant is ready.'

He sank into a reverie while Panasch wrote on the signals pad and then passed the flimsy across to the signaller. The NCO studied the paper and bent over the morse key. There was a rapid buzzing sound. A silence; then two short buzzes and the sergeant looked up at Peiper.

'Task completed, Sturmbannführer.'

'Thank you. Go off now and rest. You too, Panasch.'

Outside it was cold and snowy. Here inside there were the familiar smells of the front line soldier and his environment; unwashed bodies and clothes, tobacco and the sour smell of stale food. Peiper's head began to sag slowly forward. He felt the movement and brought his head back. The need to sleep was more powerful than his will and soon he was sleeping as a fighting man sleeps; deeply, yet ready for immediate action.

An hour later and the large red disc of the winter sun had climbed out of the plain to the east of Zmiyev and into a blue and unclouded sky. It was going to be a lovely day. Except for the sentries and those on duty in the AFVs, the whole Command was sleeping. The roar of an aeroplane engine woke them all. A fast, light bomber roared, just above rooftop level, over Zmiyev, circled and headed south-east. So sudden had been its appearance and so fast had been its speed that none had been able to determine whether it was a German or a Russian machine. Ten minutes later it roared back over a now fully alert garrison, banked, so that the black cross on the fuselage could be seen clearly and then climbed almost vertically into the sky.

The general feeling among the troops was that the pilot was a cocky bastard. At about two hundred metres altitude the plane suddenly turned onto its back and from out of a hurriedly opened hatch a man fell out. The feelings of the watching soldiers changed abruptly to horror as they watched the airman fall, and then changed again to a sense of relief as a parachute canopy blossomed and the aviator fell quickly through the air to land on the open main square of the town. He was escorted to where Peiper and some of his officers were eating breakfast. The slight figure carrying the silk 'chute over his left arm entered the room and reported.

'Herr Sturmbannführer- Schlank.'

It was the Luftwaffe officer of KG 200 and Peiper knew that he was being deliberately funny, deliberately laconic, to remind him of their first meeting. The Sturmbannführer did not rise to the bait.

'Welcome, Schlank. What are you doing here?'

'It was not possible for me to report everything I saw, so I thought I'd drop in.' The Lieutenant opened his notebook and began to read. 'The point unit of 320th Division is located just east of Liman and the main seems to be in and around Shebelinka, concentrated principally around the railway station there and occupying ground on both sides of the track. That means that the Division is spread over eight kilometres or more of ground. From what I could see it is not a very well-organised operation - but it may be a different picture when one observes it on the ground. The terrain is open and flat where the advanced guard is. Quite extensive woods dot the area where the main body is. The left flank of the Division is protected by the Donets river. The right wing is protected by a screen of recce vehicles - armoured cars it looks to me. No tanks. There seem to be a lot of horse-drawn carts scattered throughout the Divisional area. I saw several Russian columns. The biggest of these has its right wing on the Donets and is heading east to Bishkin - here.' Schlank indicated the position of the town on the map.

'This column is mainly cavalry with tank advanced guards. There's another heavy column - armour and soft skins. Its tail is in Andreyevka and it appears to be heading for Kharkov. There was one very unusual thing. We must have a pocket of men around Starobelsk, just here. There was a group of T-34s, probably in regimental strength, firing into the woods, here.' Again the pointer rested on the map. 'But I could see no sign of our men. No recognition flares were fired, but those tanks were definitely in action. Do you know of any pockets of our men that far out?'

'No, no I don't,' replied Peiper. 'If it is one of our pockets why haven't the men reported themselves? Of course, they may not have a radio but if it's a group large enough to be attacked by tanks, then it must be a fairly sizeable group. Do you think it can be part of the 320th?'

Schlank shook his head. 'Too far away and 298th Div is out of the line so it can't be any of theirs. Is it likely to be anything from the SS Panzer Corps?'

'Almost certainly not, but I'll check on it, of course. The next thing to consider is what we are going to do with you now. You can't fly out of here, so you're here to stay. Well Schlank, you're in the Army now. No more slap up meals - just hard tack. No comfy billets- just burned-out buildings or dugouts. There are no girls out here, but we've got friends, little beauties, who'll be closer to you than any devochka. We call them lice. Oh, you'll find our war a lot different from yours. But we welcome volunteers and you have just jumped from an aeroplane to join up with us, so welcome. I'll apportion you a job in my HQ, at least for the present. Later we'll find you a combat role. Now let's finish breakfast.'

After the meal, patrols of panzergrenadiers went out to determine that the town really was empty and Peiper checked his unit thoroughly; its men, machines and morale. Weapons were cleaned, everything made ship-shape ready to meet the 320th Division when it arrived. And according to Lieutenant Schlank, its advance guard could not be far away.

Chapter 8

Comrade Commissar Major Lipski and his NKVD infantry group moved cautiously towards the clearing in which the Siberians had mutinied. The politicals had been debussed some distance away from the place and had picked up the men of the cordon troops. The whole formation now worked its way into the clearing, hoping to catch the Siberians off their guard and to destroy them. In the clearing there were only dead bodies; NKVD dead whom the Siberians had killed in the first seconds of their volt together with the known Party members and activists in their own battalions. The bodies were neatly laid out in rows.

The clearing had seemed to be deserted when Lipski and his men arrived; empty that is except for the dead politicals. Of the Siberian battalions there was neither sight nor sound. No sound at all until a bird trilled and upon that signal fusillades of shots had struck down more of the hated NKVD. The politicals went to ground and were very soon pinned down. The incautious, the unwary or the daring fell to sniper fire. Among the first to be killed was Arseev; shot as he reached up to the radio. It had been no more than a second during which he had raised himself to snatch down the microphone, yet in that fleeting moment he had been seen, had been fired on and had been killed. Now Arseev lay face down beside Lipski. The Major looked at the torn-open back, ripped as the bullet in its passage had struck a bone and cart-wheeled. Secretly, Lipski rejoiced at the ghastly wound in his subordinate's body, for it was proved that the mutineers were using dum-dum bullets. Arseev's body would be a vivid demonstration of the filthy things that the Riflemen were prepared to do.

Bullets hummed and whistled through the air. The rattled politicals lay there for a long time under fire until a rumbling sound announced the arrival of the first tanks, crewed by NKVD troops. The T-34s lumbered into the clearing and in their shelter Lipski issued orders for their guns to fire high explosive shells into the trees and for the machine gunners to rake the undergrowth in which the fascist swine might be hiding themselves.

The barrage was short but intense. The guns ceased fire. A deep and heavy silence hung over the area. There was no rifle fire coming from the Siberians. Perhaps they had been driven off. Slowly and hesitatingly, the NKVD infantry stood up, watchful but gaining in confidence as minutes passed. It certainly seemed as if the Siberians had gone, but Lipski did not believe this. He knew, with absolute certainty, that some were still nearby. How many he did not know - certainly not the whole three battalions - but a determined rearguard was certainly still there waiting for the opportunity to strike. He'd flush the bastards out. He would incinerate them,

'You,' he shouted to a runner. 'Bring the flame-throwing tanks up here to me.'

The Comrade Major was right in his judgement. There was a rearguard; a small group of wounded who had volunteered to stay behind. Each of them knew that in their condition they would have slowed down and hindered the escape of their comrades. Rather than imperil the Regiment the wounded remnant was determined to hold the politicals for as long as they could.

The men of the rearguard had positioned themselves around the clearing to wait for Lipski and his men to arrive. In round fox holes or tied to tree trunks they had waited for the politicals to reach the open space. Harsh training in the Red Army had prepared them for the suffering that each was enduring. Combat experience had given them military skills, and a passionate hatred of their oppressors inspired them. The wounded men of the Siberian rearguard waited, adopting instinctively the attitudes of beasts of prey; ;patience, endurance and cunning.

Their first salvoes had dropped a lot of the NKVD but then the first tanks came and had opened fire with cannon and machine gun. Siberian riflemen, hit by shrapnel, sagged against the ropes which bound them to tree trunks, their life blood dripping onto the snow, dripping and dripping until the cold froze the drips and formed them into red stalactites hanging from the heavy overcoats. Other men, hit by machine-gun bullets, had sunk down inside their slit trenches to die lonely but unvanquished.

More T-34s arrived. The special ones that Lipski had ordered to be brought forward. These machines carried no gun but instead had a hose connected to a squat vat at the rear of the turret. These were the flame-throwing tanks.

There was a sudden and very loud hissing sound. A jet of golden fire burst through the trees and above the brilliant flames an acrid black smoke wreathed the branches. Globules of fire dripped from the trees to the ground melting the snow, igniting the dead undergrowth. As quickly as it had appeared the hissing flame died leaving nothing to be heard other than the crackling of burning wood.

Lipski listened intently. The silence annoyed him for he had hoped to hear the screaming of the Siberian riflemen caught by the blazing phosphorus. Lipski was disappointed.

'Bring the tank round another thirty degrees and flame again.' The engine revved up. The T-34 swung on its left track.

'Flame,' the NKVD lieutenant told his gunner. Fire arced for long seconds from the bow of the T-34, reaching across the clearing and into the trees.

'Stop flaming.'

Once again the NKVD group stood silent, listening. Nothing but the noises of burning wood disturbed the deep silence of the snowed-in countryside. 'Again.' Then again, and again, the flaming was repeated.

'Comrade Major,' the tank lieutenant called. 'We have now fired eighteen burst of flame. There is only enough for another couple of bursts, then I shall have to go back to refuel.'

'Yes, yes,' Lipski was impatient. 'Turn another thirty degrees and flame again. Keep doing that as long as you can. You must hit something soon.'

'Very good, Comrade Major.'

The arrival of the flame-throwing tanks sealed the fate of the Siberian rearguard. The burning compound flooded across the earth like a river, burning everything it touched. Mutineers still able to move had the choice of leaving their fox holes and being shot down by the politicals or of remaining there with the certainty of being burned to death. Rather than betray their positions the Riflemen stayed. Among them was Rifleman Paprilov. Shot through both thighs in one of the morning's attacks, he could not walk and had accepted the fact that his death was only a matter of a very short time. Part of one jet of flame that had ricocheted from a tree had struck him severely on the chest and less badly in the face.

Without hesitation or panic Paprilov had applied fresh snow to the burning flesh and uniform and then mixed mud and snow to form a creamy paste which he applied to the burnt parts of his face. The ice cold mud could not remove the pain completely but it did numb it so that he could concentrate upon treating his more badly burned chest and shoulder. These were a mess. His face had only been splashed with the burning solution, but his chest had caught a packet.

Gingerly, he craned his neck, grunting with the pain and looked down. The movement loosed wet fragments of burned overcoat and these fell away taking with them part of his shirt and string vest. Paprilov looked in horror and felt sick. His flesh was dropping off into pieces of stinking, black-edged fat; falling and falling, leaving raw flesh open to the bitter cold air. There was pain- agonising pain. He could have screamed with agony but his hunter's instinct told him that to cry out would betray the rearguard. So he kept silent, knowing that soon the NKVD would have to come in on foot to comb the woods and when they did he would get some of the bastards who had hurt him.

Moving slowly so as not to increase the pain of his frightful wounds, Paprilov slid deeper inside the fox hole, arranged snow-covered branches over the small entrance hole and waited. Noise travels through the earth and he could hear the sound of the NKVD infantry as they moved about. They were some distance away from him. The sound of their tramping around was blanketed suddenly by the noise of tank engines as the T-34s drove forward towards the trees. The vehicles halted, fired their last shells into the trees and then pulled back to refuel and to take on more ammunition.

Paprilov heard them go and although he did not know why the tanks had left the area, he knew that they would certainly return to support the infantry in the sweep. The Siberian also knew that the NKVD foot soldiers would not move into the woods without their armour. He was in no immediate danger; a quick snack would refresh him. With his burnt face there could be no question of his chewing anything and certainly not the piece of dry bread that he had found in his pocket. In the bottom of his small linen haversack there was some sugar. Cupping this in his left hand he mixed it with melting snow. Into the mixture he crumbled the stale bread and mixed the slop with a grubby finger until the whole was a soggy brown mess. Paprilov slurped it down, licking with relish the last sticky fragments from fingers and hand. The primitive food restored him quickly.

There was noise again. The tanks were returning, causing strong vibrations in the earth as they came towards his fox hole. Closer and still closer. Soon they would be upon him. He had no weapon to combat the steel monsters; only a rifle and bayonet, a few rounds of ammunition and a hand grenade. The vibrations were shaking him and he knew that one tank was driving straight at him. He decided; he would place the grenade in the tank's track as it passed over him. It might not do much damage but he would go down fighting.

The vibration of the tank tracks shook the fox hole. Earth began to pour in as the walls buckled. Soon Paprilov's legs were trapped. He guessed that the T-34 was about five metres distant, then four metres. Stand up, his mind ordered. Groaning with the Pain, the Siberian obeyed. He knew that he had now only seconds left to live but the realisation did not frighten him. His brain reasoned calmly. He must pull the pin from the grenade now- not wait until the tank had passed over him. He would hold the grenade in his right hand, place it in the track and hold it there. The tank wheels would certainly cut off his hand but, he consoled himself, I shall be dead by then. He pulled the pin and waited.

The T-34 rolled over the fox hole. Under the belly of the beast it was dark and noisy but Paprilov was unaware of it. His concentration was upon the task in hand. Two seconds had passed and then with a sudden movement he screwed his courage to the sticking point and laid: his hand holding the grenade inside the track teeth. The heavy tank wheels rolled forward and crushed his hand. The scream that rose to his throat died as the bomb exploded and killed him. The tank ran on for a few metres and then veered sharply to the left. The grenade had shattered a track pin. The links undid and the track fell away from the wheels. The T-34 was temporarily out of action and as it swung away the Riflemen could be seen- a corpse trapped in a fox hole. The stump of the right arm projected at right angles to the body. The badly mutilated face was discoloured. Grenade fragments had torn open the scalp so that blood pouring down the cheeks mingled with the mud poultice which covered half the dead face.

Lipski, running past the dead Paprilov, stopped in mid stride, turned and bent down to look at the body. That movement saved his life. A sudden crack of a rifle shot and a clapping sound immediately above his head told the Commissar that a bullet had passed only a centimetre above him. He ignored the danger. He must lead his men in and, with a shouted order for someone to get the sniper, Comrade Major Lipski trotted through the woods behind the T-34s, trying to flush out the remaining Siberians of the rearguard who had held up his NKVD troops.

Chapter 9

There is in the gently undulating country to the east of Sheludovka a village, so small and isolated that it is unmarked on all but the most detailed maps. It is called Lukovaya and from its wooden houses, set on a low hill, generations of wood cutters and charcoal burners have gone out to earn their hard living in the forests which surround it.

It was around Lukovaya that the rebellious Siberians gathered. It must not be thought that the mutiny had weakened the bonds of military discipline. If anything, it had strengthened them. The only strength was loyalty, one to the other and from all to the Regiment. The true discipline of free men, freely given, made for a stronger discipline than one imposed by fear. The Riflemen had to hold together. Each of them realised that they were outcasts from Soviet society; criminals to whose destruction every loyal Soviet citizen was bound to contribute. The Siberians knew that their lives were forfeit, that they were all living on borrowed time. From the first moment of disobedience they had been condemned. No going back; no penitence could save them from the NKVD firing squads. No betrayal by them of their comrades to the secret police would reduce that dread sentence of death to merely one of life-long hard labour in a Soviet concentration camp. Nothing but death would expiate their crime. How far the dreadful hand of Beria and NKVD would pursue their families, none knew. But they all knew with dreadful certainty that they themselves could never go home.

The realisation of what would happen struck Colonel Marenko more strongly than the others. In the time of Lenin, the Red terror had fallen on his father. In the summer of 1935 after years of exile he had barely settled down in his native city of Kiev when, as one of the first victims of the Stalinist purges, he had been sent to Siberia again, this time with his young son. No word ever came to father and son of the other members of the family; mother, sisters, aunts. Colonel Marenko never had established whether they were alive or dead. Soviet Russia is large; the largest concentration camp in the world.

Marenko sighed heavily as he remembered the time of his youth. Returned from exile at the outbreak of the war with Germany in 1941, he had fought his way forward, millimetre by millimetre, this suspect son of a political criminal father into being a first class soldier. His courage in the fighting for Moscow in December 1941 had brought him his first decoration and an officer's patent. Bloody campaigns and sickness are the ladders to rapid promotion in the Armed Forces. On the Eastern Front there was death in abundance and sickness aplenty. He rose quickly from platoon leader to company commander; and then from leading a battalion to directing a regiment. All those advances had been made in a single year, and now the whole lot had been flung away in a single outburst against that animal Lipski. All had been lost in defence of his Siberians. Nobody would insult his men, not even Stalin would be allowed to insult Marenko's rifleman. Not that he would, thought Marenko. He's not one to despise the common soldier. It is only those intellectual lice, with their university education's and diplomas, who hate the military. Stalin understands. If only we could get word to the little Father in the Kremlin, then all would be resolved. It was, he realised, a stupid idea and one which he rejected immediately. The Marshal has more to worry about than a group of soldiers in a single regiment.

Marenko called a council of war at which every surviving officer and senior NCO was present. The Colonel was worried that the council would be attacked while in session by Lipski and the NKVD Battle Group.

Don't worry, Comrade Colonel,' he was assured. 'Each battalion holds a sector of the perimeter. Sentries are properly posted and well hidden. No fires have been lit. No one would guess that we are here.'

The Colonel was confident of the proficiency of his men in fieldcraft. 'But what I fear,' he said, 'is that the NKVD will be searching for us with aircraft. Remember that machine which flew overhead when their Battle Group was attacking our rearguard this morning? Just before the flame-throwing tanks went in? I'm worried about being spotted by their damned planes.

'There is no need to worry, comrade Colonel. That particular machine was a German plane. I myself saw the crosses on its side and wings.'

'I'm sorry,' Marenko apologised. 'I am becoming quite neurotic. It's hardly surprising'. He buried his face in his hands. 'Look at the desperate situation into which I have led you. There is really no hope for us. Every man's hand is against us. If we strike east to go back home to Siberia, how long will the journey take? Will we ever arrive home? And those of us who do. How long do you think we shall be allowed to live in peace?

'We shall not be back with our loved ones for more than a day but that the Party swine will know and the same type of bastards that we killed today will be rounding us up to execute us. We can never go home.'

Colonel Marenko paused. His shoulders drooped with exhaustion and despair.

'I led you all into this. Even now, if I thought that my death would appease the Red swine I'd go out willingly to die at their hands. But now you - we - are all involved. Each day that breaks is a false dawn. It is only one day nearer to that day when we are shot down like dogs.'

Voices rose in protest. Voices loud in argument. No one blamed the Colonel. Each man present had been a keen and eager participant in ridding the Regiment of the commissars and each man was now prepared to fight to the death to stay free. The Riflemen knew that they were all in it together, that they were all comrades. Not in the sense of the hypocritical Party cant, but in the true meaning of that word. Voices rose and fell and then, above the noise of shout and counter shout, a single, bellowed word 'Quiet,' silenced them all. The noise in the room was suddenly hushed. The abnormally loud voice of a young lieutenant, Koszov, of No 8 Company - a small, fat, cheery man- had quietened them.

'That's better,' he said. The Siberian officers and NCOs sat silent, prepared to listen to him. 'Now, comrades - no, not comrades. Siberians; Riflemen. Now that we are free of the commissars, let me show you a little treasure that I hold dear to my heart. I am certain that others of you will have the same talisman as I. When the Red filth was oppressing us, just to have these little pieces of paper meant imprisonment or death Now we are liberated and in this society of free men I make my first voluntary decision. Let me show you this.'

From the lining of his fur cap Koszov drew a paper, unfolded it and held it up. It was a German Army propaganda leaflet- a Safe Conduct Pass.

'All those here who have a little treasure like this document, please show it. I need to know that before I make my proposal to this meeting.'

Most of the men fumbled within their uniforms, in secret places. Some Safe Conduct passes were in the lining of coats, others were inside boots. One or two had rolled their passes up so as to look like cigarettes. Other soldiers had flattened the leaflet and taped it under their tobacco tins. Most of the men present in the small room had these German promises of safe conduct. Not looking at each other they held up their pieces of paper, ashamed that they had been influenced by the enemy. Koszov attacked them for their sense of shame.

'Why the shame, my brothers? We each have only one life. Why should it be wasted dying for the butchers in the Kremlin? They say that we are fighting for Russia. Are we? Or are we fighting for a return to the Stalinist terror? You all remember the deliberate starvation of the people of the Ukraine? That terrible famine that the pig-eyed bastard Kruschev organised? It cost Russia twelve million people, people like you and me. Is that the Russia that we are fighting for? Well I'm not. Not any longer. Under the Reds it was fight or die. The commissars told us that we could not surrender and retain our honour, but if I have ever been in a situation where death or captivity were the only choices, then I should have chosen captivity. That's why I carried this leaflet.

'Why should I die for the Reds? They despise people like us. Am I an ant that I should allow myself to be killed at their order? I don't think so.

'I asked how many had a leaflet such as mine because I needed to know. Merely to have this piece of paper means that mentally you too have considered going over to the Germans and becoming prisoners of war. Mentally, you are already half way convinced that life is better as a prisoner; that as a prisoner there is a better chance of returning to Siberia. Am I right?

'Well then. What I propose is that we surrender as a Regiment to the Nemetski. Let us go forward as if we were going up the Line. There, once in the forward zone, we go over en masse to the Germans. I think they will win the war. When, not if, they win then we shall go home, one day, to a Russia purged of the communist butchers -'

'Don't be naive, Koszov,' a voice shouted. 'The Nemetski shoot all prisoners and mutilate them.'

'Who says they do?' the young lieutenant challenged the speaker. 'The Reds say that. What proof have we got that they do this?'

'What proof have you got that they don't?'

'None, I grant you. But I am prepared to back my judgement with my own life. Our commissars made very sure that we heard nothing but the Party's fairy stories. It is not Russia I question. For Russia I would fight to the death. I question the Soviets. If the Soviet Union is so beloved, as the Reds would have us believe, then why is it that we are attacked by Germans, Hungarians, Italians, Rumanians and God knows who else besides? Their soldiers can't all be fascists or deluded dupes. And if they are not and they're ordinary working-class chaps like us, then what are they attacking us for?

'Perhaps we're not the "Soviet Land so dear to every toiler", that the Party song says we are. Perhaps those foreigners see us as prisoners in an asylum where the psychopaths and loonies hold the keys. Perhaps all those working-class enemies who are fighting on Soviet soil have really come to free us from the prison which Russia has been since the Revolution. I'm for going over. All those with leaflets convince those who do not have them that it is our only course of action.'

Koszov spoke on and his enthusiasm and determination swayed the meeting. It was clear, he pointed out, that for the Regiment to disperse and for each man to find his own salvation was pointless. If the Regiment moved east, either as individuals or as an organised body it would mean capture by the Reds. To stay where it was would achieve nothing. To die fighting for the Soviets was out of the question. There remained only the option to surrender to the Germans. Trapped between no chance of survival and a slim hope of surviving the war, it was clear that the battalions had no other choice than to betray their country. A vote decided it; surrender.

Marenko called for maps and the group gathered round the outspread sheets.

'Here we are. The regiment is here. The nearest German line is this salient here.' His finger rested on the river Udy. 'The nearest village, south of the river, is Krasnaya Polyana. Does anybody know the area? Nobody? From the map it would seem to be a fairly easy march. What is it? About thirty kilometres. Reckon fifty up hill and down dale. A cake walk for the men. Yes?' He turned to the Intelligence Officer who had interrupted him.

'Excuse me, Colonel. I have a note from Corps Intelligence. The salient above Krasnaya Polyana is held by the SS. You know they're not gentle with prisoners- Soviet sub-humans and all that sort of thing.'

'Surely that nonsense applies only to commissars and the NKVD battalions, doesn't it? It can't apply to Line regiments like ours?' Marenko saw the doubt in the Intelligence Officer's eyes.

Well, whatever it is we'll have to chance it at Krasnaya Polyana, or else move further westwards.'

The IO broke in 'There's not much point in marching to the west. The SS hold the whole area to the east and south of Kharkov. If we want to avoid surrendering to an SS mob then we should have to march across our own Army's supply and reinforcement lines in order to reach a German army formation to whom we can surrender in safety. Consider the dangers of being caught, Colonel. Believe me we should never complete such a march.'

'In that case, then,' Marenko decided, 'we march westwards as Koszov suggested, like a regiment going up the Line. That will rouse less suspicion, for nobody would expect deserters to move *towards* the Front. At Krasnaya Polyana we go over to the SS. That's decided then. Now, from here to Krasnaya Polyana the order of march will be; 3rd Battalion in the lead. No 12 Company will patrol on the right wing of our advance. No 8 Company will do the same on our left. Mortar groups will accompany. The remainder of the Regiment will form both the main body and the rearguard. There will be no train of vehicles. We do not want carts to slow us down. We shall carry what we need. What we can't carry we do not need. Food is all that is required. Arms and ammunition we shall obtain on the march to the forward zone.

'I see from the map that there is a bridge over the river Udy. Assuming that the bridge is in our hands we simply relieve the sentries and the unit guarding that sector. They won't ask stupid questions. They'll be only too pleased to be taken out of the Line. Once we've taken over we march across the bridge into captivity.

'If the Germans hold the bridge then we'll spread out and make it look like a regimental assault. When we are near enough to be seen by the Nemetski, we stick our rifles muzzle down into the snow. To hide our intentions from units on our flanks we'll put down smoke. The platoon on each flank will be responsible for the density and size of the smoke screen on its sector.'

'It might be an idea for a smoke screen to be at our back,' Colonel. That way the NKVD Battle Police won't see us but the Germans will, because we shall be silhouetted against the smoke.'

'Yes, of course. Comrades - no, no, not comrades- gentlemen. Please tell your men what has been decided. We move at first light.

Anybody who doesn't want to come may stay here. When we move we shall hole up about two kilometres short of Krasnaya Polyana until we have established where the front line runs. Then we take over from the Red Army unit holding the place. The day after tomorrow, in full daylight, we go out in our mock attack and surrender.

'We march at dawn. Good night, gentlemen.'

Chapter 10

'Sturmbannführer!' the signaller reported. 'A message from Division.' The text was short. 'Kampfgruppe Peiper will move to Liman to contact 320th Division. Luftwaffe will advise location of 320th Advanced Guard.'

Minutes later Peiper briefed the officers and senior NCOs who had crowded into the room and soon the column was en route southwards out of Zmiyev, leaving Hennecke's group to hold the town until Peiper returned.

The strip of mud which is called a highway and which runs southwards out of Zmiyev changes abruptly from a wide ribbon of mud to one so narrow as to permit only one vehicle at a time to use it. It must be understood that the ordinary roads in the Soviet Union in those days were in no way comparable with their equivalents in Western Europe. In Russia, with the exception of the very few, all-weather, highways which linked the principal cities, all other roads were unsurfaced tracks. In rain or snow they were rivers of mud. In the summer they were dust bowls. In any season they could smash vehicle springs, could shatter suspensions and destroy totally the morale of the German drivers who used them.

The road southwards from Zmiyev, a morass of slush and mud, followed exactly the line of the Donets river. The narrow track ran along the western bank and behind the bank sheer escarpments rose. Across the river, to the east, the ground was flat, open and marshy. The eastern bank of the Donets, like that of so many of the rivers in European Russia, is five metres or more lower than the western one. From that higher, western bank the men of the Kampfgruppe could see, as they drove south, much of the terrain to the east and nearly as far as Liman.

Standing high in the turret of his Panzer IV, Peiper turned to check the disposition of his leading, armoured unit. Each tank gun barrel was pointing in a different direction. It was not a pretty sight, but it was a sign of unit efficiency that the tank commanders had adopted the correct tactical positions without having to be told. On the Eastern Front battles were sudden and immediate. On those high cliffs under which the panzer were driving, there might be any number of anti-tank guns sited. Who knew what lay around the next bend in the road? It was better to be prepared than dead.

Peiper's men were veterans and without orders each panzer commandant had taken up the correct firing angle and direction for the 7.5 cm tank gun. The Panzer IV immediately behind Peiper had its gun trained to fire along the right side of the Commander's tank. The third vehicle in line had aimed its gun so as to fire to the left of the leader's turret. Farther back in the column tank guns swung backwards and forwards, covering the high cliffs, while other panzer drove with their 7.5s trained eastwards across the Donets.

The Sturmbannführer was satisfied with his men's dispositions. He felt good. The Command was working well together. There was no enemy to obstruct the progress of his Kampfgruppe to the rendezvous. The sun was bright. It was 10.00 hours and although there was little heat in the mid-winter sun there was enough to show that the worst excesses of winter were past. Spring was not far away; summer lay ahead. The year of 1943. What would be the objectives What great battles would the summer bring? He pulled himself out of his daydreams. His thoughts came back to the lack of enemy opposition and Peiper recalled that he had expected to fight every step of the way. Instead, Soviet opposition had been limited to isolated actions. The Kampfgruppe had made good progress. Far better than he had dared to hope. A buzzing sound intruded. Once again he pulled himself out of the cold-induced dream state. A buzzing sound? An aircraft roared so low that its engine sound had overcome that of the tank engines. A quick look; a familiar shape. An ME 110. There was an orange streak in the sky and a parachute capsule trailed smoke as it fell through the clear, cold, morning air. A Grenadier from the Point Group leapt from a half-track and waded through deep snow to bring back the message. It read, '320th Division west of Liman. On your present course you'll miss them.'

There was a crackle in the ear phones.

'Division on the air, Sturmbannführer.'

'Thank you. Jochen here.'

Lachmann's North German accent came through the earphones.

'The Luftwaffe recce plane reports that you are near Taradevka. This means that you are still on the west bank. Why haven't you crossed to the east bank and why aren't you heading for Liman?'

'Lachmann,' Peiper reported, 'there are no bridges intact and the river ice is too thin to bear armoured vehicles. At best it will take only light carts. You must tell 320th to turn south. I suggest as the rendezvous the road which comes out of Liman and passes across the river. Map reference Square J, Point 204 364. There's a big bend in the Donets there. It should give us excellent observation. According to the maps there should be a bridge there. If there is, I shall cross over to meet 320th. If not they will have to come across the ice to me.'

'Understood, Jochen. I'll inform 320th. There's no wireless link with them so I'll use the Luftwaffe to drop a message. Out.'

Peiper's Kampfgruppe roared on through the empty village of Taradevka, rolling southwards until it reached the eastern road which ran from Liman across the Donets. There was no bridge across the river. There had once been a bridge - a wooden one. Now only fire-blackened poles projected through the ice, like decaying teeth, showing where the bridge had once spanned the river. Peiper checked his watch. Midday. He called for a runner.

'Tell Company Commanders we shall eat here. Fifty per cent of the men and vehicles on standby at any one time. Companies to take up good defensive positions. We may be here for some time and we do not want to be surprised by Ivan.'

Soon there was the smell of cooking food in the winter air. The hungry young soldiers ate and drank with speed, but however deeply they drank, however strong was their concentration on the food, their weapons were always to hand. The simple meal was soon over and in the cold air some men relaxed; others kept guard. Peiper, isolated by the loneliness of command, looked eastwards towards Liman, which he could identify only as a grey smudge on the far horizon.

As early as 13.30 hours the sun had passed behind the west bank cliffs and the temperature sank quickly. The sun's rays shone almost horizontally, illuminating in a golden glow the whole of the open ground across the Donets. Far away in the east, twinkling points of light attracted the Commander's attention. Some of them, thought Peiper, might be reflections off the snow, but those - a mass of sparkling lights which were moving from right to left along the line of the road - those can only be vehicles. They were still too far off for him to identify the source of the lights or to isolate them from the blinding glare of the sun on the snow. Whatever or whoever they might be, he thought, we had better prepare to meet them, for those lights might well be an enemy force.

'Runner. Inform Company Commanders that a group is approaching from the east. All units will stand to with one hundred per cent manning and vigilance. Tanks are to load with HE. It is to be considered that the approaching column is an enemy one. No firing until I give the orders.'

The runner trotted away. Peiper looked towards Liman again. In the cold air the images became clear in outline and as they drew near to the river bank they became distinct and identifiable. The Sturmbannführer could see clearly now. There was a Horch Staff car, a half-track escort and an accompanying SP. The small column was made up of German vehicles; the divisional headquarters of 320th Division. Peiper watched as the vehicles swayed and lurched finally to halt at a point some four hundred metres from the river bank. Soldiers leaped from the half-tracks to take up all round defensive positions. Then a fur-coated figure climbed from the Horch car. Through his binoculars the Sturmbannführer saw that it was Postel, the General Officer commanding the 320th Division.

The tall, erect but corpulent figure walked down to the river bank. Postel cursed as he saw only the fire-blackened timbers, all that remained of the bridge across the Donets.

'Damn and blast. The bloody bridge. If we had just one thing which had gone right for us. I've got no Engineers to build a bridge even if we had materials. Not that there is any time. And where the hell are those bloody SS men who were supposed to be here?'

General Postel swung his glasses quickly from right to left along the western bank and in his haste saw no sign of those who should have come to escort him. The SS had learned from the Russians the art of camouflage and of staying under cover. Until their Commander declared this column to be a friendly one, then each man of the Kampfgruppe was hidden and was looking through the sights of his weapon. The Kampfgruppe vehicles were concealed behind tarpaulins over which snow had been carefully thrown. General Postel in his hasty sweep of the far bank could see no sign of the unit that he had been told would be at the river to meet him.

'Unreliable bastards.' He swore again and again. 'Bastards. Bastards.'

Peiper, now certain that this was truly part of 320th Division, gave the order to fire the recognition signal and soon the bright rocket had burst and hung, suspended above the General's divisional headquarters, beneath its brightly coloured 'chute. A red rocket sped from east to west. The challenge had been made and answered. 'Haaaallooo,' shouted General Postel from the river bank. 'Where is Sturmbannführer Peiper?'

The SS commander scrambled down the high western bank and onto the ice of the Donets river.

'Here, General. I shall be with you in a minute.'

The reception he received was a hostile one. Why had he not come across into Liman, was the first question which was flung at him. What was he doing on the wrong side of the river? Didn't he obey orders? Didn't he realised that his disobedience had caused sick and wounded men extra suffering? Didn't he realised that the 320th was at the end of its tether? General Postel waited for no answer but demanded that the Kampfgruppe vehicles should be brought across the river there to wait and to be loaded with wounded. General Postel under normal circumstances was an articulate man. When aroused emotionally he was bold fluent and sarcastic. He had a way with words and his reputation for using language beautifully was known throughout the Army. The citations he wrote were classical; his reports concise and fluent. He faced Peiper as they stood on the river bank, raving and ranting at the SS man.

To be fair, Postel had borne the burden of his encircled unit for weeks. He had seen its strength bleed away in the terrible trek that it was making through the Soviet lines. With a growing tally of wounded, short of transport, ammunition and food, only his great strength of character had borne the Division along through the misery of its encirclement. Now, relief was at hand and the General's long pent up feelings could be vented. The victim of his tirade was the young SS officer who stood in the dirty snow facing him. Peiper, who had no way with words, waited until the General paused at last.

'General. This is the only place that I could meet you. Like you, I did not expect the bridge to be burnt. If it had been intact then I should have crossed the Donets and advanced upon Liman. I was not aware that it had been destroyed. Now that I am here I cannot bring my vehicles across to you. The ice is too thin to bear the weight.'

'Nonsense,' retorted Postel. 'You SS clowns can't bloody well be bothered. I'll show you that the ice will bear the weight. Riedl,' he called to an aide-de-camp. 'Tell the driver of the SP to take his machine across to the west bank. Watch this,' he ordered Peiper.

The armoured vehicle with its 5 cm gun edged slowly down the low eastern bank. The tracks slipped, gripped, slipped again and then found purchase. The SP touched the ice, skidded, was straightened up and began slowly to crawl across the frozen surface. There was a sudden loud cracking sound. Around the vehicle the ice had split and then with a frightening suddenness the machine disappeared completely. No one came out through the black and gaping hole which now defaced the river's white surface The crew had died with their SP.

Postel really did feel that the Fates were against him. The encirclement, the running battles with the Reds; the long march through enemy-held territory; the diversion from west to south to meet Peiper's Kampfgruppe. The bridge which had been burnt down and now the too-thin ice. He felt that he would go mad with frustration. Postel forced his temper under control and turned again to Peiper.

'Yes, well the ice is too thin to carry the weight of the armoured fighting vehicles. This means that my men, my tired, exhausted men, will have to cross the river on foot. Well, for a start they will not be able to scale that high western bank, so I want ramps excavated. These will be made at a number of places along a width of river bank of about two kilometres. That way the greatest number can cross at any one time and without undue bunching. Sturmbannführer, you will get your men busy on that. Now about the doctors. How many do you have with you?'

Peiper explained that the medical teams had been left at Krasnaya Polyana together with the rearguard, but that sufficient trained medical personnel were with the Kampfgruppe. This news did not please the General.

'I have nearly two thousand wounded men here. Do you realise that?' he demanded. 'What's the use of your main dressing station being miles away? This is a *Schlamperei*, a slapdash cock up. Right. I shall set up my TAC HQ here on the eastern bank. I shall put runners out to guide my units as they come in. The first lot will be a fighting detachment, then the walking wounded, then the serious cases and finally, my other fighting detachment.

'Your men, Sturmbannführer, will now take over the responsibility for local defence of both banks until my fighting troops arrive. Get your men properly deployed. Get others making easy approach ramps on the western bank and get your medical teams ready. Then inform Army that you have made contact.'

'I have already informed my Corps Commander that a link-up has been made,' replied Peiper. 'My men are already deployed and orders have already been given for my Grenadiers to begin digging the ramps.'

'Very well,' Postel grunted. 'Now all we have to do is wait for my men. Your lot can get busy.' And with that the General commanding the 320th Division climbed into his staff car and lit a cigar. The time was 14.40 hours.

Soon the Grenadiers were digging the ramps and they worked with a will. The exercise kept them warm and occupied their minds so that they did not think too much about the danger in which they were placed. Grenadier Bauer dug expertly and tirelessly. Mechanically, he thrust the wide metal blade deep into the river bank and brought out the shovel heaped with clods of the frozen earth.

Peiper checked the time. An hour had passed. He was becoming impatient and nervous. The delay was jeopardising the whole operation. The essence of such a raid was speed. In and out; fast. For a Kampfgruppe to remain immobile for hours in one place, inside enemy territory, was to invite trouble. It was obvious that the Ivans knew all about the operation to rescue the 320th and would probably trail the broken Division to its rendezvous with his Kampfgruppe. He knew that even if the Soviets did not attack him immediately, they could ambush the Column at any time and at almost any place they chose between the western river bank and Krasnaya Polyana. He could think of a dozen first-class positions from which to carry out an ambush. He walked up to the Horch staff car. Postel looked up.

'Yes?'

'I was wondering if you had any news of where your men are exactly?' Peiper asked diffidently.

'Do you know what my men have been through?' the General exploded. 'I have already told you that we have a lot of wounded with us. Even the unwounded marching groups can achieve barely a kilometre an hour. The lightly wounded can achieve even less.

'How fast could you move on frost-bitten feet, eh? Tell me that. My men are coming as quickly as they can. They cannot bloody well fly you know. You must learn to be patient. It is the most difficult of all attributes which a good commander must have...Yes, what is it?' There was a movement at Peiper's elbow. Riedl, the General's aide-de-camp, had come up to the car.

'General, the combat group is approaching. The head of the column is quite close, now.'

'Thank you, Riedl.' Postel got out of the car. The Army man and the SS commander stood and watched the first companies of the advanced guard as they approached. Postel fumbled inside his fur coat. 'My poor men, my poor men,' Peiper heard him murmur over and over again. The SS commander turned and saw tears running down the General's face. Postel was still fumbling inside his coat and produced at last not a handkerchief but a monocle which he fitted firmly into his left eye.

'Useful thing a monocle, Sturmbannführer,' he told Peiper. 'If you have a window in your eye they can't see that you are broken-hearted. A monocle,' he went on to explain, 'controls the face muscles. Hides the emotions. See?' His eyes still brimmed with tears but his face was immobile. 'Works like a charm. Ah, here are the first group now. Staff Officers to your duties,' and these men hurried forward to guide the groups to their crossing points.

The first detachments were from 585th Regiment and Peiper looked carefully at the men as they plodded past him. They were moving well and were still fighting troops. They were scruffy, certainly, but they were not a demoralised rabble. A military police group with the advanced guard marched out to be posted as guides to lead the other units of the Division to the crossing points on the eastern bank. Small queues of silent infantrymen built up at each point, each man waiting until it was his turn to climb down the Donets river bank and onto the ice.

'Not too many on the ice at any one time... Spread out ...Keep artillery distance between each man...' Officers' voices.

Voices with authority. Voices which kept control over men who obeyed without question the timbre of the voices.

The last companies of the fighting echelon passed the two commanders. There was a long pause. Nobody could be seen on the road. Peiper turned to see how well the controls at the crossing points were working. There was a delay. It was proving hard for the tired infantry men to climb the western bank, even though shallow ramps had been dug. Peiper spent some minutes issuing orders and then turned back to stand beside General Postel. The SS officer looked up the road. A straggle of men came round the bend and at the sight of them Peiper's heart sank. These were not like the marching, fighting detachments which had preceded them. These were the walking wounded.

'Oh Christ,' Peiper's voice was rough with shock and emotion. 'Oh Christ. It's Beresina all over again.'

Memories leaped into his mind. Recollections of figures seen in paintings depicting the retreat of Napoleon's army from Russia in

1812. The agony, the horror of that retreat was not one that the SS officer had thought ever to see. Yet its parallel was here. The agony was here, imprinted on the faces of the German soldiers who were hobbling, staggering or crawling across the open steppe. And these were the walking wounded. There was little pretence of a military formation. Their columns had spread so wide that they extended across a great width. Acres of unbelievable suffering were passing Peiper and General Postel.

The calvary of misery and pain moved at a snail's pace towards the river bank. Peiper was downwind of the wounded and there came to him, from them, a stench of decay and of defeat. Prominent among the many smells was the familiar cloying sweetness that means gangrene and also the sour-meat smell of suppuration.

'Beresina. Oh God.' The thought burned in the Sturmbannführer's mind as he saw and smelt the terrible procession of half-crazed men who staggered past him. Many had no weapons. Others were using rifles as walking sticks or as props, to drag their feet, bound into grotesque bundles of stinking rags, through the freezing snow. A pathetic, dog-like fear burned in their eyes; the fear of being left behind.

There was a noise coming from the wretched mob of decaying men. Peiper listened. Could these poor wretches be singing? It was no song but the expression of pain, sounds of agony being wrung from men who were dragging their wounded limbs across the winter wastes of the Russian steppe. Slowly the acres of agony seeped past. The last men crawled towards the river bank where SS stretcher bearers were already helping the wounded to reach the ice. In the snow to the right of where Peiper stood were the visible evidences of the Via Dolorosa which had been trod by the walking wounded of the 320th. Blood trails; thick smears of pus. There was a black slime that glistened in the sunlight. There were scraps of cloth, deep imprints in the snow where men had fallen and had dragged themselves - or been dragged - to the river bank.

War and its attendant horrors were not unknown to Peiper. He had lived and had fought through the first terrible winter on the Eastern Front. But never had he seen anything so frightful as that spectacle whose last sufferers were even now crawling, stumbling and swaying as they inched forward towards the western bank.

'If you thought that was bad, then brace yourself, Sturmbannführer,' Postel said. 'Those whom you have just seen are the walking wounded; the lightly wounded. The serious cases are a lot worse.'

And so they were. Half an hour later, when the head of the column came into view, there was absolutely no pretence at military order or discipline. A mass of men and carts rounded the bend in the road and began to pass the silent officers. Peiper saw first of all a mass of panje carts loaded with bodies - for all that Sturmbannführer knew they might all have been dead bodies. One man riding on a panje horse personified the horror of the whole. He was holding on to the mane of the horse with one hand. Where the other hand should have been was a dirty, blood-encrusted bandage. His head fell backwards and forwards with the animal's motion. He was to all intents and purposes, dead. Only the spirit kept him still in control of the horse.

The riders in the carts were the fortunate ones - the fortunate ones; good God! At least they were riding and body warmth kept the inner layers of bodies from freezing. Those who rode in the carts were indeed the fortunate ones. There were others less lucky. Bundles of rags were being towed behind the carts and as he saw the first of these Peiper realised with horror that each bundle was a badly wounded man who was being dragged through the snow as if he were a sledge. Each panje cart towed a group of five or more of these human sledges. Hollow eyes blazed from sunken sockets. Others showed no comprehension of what was happening. They were too far gone to comprehend the indignity. Other eyes were glazed and sightless in death. Those shapeless bundles which were still living men could only be recognised as such by the small and shallow puffs of steam which issued from their parched mouths. From some mouths no vapour came. These were the poor devils who had rolled over and who were being pulled along face downwards in the snow. Peiper could stand no more.

'General Postel, I must protest. This is inhuman,' he burst out.

'An animal should not be allowed to suffer like this. To do this to German soldiers is offensive.'

'What the hell are you talking about?' demanded Postel. 'We have not been on a sodding ramble round the Black Forest, you know. We've been cut off for weeks now, fighting our way through the Russians without,' he emphasised the word 'without help and without much motor transport. What the bloody hell did you expect, a Potsdam parade, all goose-stepping and snappy arm drills?

87

'No, General, but neither did I expect this shambles. We in the SS have other standards.'

'Oh yes,' retorted Postel. 'We all know the SS ethos. We've all heard that your officers give the *coup de grâce* to those men too badly wounded to survive. We've all heard of it. We in the Army don't do that. We try to get our men back.'

'Like that; like those poor devils?' Peiper demanded. He was almost incoherent. 'In the SS when a man won't make it back to our lines, we leave him with a pistol. If he is too far gone to use it on himself then we do it for him. Yes, we kill him. He dies with dignity. It saves him lingering on and dying, perhaps, under torture at the hands of the Ivans. More importantly, it means that his unit is mobile, that it is not being held back by wounded men who can't keep up. What you are doing is a criminal act and I hereby register the strongest possible protest.'

'Balls, Sturmbannführer. Our ethos is to give the man a chance to live. Wounded he may be. A cripple he may be for the rest of his life if we get him out. But he is a live cripple in Germany and not a birch cross in the stinking soil of this bloody awful country. Your protest is noted, Herr Sturmbannführer,' the General concluded stiffly. There was a heavy silence between the two men, each silent with his own thoughts as they saw the straggling lines of slow-moving panje carts crawling towards the Donets loaded with their cargoes of paraplegic, blinded and shattered bodies.

At the river bank a crisis had developed. Despite the staff officers, despite the guides directing the marching columns to their crossing points, despite the organisation, the carts of the badly wounded had come to the river before the lightly wounded had all crossed. A mass of men and carts milled around the crossing points. No priority was given. Now that they were so near to safety, fear of the Ivans had broken the straining links of discipline. Postel's men knew that once across the ice and they were in good hands. Nothing and nobody would stop them reaching the western bank. The demands of comradeship, the feelings of compassion were forgotten, discarded, rejected, as each sought to climb down the eastern bank onto the frozen surface.

'Good God, the situation is getting out of hand,' thought the General. 'Riedl,' he called to his aide, 'sort out that bloody mess - no not with threats of pistols, you oaf. If you fire a single shot you'll cause a first class panic. Sort them out. Clear the ice. Get the Military Police onto the job. Only one cart at a time at any one crossing. Fifty pace intervals. No foot troops, repeat no foot troops, or lightly wounded are to cross until the badly wounded are over. Ah, here's the rearguard and the transport,' he said as the remnants of Stumke's battalion, its men on full alert, watchful in the trucks, crunched towards the Divisional TAC HQ.

'Ah Stumke. Get your men out of the trucks. They're fresh now, are they? Good. Get them into all-round defence. The crossing is taking more time than I expected. When the last elements have crossed we'll destroy what we cannot carry. Don't burn it. Smash it. An SS Kampfgruppe is on the far bank. They have taken over the defence of the western bank and when you are finished here and have rejoined us on the western bank, then the SS will take over command of the whole group. The Sturmbannführer intends to leave a small bridgehead of his Grenadiers here all night; an outpost. So drive the lorries into a perimeter position and then hand them over to the SS. You will form the Division's rearguard here until the SS Kampfgruppe comes over. Well done, Stumke. You've done a grand job. Carry on.'

The men of Stumke's 1st Battalion turned out into the snow and set up machine-gun positions. Their weapons groups formed a small semi-circle as they settled down to guard their comrades against any Russian attack.

Peiper felt that his duty now lay with his own Kampfgruppe. He left the General still standing, sad-faced and defeated, on the eastern bank and returned to his SS men.

'Runner, please ask Doctor Stranjc to come to me.'

While waiting for the Medical Officer to arrive, Peiper decided on a course of action. Soon it would be dark. By that time the light and badly wounded should have crossed. Only the unwounded men and the rearguard of the 320th would still be on the other side of the river. These could come across in their own time. The 320th was exhausted so no move towards the German lines would be possible until tomorrow. What was important now was to carry out the most vital operations. The lightly wounded would be made as comfortable as possible for the rigours of the journey which lay ahead. For the unwounded soldiers of the 320th a night's sleep and hot food would restore them. Taking into account the old patrol maxim, never come back to your own lines along the route by which you left them, then the drive to Krasnaya Polyana would have to be across country. This would also have the advantage that it would be a direct route and should be faster than by road. The disadvantages were that cross-country driving would burn up more fuel and it would submit the wounded to more suffering as the vehicles bumped their slow way across the steppe. Could he save the badly wounded the pain of a cross-country drive? Yes, he would have them taken off by aircraft. At least one JU could land on the snow to take out the most badly wounded.

'Sturmbannführer.' A voice called him from his thoughts.

'Ah, Stranjc. Thank you for coming. Straight to the point, now.

What is your assessment of the medical situation?'

'My assessment, Sturmbannführer?' Stranjc was fighting to control his emotions about the problem that had just been passed to him.

'Firstly, I must say that never in my life have I been faced with anything like this situation. It's ghastly. There are more than three hundred grievously wounded among the two thousand plus casualties. At least fifty of those three hundred will die before we can get them onto the operating tables. I can tell you now that we'll lose another lot under, or as a result of, the knife...

'Not one of the cases I have seen in my first inspection would be operated on in the normal conditions of front line life. They are all too weak. You are aware that many of the frostbite cases are gangrenous?'

'I had suspected as much,' replied Peiper. 'But we must get back to Krasnaya Polyana. It is clear that the 320th cannot be moved tonight, so we shall stay here until tomorrow. If I give you until 08.00 hours tomorrow morning, will this help? Will you be able to do anything?'

'Frankly, Sturmbannführer, the answer must be - very little. I have not yet seen all the cases, so I do not know how many are life and death decisions. The medical officers of the 320th don't know either, or they won't give me a figure.

'Then, of course, I cannot operate in the dark. I need light. If you can give me light, hot water and a couple of hours to prepare, then I shall have a clearer picture and will make a start on the amputations. I expect there will be a lot of cutting, but I'll do as many of the most urgent cases as I can. My stretcher bearers will assist.'

'Light,' Peiper assured him, 'presents no problems. We'll use headlights from some of the heavy lorries shining into a tarpaulin tent which will form the operating theatre. I should not think that the light from the electricity generators would give sufficient illumination, but some generators can be used to produce the hot water you need. Let your medical teams do the diagnosing. I want you and the other surgeons to rest. Begin operating about 22.00 hours tonight. Finish at 06.00 hours in the morning. Then the rest of us will load up and we'll all be away.'

'You must understand, Sturmbannführer, that I must formally protest. The men on whom we shall operate will be in no state to be moved, but I understand the military necessity and my protest is, therefore, that of a medical man and not of a soldier.'

'Thank you, Stranjc. We might be able to air evacuate the worst cases tomorrow, but this is not certain. We may lose all the men you operate on tonight as a result of post-operative shock. I hope not. But to me the most urgent problem is the mass of men who will have to spend the night in the open, or in the trucks. In your opinion do you think that they will be able to last the night?'

Stranjc was positive. 'I have no doubt of it. They know that they're nearly home and that knowledge will open hitherto untapped sources of determination to survive. They will need food and hot drinks, of course. These you will have to issue perhaps, all through the night. I warn you it will be costly on fuel.'

'That's the least of our problems, Stranjc. The Luftwaffe can air lift it. Go now and rest. Send the officers to me for O Group please.'

When Peiper's subordinates had gathered he told them of his decision not to move out until next morning. There were voices which spoke out against the delay. Only a matter of hours, it was argued, separated the column from the houses and the warmth of Zmiyev. Other officers asked why a stop should be made at Zmiyev and demanded that the Kampfgruppe press onto Krasnaya Polyana so as to finish the mission. Peiper raised his hand.

'Comrades. We cannot submit those comrades of ours to such a strain. You have all seen them. Well, would you put your men through such an ordeal? Of course not. Tonight,' he went on, 'we shall let the 320th rest. We shall be on full alert, both on this western bank and also on the eastern bank.

'Schlank, I want you to lay on an air drop. What we need is petrol, cooking fuel and concentrated rations. If there are any Luftwaffe medical men who would like the practical experience of battlefield surgery, then they are welcome to join us. I do not know aircraft loading capacities but we want petrol enough and to spare. I want the first drop to come in tomorrow, first thing after full light. The lorries will use up a lot of petrol to light up the operating theatre and the generators. So, arrange it will you, Schlank, and also establish whether the JUs can land here so that the most serious cases can be taken out. Let me know about that point please. It's important.

'Right. All round defence. Full alert tonight. There's no moon, just the weather for Ivan to come sniffing round. Don't shout a challenge, open fire. No tracer. Leave them out. Remember, anything out *there* is *them*. But don't let your men fire at shadows.

'The cookhouse will be open all night for the issue of hot drinks. Well, you know your sectors, so thank you, gentlemen. Good night.'

Eight lorries were driven to a flat part of the western bank and set up so as to form three sides of a small square. Heavy tarpaulins draped over the trucks screened them to the east, to the north and to the south so that no light showed. A less heavy tarpaulin was the fourth - the western - wall. Behind that western tarpaulin wounded were already waiting, lying on stretchers. A series of light tarpaulins joined together were dragged across the tops of the lorries so as to form a roof to the operating theatre. A collapsible field operating table was erected and buckets set out-to receive the amputated limbs. A number of low-powered bulbs already burned inside the tarpaulin tent which smelled of wet canvas, disinfectant and blood. The generator light was poor but when the time came to operate the headlamps of eight trucks would fill the theatre with light sufficient for the surgeons to work.

The ante-room to the theatre - a screened-off patch of snow - was ready. The anaesthetist's equipment was set up. In one corner of the operating tent was a field kitchen, filled with hot water whose steam was beginning to warm the air inside the tent. Instruments stood ready under paper gauze. The surgeons who would operate slept fitfully in their cold trucks. The whole Command was prepared to meet the tests of the coming night. Outside, in positions cut out of snow, the Grenadier sentries peered out into the dark February night and counted the minutes to relief.

Chapter 11

Half an hour after the hospital had been set up, Peiper made a tour of inspection of the Kampfgruppe. When his vehicle was halted there was a total and absolute silence. No sound could be heard; not even that of the trucks whose headlamps, powered by their powerful engines, illuminated the operating theatre. No sound betrayed the fact that in the snowy bridgehead there lay several thousand German soldiers waiting for day to dawn and for the chance to break through and rejoin the main body of their own Army.

'Driver advance.' There was, once again, the familiar crunch of snow under the vehicle's wheels. Driving at night was by compass bearing and by speedometer for there were neither signs nor landmarks in this icy wilderness. Peiper's car drove south-westwards for two kilometres. A blue light showed dim in the dark night. It was a torch held by an outpost Grenadier. The panzer force was protecting the Kampfgruppe. The armoured fighting vehicles were set out high on the cliffs of the western bank, dominating the ground on all sides. On either flank of the armour lay the SS Grenadiers shivering in their snow sangars. The line of their machine-gun posts ran in a shallow bending arc back on either flank of the panzer line to touch the Donets.

The night was a bitterly cold one. Even though there was no east wind the cold was still intense. The Grenadiers who were not on sentry duty sat huddled together in groups, gaining warmth and comfort from their close packed bodies. No one slept. There were fitful dozes; a brief nodding off now and again. That was all. Frost settled on overcoat shoulders, stiffening the material. The cold at the top of the body moved slowly down to meet the cold that was coming up from the frozen feet and through the frozen legs.

Sentries were changed every half hour. To have ordered a man to stand an hour in a hole without a hot drink would have been to condemn him to death. After half an hour the cold dulled the senses to such a degree that the mind saw enemy soldiers who were not there; or one sank into a lethargy, then into a light doze, a deeper slumber and then into a sleep of death. Throughout the night two-men ration parties from the perimeter detachments crunched their way to the field kitchens to collect back packs; giant thermos containers of tea or ersatz coffee. The scalding hot liquid, issued at frequent and regular intervals, kept the troops alive.

Peiper looked, finally, into the makeshift operating theatre. It already smelt of pus, of gangrene, blood and diesel fumes. The half-melted snow around the operating tables was now a red mush in which there were buckets filled with dirty clothing, soiled bandages; with amputated limbs; fingers, hands and frost-blackened feet. The Sturmbannführer's entrance brought with it a draught of icy air. Stranjc felt it, looked up and saw the young commander standing lit by the beams of the vehicle headlights. The doctor gestured wearily towards the buckets filled with pieces of human beings and shook his head.

'We have already lost twenty before we could start cutting. My team have just carried out its fifteenth major operation. This is not a hospital. It's a factory reduction line, where defective parts are removed. It's not surgery. It's butchery. And the poor sods we're cutting up thank us for our help. Oh Christ, it's all so terrible. Never, never could I have believed that such misery could exist. God knows I am no defeatist - I'm patriotic enough, but does Hitler really merit this sort of sacrifice?'

There was no answer that a fighting soldier could give to the surgeon's rhetorical question. War is war, thought Peiper, and was angry again that he felt the need to justify that fact, even to himself. He walked out of the operating theatre and the cold night air struck him like a blow. He had a sudden thought. The river ice will have thickened. Perhaps it will be strong enough to bear heavy weights. Some of the 320th's vehicles, as yet undestroyed on the eastern bank, might yet be brought across. A winching party might be organised. The exercise would keep the men warm and it would help to take their minds off the waiting and the freezing. If the task was successful the lorries would provide additional transport for the men of the 320th.

They were not enthusiastic. They were lethargic with cold, but under the barking noises of the NCOs were soon working with rhythm and in unison. The trucks, lightened of everything that could be taken out of them, were winched across the ice, which, although it groaned and protested, remained intact. Before first light twenty lorries had been hauled across, manhandled up the western bank and camouflaged.

Stand-to at dawn brought no storming Russian attack and Peiper, standing on his vehicle's turret, surveying the ground in every direction, could see no sign of the enemy. They might just as well have been the last people on earth - it was so desolate. No movement, no sign of any life other than that of the Kampfgruppe.

'Schlank.'

'Sturmbannführer?' The Luftwaffe officer, feeling himself to be a comrade among comrades, had adopted the SS method of reporting just rank - omitting the prefix 'Herr'.

'Where's the air lift? Your JUs should be here by now.'

'Not yet, Sturmbannführer. I ordered them for eight. There are still fifteen minutes to the hour.'

'Well, let's hope they're not late.'

For a few minutes the two officers stood side by side under the white camouflage sheets which covered the vehicles.

'Have you breakfasted yet, Schlank?'

'Not yet. I'll go after the air drop. What about you?'

'I've had no time,' Peiper told him. 'I'm off now to see how the surgeons are coping. They've been at it all night long.'

'None of us has slept much and you probably not at all,' said Schlank. 'You drive yourself too hard, you know.'

'It's a hard war, Schlank. It has been from the first day we entered this terrible country. It's a bloodsucker, a leech, this Russia. It sucks us dry. It really is a frightening thing just to look at the atlas. To see how tiny is our Europe compared to this giant of a country which we will conquer, one day. It's terrifying.'

Then, as if afraid that he had allowed his deepest feelings to show, Peiper turned abruptly away and hurried down the steep cliffs to the hospital area.

Orderlies were clearing away the last traces of the night's work. The air still held the stink of hospitals - the smell of disinfectant and fear- but the equipment was packed away. Peiper looked around him and saw a line of bodies along the wall of the tent. A sergeant noticed his glance.

'We lost twenty-eight. Forty others have been reported as having died in the night. There are about five others who won't make it past midday. It was a waste of time operating on such hopeless cases, but the doctor insisted. I thought a pain-killing overdose would have been a better solution, but the doctor fought to save them. He's sleeping now. He gave me orders to be ready to march at eight. We're nearly ready now, Sturmbannführer.'

'Thank you - ah, aircraft. That will be the air drop.'

Peiper hurried outside, waded through the snow of the steep cliffs to stand with Schlank as a chain of ten square-winged JU 52s circled above the camp site at about five hundred feet. Schlank pulled a Very pistol from his pack, checked the cartridges, inserted two and fired them. A brilliant white light hung suspended and below it blazed a fiery red flare. The leading JU waggled its wings. Bundles came flying through the air. Some with, some without a parachute. They fell into the snow. Nine aircraft, their mission accomplished, then flew back westwards. The Staffel commander's plane levelled out, dived to less than a hundred feet, flattened out and throttled back to just below stalling speed.

'He's checking the ground,' explained Schlank. 'He's going to land. Oh, oh...' There was a long period of silence. 'Come on, come on - done it,' he cried as the metal machine rolled through a cloud of snow flung up by its own propellers and then stopped. Groups of men jumped out and ran towards Peiper and Schlank.

'*Servus* Otto,' the leading man greeted the Luftwaffe Lieutenant.

'Good God. *Gruss di*' Willi.' He turned to Peiper and explained. 'These are Luftwaffe medical officers. Permit me to introduce my brother, Hauptmann Willi Schlank. Willi - Sturmbannführer Peiper.'

The two men saluted formally and then shook hands.

'Good of you to come' - Peiper had no small talk.

'Glad to be of some use.' Willi was another who had difficulty with words.

'How many wounded can you take?'

'Depends on whether they're lying, sitting or mobile.'

'Lying. '

'Stretchers take up more space. Can they lie on the floor? They'll need plenty of blankets, it's very cold in the machine. Without stretchers and packing them in - fifty. On stretchers - thirty.'

'Then we'll take them off the stretchers. Runner.'

'Sturmbannführer. '

'Tell the senior medical officer to begin loading the worst cases. No stretchers. The plane will hold fifty.'

Turning back to the Luftwaffe captain, Peiper asked whether there would be any space for walking wounded. Five - perhaps, ten, no more. They had to have orderlies and nurses to tend the wounded.

'Nurses?' questioned Peiper. 'You mean women?'

'Of course, Herr Sturmbannführer. Permit me to introduce Sister Gertrude.'

96

Peiper looked at the bundled shape in the uniform that stood before him. There was nothing to show that this was a woman, not until she flung back her parka hood to show the coiled plaits at either ear.

'Sister Gertrude.' Peiper bowed over the outstretched hand. 'Why do you risk yourself in this way?'

'We are all in the war together, Herr Sturmbannführer. There is no place safe anymore. The Front is everywhere. German cities are targets. Also I came to see Otto- Leutnant Schlank. We are to be married on our next leave - in April. *Servus* Otto,' she finished softly.

'Oh forgive me.' Peiper blushed like a schoolboy. 'You will want to be together or,' as he turned towards Schlank, 'do you want to go back with the aeroplane? I can order you to go.'

'Thank you Sturmbannführer.' Schlank was firm in his resolve. But no. We've come so far. It's only a matter of days before this mission ends and then Gertrude and I will be together again.'

'Your decision,' affirmed Peiper. 'Right, how's the loading coming on?'

He gnawed on a dry biscuit and drank bitter ersatz coffee as he watched the wounded being loaded. Each man was muffled up with blankets. Before he was loaded a Luftwaffe doctor pulled down the blanket and looked at the face of the patient. At a gesture he authorised the boarding or, with a negative wave of his hand, sent the man back to the Kampfgruppe.

'Those who won't survive the flight are not taken. It's a waste of space otherwise,' Willi Schlank whispered to him. 'Ah,' he said as he saw the MO waving to show that loading was completed. 'They can take ten walking wounded. I'll say my farewells now.'

The Luftwaffe medical team entered the corrugated fuselage of the JU 52, the idling engines roared into life, clouds of powdered snow almost hid the green-painted machine and then rolling, swaying, groaning and whining, the overloaded Junkers rolled forward, was spun round and then driving through the tracks which it had carved in its landing struggled to gain power for the take-off. At the end of a long, long run light finally showed below the undercarriage wheels. She was airborne. The plane circled, waggled her wings and straightened up to make a course for base.

All eyes were fixed on the German transport. No one saw the little Russian Yak fighter which dived out of the red sun and with a series of short bursts riddled the transport plane from tail to engine. The huge machine swung wildly, the port engine burst into flames. The plane climbed, dipped and swerved again as the Russian fighter poured burst after burst into it. The Yak climbed high into the sun, the pilot delighted with the ease of his early morning 'kill'. His victim seemed as if it were about to land on the snow tracks from which it had lifted off only moments earlier.

Schlank watched in horror. 'The landing speed is too high. He'll crash.' At less than a hundred feet altitude the aircraft suddenly turned over, flew upside down straight and level for a second or two and then plunged into the ground. There was a huge, soft whooping sound, a sudden surge of heat from the billowing flames and black smoke rose straight into the air. The heat of the fire beat back all rescue attempts. No one could have survived the bullets, the crash and the fire.

'My dear Schlank- ' Peiper began.

'It's all right, Sturmbannführer. He's not the first brother that this war has cost me. I've lost comrades too, who were closer to me than brothers, even closer than Gertrude. I hope she died quickly...Now it's all gone. All my future gone in that stinking, burning aircraft.'

There was nothing that could be done.

'Battalion runners to me.'

The young men reported to Peiper.

'My compliments to unit commanders. We move out at 10.30 hours. The time is now 09.35. O Group at ten. Right, away you go.'

The O Group was brief. Peiper outlined the route back and gave details of the march ahead of them. The 320th would move in the centre. The wounded and the Div commander would be placed between the still active companies. The column would be headed by a squad of tanks. Other armour and half-tracks would guard the flanks. SPs would have a roving commission and would deploy quickly to meet any threat. The flank units would be spread like a fan on either side of the 320th column. Bounds were set at which halts would be made for tanking up, changing drivers and issuing hot tea. Accurate aircraft recognition was essential to prevent the column being surprised as it rolled towards Zmiyev.

The aeroplane fire had lost its fiercest heat when Schlank went to say farewell to his bride and his brother. Some ten paces from the still burning wreck he halted, saluted, prayed silently, crossed himself and returned to the half-track in which he rode.

Peiper was the last to leave the area. His eyes took in every detail. The burning aircraft, the rough cross marking the mass grave in the snow under which now over sixty of the 320th lay. He gazed at the trampled and bloodied slush already freezing over, and on the far side of the Donets saw the shattered bits and pieces of panje carts, the dead horses - shot to prevent the Russians using them - and the skid marks on the eastern bank where the 320th's self-propelled guns had been deliberately driven into the river.

'Driver- rejoin the column and take me to my panzer.'

Kampfgruppe Peiper was on its way back to Krasnaya Polyana.

Chapter 12

In the debriefing hut of the advanced airfield at Rubshova, just to the east of Izyum, the pilot of the Yak was recounting the story of his 'kill.'

'I was carrying out a recce to find some group of Siberians that have got lost or something, when suddenly there was this big Nemetski kite taxi-ing along the ground. Dark green against the snow; it was absolutely distinct. I didn't need to see the fascist crosses to know it was one of theirs.' The pilot was excited. He was reliving the encounter.

'I came out of the sun just as he gained height and I swung in a tight curve left to right and peppered him. There was no upper fuselage gunner.

'His port engine caught fire. I did a flip over because I thought he was trying to land so I gave him some more bursts. He turned over onto his back, crashed and caught fire. It's a "kill" all right. An outright one - not a possible - and it's all mine. The wreck will be on the west bank of the Donets just west of Tardevka.'

'Thank you, comrade.' The elderly Intelligence Officer knew that the enthusiasm of inexperienced pilots often caused them to claim victims, which they had not 'killed.'

'Go out again, find your "kill". Locate it and then bring me the exact references.'

An hour later the Yak pilot was back.

'No doubt at all. Just where I said. Here,' and he located the place on a map. I think I found the missing Siberians, too. There's a column moving across country in the direction of Zmiyev.'

Lipski looked at the Corporal of the Siberian Rifles who stood rigid at attention before him.

'I expected you to be here before this, you know, Comrade. Also, I should have expected that you would have given warning that a fascist clique was running the Rifle Regiment. The Party lost a lot of men because we had no prior warning. You've failed the Party and me, you know that? Well, you'll not get full Party membership. Well not yet anyway. Work hard and I shall recommend you myself. Right now, tell me again.'

Slowly, as in a dream, Corporal Bubnov of 3rd Battalion - a secret informer for the NKVD, an agent planted among his regimental comrades and, therefore, a traitor to them - repeated his story.

How he had left his sleeping comrades and how he had struck back into the Soviet lines there to unite, eventually, with Lipski's group.

The officers of the Siberian Regiment - 'fascist officers', he was sharply reminded, one had to get the terminology correct for the writer who was taking down the statement- well, they had had an O Group in Lukovaya and had decided to march to Krasnaya Polyana where the Regiment would surrender to the Germans.

'Unit morale?' queried Lipski.

'Very good. The men support the fascist officers,' replied Corporal Bubnov, 'and each man has a surrender pass for when they go over to the Nemetski.'

'Are you sure they will head for Krasnaya Polyana?'

'Yes Comrade Major. The Regiment will move soon so as to be in position near the village of Krasnaya Polyana and will wait for full daylight before it goes over tomorrow.'

'Right. Then we shall get to Krasnaya Polyana today and prepare a reception for the mutinous bastards. Runner, O Group in five minutes.'

When the NKVD officers and NCOs were assembled, Lipski briefed them. He touched upon the use by the Siberians of dum-dum bullets and cited the death of Major Arseev as an example of that crime. Patiently the group waited. The Comrade Major would come to the important details of the mission in good time.

'We move out as quickly as possible for Krasnaya Polyana and relieve the Red Army unit there. From all accounts it seems they're a dozy shower. They've left a bridge there in the hands of the fascists. We don't know exactly where our line runs in that area but we shall take over the sector, attack the fascists and then wait for the Siberians to come. They will throw down their arms thinking they are surrendering to the Germans. Instead they will be walking into our machine guns. Try to take the officers alive. Particularly the traitor Marenko and a Lieutenant Koszov. He seems to be some sort of ringleader. The rest we can kill. We'll move from this place to Skripoi and then across country to Krasnaya Polyana. At best speed we should do it in six hours. Ready to move out in thirty minutes.'

Punctual to the minute, the NKVD column was ready. Lipski climbed into his Zis near the head of the column. Not quite at the head. In front of his staff car were four motor cyclists. Horns blaring, headlights blazing, they drove at high speed. At the sound all units on the road halted and pulled over. The NKVD column, demanding and receiving absolute priority, raced up the Skripoi road en route to Krasnaya Polyana.

Dawn stand-to in the Siberian camp brought no attack. 3rd Battalion reported a Corporal Bubnov as absent from his Company and it was accepted without question that the silent, introspective NKVD had deserted to go back home. There had been other losses during the night. Five men had taken their own lives. None knew whether it was the shame of their betrayal of Russia that had driven them to suicide. Was it, perhaps, a knowledge that they would never get back to Siberia again or was it the terrible 'Siberian Kiss' - the sweeping, all consuming, destroying neurosis which the loneliness of the eastern wilderness bred within the soul of each and every one of them, and which often drove men to suicide or drink.

The Companies of 3rd Battalion, forming the advance guard, waited silently until the detachment which had been detailed to guard the flanks had moved out. The Regiment was ready to march.

'The Siberians will advance,' Marenko shouted. 'The objective is Krasnaya Polyana. Forwards.' The tall Riflemen stepped off. 'I don't like their silence,' the Colonel said, turning to his aide.

'Nor do I, Colonel. There's something wrong. A song should help,' and turning round he shouted in a high voice, 'Comrades, a song to lighten the journey.'

Four voices broke into a Red Army chant. It was drowned in a barrage of whistles and shouts. A single tenor voice began a song, long forbidden by the Party. The march of the Tsarist Siberian Rifles. It was a song which they all knew and which was remembered more for its melody and harmony that for its words. No one had sung it in the open, publicly, since 1917. The tenor voice sang on and on until it reached the chorus.

For God, and Tsar and Russia we'll fight on till life is spent,
We are the Tsar's Siberians, the Baikal Regiment.

Suddenly like the breaking of a dam came a thundering as the whole column took up the words of the reprised chorus. The voices of tenors, baritones, basses and those with no voice to boast of blended in harmony as the forbidden words to a forbidden song rose and echoed through the clear, cold air.

The men stepped out, marching briskly, proud of their Regiment, proud to be Siberians, proud of the freedom that the name implied.

'They're in good heart again, Colonel.' Marenko nodded happily.

His Regiment was on the road to Krasnaya Polyana.

Chapter 13

Hennecke's group was on full alert as the advance guard of Peiper's column roared into Zmiyev. When the Sturmbannführer had entered the house in which Hennecke had his headquarters, the reason was explained.

'There's been a lot of movement here today,' Hennecke began. 'A mass of infantry - I thought they were Guards by the look of them, about two battalions strong. Bloody big blokes all of them. They marched through here less than an hour ago. I'm surprised you didn't see any sign of them on your way up. From the look of them they were assault troops. There was no unit transport, not even a single cart. They carried the lot and they marched through here singing like an opera chorus. One of them must have dodged the column. We found him when a recce was made after the Ivans had marched through and away. He had a surrender leaflet on him and I think he wants to stay with us. I'm not sure, though. None of my blokes have that much Russian. They all know the usual "hands up, come out", you know, basic military Russian.'

'Don't worry about that,' Peiper assured him. 'I've got interpreters. I've even got some Ivans who went over to the 320th. We'll soon find out who that lot were. Did you see which way they were heading?'

'They took the northern road towards Krasnaya Polyana but, of course, they could always cut across country westwards to Merefa. I'm not certain.'

'Anything else?' Peiper asked.

'Yes, there's been an unusual amount of air activity. Their aircraft have been active all day and one of our Luftwaffe recce planes reported a big armoured column moving north about ten kilometres to the east of us.'

Peiper assessed the Intelligence. 'Right, very good. None of the things reported represents an immediate threat.' He began to work out the sequence of events in his mind. He had seen no signs of any enemy, other than the trampled snow of marching infantry. Since the loss of the JU earlier in the day he had heard and seen nothing alarming.

'We'll rest here for a short while,' he told Hennecke and then turning to his adjutant ordered reports on the state of the wounded and the other men of the 320th. He knew his own men. Tired they might be, but they could still keep going long after other mobs had stopped. He didn't have to worry about his battalion. It was the other showers that concerned him. Half an hour later the reports were in. The men on whom operations had been performed were the worst off. Two seriously wounded, non-operation cases, had died during the journey. The 320th needed a rest. Its men were in a state of post battle, cold weather shock. Peiper made his decision. Although it was only a couple of hours drive to Krasnaya Polyana, the time was past midday. Within a few hours it would be dark. Better to quarter here for the night and begin with an early start on the morrow.

'We shall stay overnight here. Occupy only streets on an east-west axis. Use only the room facing the street so that if any light shows then it won't be seen by the enemy. Not that any light will show. I want a tight blackout. Cooking will be by field kitchens only and they will be driven into houses. Cooking will take place inside the houses. There will be no open fires. Double sentries to be set. All vehicles will be fully camouflaged. One hundred per cent alertness.'

The young commander went on to explain that at five in the morning he would call forward from Krasnaya Polyana the soft skin column and the medical officers in the rearguard detachment. Leaving only No 13 Company to keep the bridgehead, the remainder of the rearguard would drive down to Zmiyev escorted by the Divisional Defence Platoon. If the column from Krasnaya Polyana moved at five it should reach Zmiyev at daybreak. An hour to check on the wounded and to redistribute the men of 320th and the return journey could be undertaken and should be completed before midday.

Having been told that they were staying overnight the men of the Kampfgruppe worked with a will. It was already three in the afternoon and it needed only an hour to full darkness. When that time came there must be no chink of light, no smell of smoke to betray the presence in Zmiyev of the German units. A few hours later only the watchful sentries were awake. In hovels and huts the Germans thawed out. They endured the tormenting itch of lice and other vermin; the pain that accompanies the thawing out of frost-bitten fingers and toes; forgot the heavy dull ache of constipation - pleased to endure all those things to escape for just a few hours from the terror of the cold.

In the house which held the officers of 6th Red Army Intelligence Department, Colonel Satrushkin was working on a puzzling question - what was important about Krasnaya Polyana? There was something going on there, but he could see no reason for the activity.

First there had been the sudden attack by the SS days ago when some sort of armoured detachment had attacked the local Red Army garrison in the place. That SS unit was probably Peiper's detachment which partisans had reported had left the Alexeyeva Kolkhoz. But why should a skilled commander and a strong Kampfgruppe be sent rushing southwards into a void? It could not be to rescue the dying remnants of the 320th Division. No, it could not be that. There was no military advantage to be gained by wasting a fine formation of first class troops to bring out what was really, at best, a shattered remnant of a second-class division.

Satrushkin checked his files. No report on the whereabouts of the 320th had been received for two days. Not since the Siberian Riflemen, Marenko's regiment, had gone into the attack. Since there were no further reports from Marenko then this must mean that the fragments of the 320th had been wiped out and that the Siberians were now resting out of the Line.

But whose were the columns that had been reported from aerial reconnaissance squadrons? There was some sort of activity - a marching column which had passed through Zmiyev and was reported to be heading up the road to Krasnaya Polyana. Here was another report of a second column of vehicles moving on Zmiyev and which, from its location, must be another unit of 6th Red Army. It, too, must be heading for Krasnaya Polyana, for if it moved farther to the west then it would be trespassing on the territory of 1st Guards Army. Then there was that third column of armour and trucks which had cut across the boundaries of two Army Corps at Skripoi and was reported to be moving across country towards Krasnaya Polyana. Three columns and none of them identified. All heading for the same place.

Why, why? There was nothing there. Militarily, the Germans were pulling back around Kharkov. The STAVKA of the South Western Front had ordered 6th Army's main thrust to be made at Rogan, miles to the north of Krasnaya Polyana. Yet there were three columns heading for the latter place and he was not in wireless contact with any of them. And where the hell was Peiper?

Satrushkin was concerned. The moves were illogical. There was no balance in them. They were uncoordinated and his being out of wireless contact with them meant that the movement of the columns was uncontrolled. The Colonel decided he would raise the doubts he felt during the nightly review of the military situation. Other officers might call him an old woman for such fears. After all, what were a couple of columns heading for an unimportant village, when an offensive was in operation involving nearly one and a half million men? Of course, Satrushkin considered, Peiper might be recceing the ground for the opening of a new German south-eastern drive designed to take pressure off Kharkov. From all reports the madman Hitler had ordered his SS to hold the city to the last, and they, his Praetorian guard, would be certain to obey him without question. Yes, concluded Satrushkin, the SS will soon mount a diversionary attack south-eastwards, spearheaded by Peiper. But the question remained - who were the three columns? He would clear it with his superiors at STAVKA. Always guard yourself, he thought.

Chapter 14

Lipski drove his NKVD group hard. The lorried infantry had been reinforced by Secret Police detachments taken from rear echelon duties. His handful of tanks had been increased by commandeering those of Army units and by replacing the crews with his own men. Close-support artillery had been added to the Battle Group's strength so that it was a well armed fighting force which, before midday, roared up to the TAC HQ of 2nd Battalion 684th Regiment, the Army detachment holding the line outside Krasnaya Polyana.

'Please report to your commander that I have arrived,' Lipski told the battalion adjutant, 'and that I should like a meeting with him as soon as it can be arranged.'

Minutes later the infantry Colonel came into the room where Lipski was waiting. There was the usual exchange of courtesies and then the question, 'What can I do for you, Comrade Major?'

Lipski decided on a bold lie.

'STAVKA of the south-western Front intends to make Krasnaya Polyana the start line for a thrust towards Kharkov. The operation is, of course, absolutely secret. You understand? It is clear that your 2nd Battalion cannot recapture Krasnaya Polyana without help. That help is my group. You will launch a frontal attack against the fascists holding the place. The whole point of the operation is to hold their attention to the front while my group comes in from the flank and captures the place - What?' he burst out as the Colonel interrupted.

'You are asking us to be targets in a shooting gallery, Comrade Major. We've been in action since Stalingrad. This is supposed to be a quiet sector of the Front. I must formally - '

Lipski silenced him with a gesture. 'I am not asking you to do me a favour. I am ordering you in the Party's name to carry out your duty. Every bloody Army unit I come across gives me the same chat. They're all tired and under strength. It's not shortage of numbers, it's lack of Communist morale. It's defeatism. I'll sort it out, don't you fear, and all those who have been infected will be destroyed. Do I make myself clear?'

The Colonel nodded miserably. He knew that NKVD terror struck regiments and destroyed great numbers by summary execution. Near Kiev in the autumn of '41 a whole infantry division of Ukrainians who had refused to go up the Line had been surrounded by the NKVD. The execution squads had shot every man in the division from Commander to a drummer boy recruit. The blood bath had lasted a week. And that had not been the only example of such butchery. If the politicals could wipe out a whole division then the shooting of the few officers of 2nd Battalion would be no problem. The Colonel understood Lipski very well indeed; attack or be shot - those were the alternatives.

'I should like to check with Regiment and with Division,' he began.

'You make any move to contact anybody and you will be dealt with now; here and now. I told you it was a secret mission. Are you stupid or something? It's secret, so you don't go around blabbing to people and asking silly bloody questions. I shall assign one of my people to you. He will monitor your every move. Every word you utter. One word out of place and you go West. But not alone! Oh no! Your family; wife, children, mother, father - anybody even distantly related to you, will suffer. Do you understand now?'

The Colonel tried desperately to maintain his stand.

'There should be some authorisation. An order to quote for the War Diary. Something in writing- '

The buzzing of the field telephone interrupted him. It was Regimental Headquarters on the line.

'Yes?' he barked into the mouthpiece.

'Regiment here. A message from Colonel Satrushkin of Army HQ. He's the Intelligence Officer there. Satrushkin says that something is going to happen at Krasnaya Polyana. Collaborate with all our units in meeting the situation, whatever it is. Absolute discretion. Message ends.'

The Colonel turned to Lipski.

'Comrade Major. Forgive me. Army Intelligence has confirmed that something is going to happen here. I am to co-operate in every way. Comrade Major, I would ask you to accept my deepest apologies and to excuse my attitude. It's tiredness, you know.'

Lipski was baffled at the development but did not show it. Luck was with him. He'd have that Siberian bastard and his bloody officers. Nothing could fail him now. The Commissar flung in his trump card. He was a good judge of men. He knew that the Colonel could be influenced by concessions made to his men.

'I'll tell you what I shall do,' he began in a conciliatory tone 'When the attack is over, I shall come back here and write out not only the complete authorisation but also a citation or two and a recommendation that will get your battalion out of the Line for rest. How does that strike you?' He continued in a confidential tone, 'It's only a mock attack really. We are not even having a barrage. Really your role is to make a demonstration. That is all. One more effort and then you'll be out of the Line, at least for a couple of weeks. You agree? Right, it's 14.00 hours. Give my boys an hour to reach position. My man with you will tell you when to set off and when to stop and come back here. Couldn't be simpler, could it?'

Shortly after 15.00 hours there was a crackle in the earphones of the NKVD signaller whom Lipski had left at 2nd Battalion's headquarters.

'The Comrade Major reports himself in position. Your battalion,' he told the Colonel, 'is to begin its attack in ten minutes time and is to continue to move towards Krasnaya Polyana until ordered to stop. The Major wishes you good luck. Message ends.'

The 2nd Battalion took up no rigid formation for the assault. Rifle Companies were in loose order and formed two extended lines. At the Colonel's waved hand the first line stepped off. There was no thrill of battle, no enthusiasm. All ranks knew that it was going to be a sticky, bloody job. They were living targets. Still, it shouldn't last too long. It would be dark in an hour.

The SS men of the rearguard stared incredulously at the sight of the straggling lines wading silently through the snow towards them.

'They're not making an attack. They are just making a gesture. The poor sods must be some sort of bait.' The mind of the young Lieutenant commanding the Divisional Defence Platoon considered what sort of dodgy trick the spiritless infantry assault could betoken.

'Right lads. Wait until two hundred metres then blast them.'

The Russian infantry trudged on anticipating with every dreary step the fusillade that must come. Those who marched in the front rank of the right flank Company could see the black muzzles of a Flak Vierling, a four-barrelled, cannon-shell firing, anti-aircraft weapon, as its barrel swung ominously, traversing across the short front. The infantry saw the movement stop. The gun pointed straight at them. They knew that when those four barrels opened up the rain of cannon shells would blow them all away. Still the line trudged on through the deep snow, the faces of the soldiers hidden in clouds of steamy breath as they panted with the effort. A voice began to pray aloud, '*Nash Otets...*' The opening words of the Lord's Prayer were blanketed out by the shattering roar of gunfire as the German line opened up. The range was exactly two hundred metres. The men of the SS Defence Platoon were well armed, skilful veterans, holding a good defensive position. Like corn to the sickle the Red Army men fell. The first rank vanished almost completely and huge gaps were torn in the second wave.

'Where are those scabby Politicals?' the Colonel demanded, his face blanching as he saw his Companies wither and perish. Even as he asked that question there was in the rear of the SS Platoon a thunder of gunfire and the NKVD troops burst into the huts which made up the hospital area. Lipski's group had struck the Defence Platoon from the back. The fighting while it lasted was bitter and intense. Close quarter combat ended the fray as Soviet entrenching tools gashed and tore SS faces and bodies.

'Line the bastards up,' Lipski ordered, when all resistance had ended, 'and let's have a report. But first tell the 2nd Battalion to return to their own lines. We don't want those infantry clods hanging about here.'

From the reports received it was clear that complete surprise had been achieved. The Germans had concentrated totally on the frontal assaults. Sixty-two SS men had been killed. The remaining ninety seven, chiefly drivers and medical personnel, had been taken prisoner. Losses to the NKVD troops had been fifteen killed and eight wounded. Lipski neither knew nor cared how many men the infantry battalion had lost. He gave instructions on the disposal of those who had been captured.

'Take our wounded away and patch them up. Remove them to one of *our* hospitals not to an Army one. Now for the Fascist Nemetski. Those who are drivers dig out their eyes. If they believe in God then he will let them see again. Blind the first one in front of all the others so they know what is to be their fate. When the last one is done, knife the bastards to death.

'The wounded you will hang from trees. Pour petrol into the jackboots and while they are strangling to death on the rope, set fire to their feet. The medical ones we shall give a Lenin's coffin. Tie them up and pour water over them. It's freezing already. They'll be well and truly iced in by dark.

111

'Now for the officers. Peg them out. They are to be castrated and their throats choked with their own balls. Let the bastards bleed to death.

'The object is to psychologically dominate the enemy and in particular the SS. When their regimental headquarters receives no report from the garrison here they'll send out a patrol and those men will see the lesson which we teach to those who dare to invade the great Soviet Fatherland. Soon the SS will fear to be taken alive and we shall have won the psychological battle.'

'Should we interrogate the prisoners first, Comrade Major?' asked a young lieutenant.

'Superfluous.' Lipski rejected the idea. He was not concerned with stray pieces of information torn from a German soldier by Standard Interrogation Procedure No. 4. Lipski wanted to catch the Siberians and to lay their bodies alongside the SS, to make it seem as if the Riflemen had committed the atrocity. He knew that once the word was passed among the SS units that the Siberians had murdered and mutilated hospital staff, then not one of them who fell into SS hands would ever live to see a prison camp.

Lipski settled himself down in what had been the living caravan of the senior medical officer. He looked around him. They lived well did those SS swine. Carpet on the floor. Doubtless stolen from a Russian family. Slowly he deciphered the words on the bottle of drink that stood on the table. 'Slivovitz' - a spirit, like vodka. Stolen, of course. There was champagne too. Obviously looted. He opened a bottle of Moët et Chandon across whose label was the stamped legend, 'Reserved for the German Armed Forces.' Lipski thought the champagne to be insipid muck, just like the decadent scum who drank it. He opened a small medical chest and began to examine the surgical implements which lay inside it. He felt the edge of a bladed scalpel. A thought came over him. He'd always wanted to be a doctor; to carry out an operation. Now he had patients galore on whom he could experiment, to demonstrate his obvious skill with a surgeon's tools.

'Bring in a prisoner; a driver. Anyone will do.'

A few seconds later the bound figure of a sergeant of Divisional Transport was flung in through the caravan door.

'Kneel him down there,' Lipski ordered the two NKVD men who held the prisoner between them. 'Hold his head up. You,' he addressed one of the escort, 'hold his upper lid away from the eye ball.'

The Commissar took up the scalpel and swiftly cut off the German NCO's right eyelid. The sergeant screamed. High pitched and terror laden. His unlidded right eye stared white as he threshed between his guards.

The next incision was less swift and neat because of the SS man's violent struggles, but it was done at last.

'I first saw our Spanish comrades do this to the Fascists during the Civil War there. They had some charming novelties. What surprised me then, and does now, about this operation, is how little blood is shed.' Lipski casually smashed the sergeant across the head to stop his screams. He picked up the scalpel again and leaning forward so that he stared into the lidless eyes said softly and in bad German, 'The lights go out.' Slowly he pushed the scalpel into the sergeant's left eye. There was a thin, gushing stream of black fluid as he withdrew the probe. The screaming which had filled the small caravan suddenly stopped. The German sergeant had died of shock.

'Pity that. I should like to have seen his reaction to being without sight. Show his body to the others. Blind them. Don't worry about cutting off their eyelids, just stab them in the eyes. Start the other things too. We must be ready to move soon so as to be in position when the mutinous Siberians come in. They should be coming over tomorrow morning. Right, start on the SS swine now.'

Lipski paid no heed to the frightened screams that sounded in the area. The men of the SS regiment holding the line on the far side of the river would do nothing until the daily report signal was overdue. So he had no need to worry about interference from the Germans. The Russian infantry battalion, if they heard the screams, would decide on discretion. So his men were free from interference.

The Commissar was soon engrossed in magazines that he had found in the caravan. A great number contained untouched pictures of young German girls, completely nude. What he was reading were naturist magazines, but Lipski saw them only as sexual stimuli and felt the old familiar urge as he looked at the firm breasts and the downy pubic hair of the young teenage girls. The Commissar promised himself that in occupied Germany he would feast on the virgin flesh of young, very young, Teuton girls. His erotic thoughts were suddenly interrupted by his adjutant coming to report that the last mutilation had been carried out. Pausing to look just once more at the full firm breasts and blond pussy hair of one young maiden, Lipski left the caravan to prepare his Command for all-round defence and for the arrival of the Siberians in the morning.

113

Chapter 15

Shortly after 10.00 hours on the morning following the massacre of the SS detachment, Marenko went forward with his adjutant to the TAC HQ of the 2nd Battalion 684th Regiment.

'We are under orders to capture Krasnaya Polyana,' he began. A gesture from the infantry commander silenced him.

'I know all about that. Army HQ suspects that something big is brewing up there. One unit went in to take it yesterday. My own battalion was cut to pieces making a demonstration to draw the German fire. I don't know if that mob that went in yesterday captured the place or not. Certainly, they've sent down no patrols to liaise with us and so I suspect that their attack failed. They left a man, a signaller, with me but he took off during the night. The Nemetski up there are bloody good. I wish you blokes luck.'

The Colonel asked no question of Marenko - on an operation seemingly as secret as this one, it didn't pay to be too inquisitive. He still had Lipski's warnings in his ears. Marenko, for his part, was pleased with the news. In some mysterious way the road forward was open. There was no need for concealment or smoke screens. His men could just march straight up the road and be taken captive.

What the commanding officer of 2nd Battalion made of the Siberians cannot be known, but he watched, nonplussed, as Riflemen pioneers tramped past him carrying placards. The wording on them was in German. The battalion Intelligence Officer spoke that language and the Colonel called him over.

'What do the words read?' he asked.

'That big one says, "German brothers, do not shoot; we are all comrades" and the little ones read, "Peace", "Brotherhood", "Comradeship". What do you make of it, Colonel?'

'Damned if I know. Some fiendish NKVD trick, I suppose. That lot last night were NKVD.'

Marenko marshalled his Siberians as if for a parade. The home-made banners were held high, dominating the centre of the first line of soldiers. The smaller placards with their one-word messages dotted the front line. By 11.50 hours everything was ready. The ranks of Riflemen stood silent. Marenko marched to the front of his regiment, drew his sabre and turned to face his men.

'For Russia,' he cried. 'For Freedom. Shoulder arms. By the centre, Siberian Rifle Regiment Baikal, advance.'

The lines were ruler straight as the tall, overcoated men marched across the trampled snow. At about two hundred metres from the defensive positions at Krasnaya Polyana, the dead of the previous evening's attack by 2nd Battalion lay thick on the ground. They were clearly visible. There had been no snow for a whole day. Stolidly, not seeing the cramped hands and frost-blackened faces, the Riflemen marched until Marenko waved his sabre again. The long lines halted.

'Plant your rifles muzzle down in the snow. Lieutenant Bablik, shout out in German that we wish to surrender. Now everybody, raise your hands in the air.'

The lines stood silent, brown-overcoated figures sharply silhouetted against the white snow and less than two hundred metres from the muzzles of the NKVD rifles.

'The God of my Fathers,' Lipski exulted, 'that is if I believed in Him, has delivered the enemy into my hands.' Then he said to the waiting men, 'Targets like this don't often come a fighting soldier's way. So make the most of this opportunity. Fire.'

The whole centre of Marenko's regiment vanished as if wiped away, but the units on the flanks, escaping the first shocking volume of fire, ran back for their rifles and with the inherited hunting skills of generations to aid them, soon took up positions from which they returned the fire of the NKVD men. A sudden cry rose and ran from man to man of the Rifles.

'They are not Nemetski. They are Soviet NKVD men. They are politicals. It's a trap. Death to the Red swine.'

Fury built within them. Fury that burnt and burnt at them until, almost spontaneously, the whole Siberian line rose and with bloodcurdling cries hurled itself forward against the positions in which Lipski's men were lying. There comes a point in every battle when the defenders realise that for all their weapons the enemy will overrun them. With that knowledge comes the knowledge that death is imminent. It is then that the weak begin to waver and turn away, that fire slackens and dies as the huge shapes of the attacking infantry loom up, menacing and, apparently, snorting fire. The NKVD troops, not veterans of battle as were the Siberians, began to waver.

The Riflemen overran the first positions in the snow and rolled over those to storm the houses. The politicals who offered to surrender were given a treatment known in the regiment as the 'Partition of Siberia'. One Rifleman held one political's arm. A second held the other. A third huge Siberian chopped the victim from crown to crotch with vicious strokes of the huge machete-type weapons which they carried.

Obsessed with the need to make the politicals suffer, the Siberians did not see the screen of tanks until a thunder of guns and the explosion of shells burst among them. To advance was to die and, despite their hate and the blood lust that was upon them, the Siberians were forced back, out of the hovels of Krasnaya Polyana and down the long, slight slope across which they had advanced, back in retreat towards the positions held by the 2nd Battalion.

'Shoot them, kill them,' Lipski exhorted his men. 'Wipe out the counter-revolutionaries. '

However hard the NKVD troops tried to carry out their commander's orders - and they killed a lot of Siberians - most of the Riflemen escaped into the shelter of the woods and there regrouped. Marenko, slightly wounded, had survived. Koszov, the loud-voiced Lieutenant, was among the fallen. The Regiment was bitter and angry and its soldiers, gathered under the trees, smoked and cried and swore revenge.

Sensing the mood of his men, Marenko ordered a renewal of the assault, but before it went in his best shots would snipe the political swine into a panic. Then, when they were really jumpy, the battered remnants of his Riflemen would crawl forward and rush the Red enemy. Patience was needed. Patience and the ability to lie for hours in the snow. Both of those attributes his men had. The first snipers went out. The remainder of the Regiment prepared itself to carry out a second attack, on the hour, as was laid down in Field Service Regulations for the Red Army; 1935. Old habits die hard.

Lipski checked the dead Siberians. He did not find Marenko but Koszov's corpse was brought in together with those of other subaltern officers. Pistol shots sounded in the village and on the snowy field. The NKVD executioners were shooting to death the Siberian wounded. Three-men teams - an officer and two privates checked each body. The wounded were shot before they could speak. Lipski wanted no evidence against him to be heard. The wounded were silenced for ever. One such team bending over a badly wounded Rifleman suddenly fell over and lay still. The air above the battlefield was filled with whistling and crackling sounds. There were cries for medical orderlies.

'What's happening?'

'The Siberians, Comrade Major. They must have forty or more snipers out there.'

'What are you doing against them?'

'Our best, Comrade Major, but those devils are trained and expert hunters. We can't locate them.'

'Can't you use tanks, flame throwers, artillery?'

'To do what, Comrade Major? We can see no targets to fire at.'

'So, we just sit here waiting to be killed?'

'I have the feeling, Comrade Major, that the sniping is of nuisance value only. The Siberians will attack again very soon.'

As if to confirm that belief a runner came trotting up to report that scouts in the skirmish line had seen the Siberians preparing for a fresh assault. Lipski repeated his simple orders. .

'Kill them all.'

Chapter 16

Those bloody Ivans, thought Peiper. The Sturmbannführer was annoyed. The Reds were jamming the radio frequencies. Something big must be in preparation. Some major troop movement, perhaps. Attempts by the signallers with his Kampfgruppe to contact their comrades with the SS rearguard in Krasnaya Polyana had been unsuccessful. The wireless operators in the village had not answered the calling up signs which his men had been sending out for hours. Nor was he in touch with Divisional Headquarters. If he had been it would have been a simple matter to ask for a patrol to be sent to Krasnaya Polyana with an order for the columns of lorries and ambulances to drive down to Zmiyev. But the bloody air waves were all jammed. Not one of his sets could contact anybody on the German side of the Line.

The Sturmbannführer had to make a quick decision. It was imperative that he move the Kampfgruppe without delay if he were to bring the 320th quickly into safety. He had been depending upon the doctors in the SS rearguard to help his own overworked staff under Dr Stranjc. And it was not just the medical teams that he needed but also the lorries and the ambulance columns to carry the wounded in less crowded conditions. The convoys should have reached him by daybreak. It was now long past that and time was speeding by.

'Try to contact the rearguard in Krasnaya Polyana and then see if you can raise Division,' he told the wireless operator on duty. Fifteen minutes later the reply came. Nobody was answering calls. The jamming was total, a complete black-out of communications, the signals officer explained. The Soviet interference might last a day or two. They might keep it up for a week. One never knew.

'Thank you. Well, it's obvious that we cannot wait for the lorries from the rearguard so we shall set off ourselves within half an hour. Runners, please inform unit commanders that we drive off in thirty minutes. Kampfgruppe Hennecke will form a recce detachment as we advance towards Krasnaya Polyana and that group will drive out in ten minutes time.'

Those instructions had been given at 08.00 hours. Now, at 10.30, with the whole group running smoothly across country, a runner had come in from Hennecke. Peiper jumped from his panzer onto the snowy road surface to receive the report.

'Kampfgruppe Hennecke reports,' began the young soldier gasping for breath.'

'Slow down lad; take a deep breath,' Peiper ordered. 'Get yourself calm. Ready? Now begin again.

'Sturmbannführer. Kampfgruppe Hennecke reports that fighting is going on around Krasnaya Polyana. A Russian infantry attack was being made against the place when I left to report to you, but it seemed that the attackers were being driven back. Groups of them were withdrawing into the trees, here,' and he pointed to a point on the map. 'Kampfgruppe Hennecke would like your instructions, please.'

Peiper considered. If there was fighting for Krasnaya Polyana the place must still be in German hands. He could advance across country towards the village but it was still necessary for his group to pass through the streets of the village if the vehicles were to reach the narrow river bridge across which they must pass.

'Unit commanders to me. Runner, stay here for a moment. You can take back to Obersturmführer Hennecke the decisions that we make here.

'Now gentlemen,' Peiper began when his officers were assembled 'the runner here from Hennecke's group reports fighting at Krasnaya Polyana. Our rearguard must be under pressure. I, therefore, intend to advance to support our men in the village by reinforcing them. Once we have linked with our rearguard then we and they shall form a shield between the Reds and the bridge. Behind this shield the 320th will cross the river.

'We shall move out now. Tactically disposed. As we approach Krasnaya Polyana the armour and half-tracks will advance in standard formation. I intend that we come in against the Reds in the wood here, enfilading them. While we hold their attention, and while they are trying to deal with us, the 320th will pass behind us into Krasnaya Polyana, across the bridge and into the 1st Battalion's sector.

'Then we shall carry out a fighting withdrawal, leap-frogging back. Any questions? No? Right, we move out in five minutes.'

The runner returned to Hennecke's group and behind him the battle squadrons of Peiper's group drove out to undertake the advance upon Krasnaya Polyana. Hennecke waved the Commander down and when the tank was halted scrambled up onto the turret.

'The Reds are making another attack against our rearguard in the village. See them there.' He pointed out the long line of

119

Siberians as they carried out the second attack of the morning. Peiper realised that his first plan had to be changed. He would not now attack the Reds in the woods. Instead he would come in behind the Siberians and crush them between his own vehicles and the SS defenders of Krasnaya Polyana.

'Panzer advance.' The vehicles drove in line ahead. At his signal they turned into extended line abreast so as to come in at the back of the Red infantry. Peiper detached part of his Command to move towards the woods and to begin a bombardment to hold down any lively defenders among the trees. He held back his main panzer line until the small group was in a position to bombard the trees and then waved his arm. The line of Panzer IV and half-track vehicles rolled across country to Krasnaya Polyana. The Siberians were caught like meat in a sandwich.

Relying only upon hand signals and Peiper's urgent pumping motion, the line of vehicles was brought into the charge. NCOs banged on the steel walls of the half-tracks to alert the Grenadiers inside them. They grasped their weapons, held hand grenades ready and prepared themselves for action. From his tank, located in the centre of the panzer line, Peiper checked and saw how his group was disposed. A wave brought the vehicles of No 2 Platoon into tighter grouping and soon the Sturmbannführer was satisfied that his armour was properly disposed. Each machine in the single extended line of tanks and personnel carriers was in its correct place and had begun to thrust into the back of the Siberians still plodding forward, trying to reach the politicals.

A runner brought Lipski the information that German armour was moving towards the village. The Commissar looked through his binoculars at the Kampfgruppe and saw first the detached unit facing the woods. Lipski swung his head and saw that the main German group was behind the attacking Siberians. It was clear that the fascists would overrun the Siberian traitors and would continue onwards into Krasnaya Polyana. His own course of action was clear. The politicals would be pulled out of the village. He could not risk his group being involved in a long and costly battle. All Lipski's actions since the Siberian mutiny had been made without authorisation from a higher source. On active service a certain casualty rate was inevitable, but a pitched battle with the SS would cause his group losses too great to be hidden. Some nosey bastard would be bound to ask embarrassing questions about the private vendetta he was engaged on. No; he must pull the group out of Krasnaya Polyana without achieving the ambition of destroying the Siberians. A plan suggested itself. He directed men to remove all the NKVD dead and to load them in trucks. No political must be left in the battle area. None of his group was to be found. When that was done he gave instructions for some of the Siberian dead to be brought forward and placed around the mutilated bodies of the SS as if they had all been killed in the fighting. It was crystal clear. When the fascists came upon the scene they would hold the Siberians responsible for the massacre. Perhaps, he reflected, he would not see the bastards butchered as he had hoped, but he knew for a fact that the Nemetski would make the Riflemen suffer.

'Let's go,' Lipski ordered and, pausing only to stuff inside his tunic a copy of the German Health and Beauty magazine, he led his men eastwards towards Shmarokva.

At a hand signal Peiper's tanks opened fire with cannon and machine gun. Another signal and the panzer closed up, changed formation into line ahead and drove towards the low buildings of Krasnaya Polyana. The German half-tracks still in line abreast hunted the groups of Siberians and shot them down as they ran back down the shallow slope towards the woods. The Riflemen's assault had been crushed. Then the half-tracks rejoined the panzer and the whole swept into the village expecting with every passing second to be greeted by the SS rearguard.

The emptiness of the place was unusual and disquieting. Peiper jumped from his tank, stood hands clasped behind his back considering the situation. He looked up at a sudden yelling. Grenadiers from the escort of half-tracks who had dismounted to sweep the village were shouting and screaming. Against all orders, against the requirements of discipline, they had not taken up fighting positions but were standing instead gathered in gesticulating groups. They had found their dead and mutilated comrades in the ice coffins. Seeing the dead, Peiper knew why there had been no response from this little outpost to his wireless signals.

'Sturmbannführer, we have found some more. Hanged and burned.'

Another voice shouted out, 'Christ Almighty, they've blinded this lot.' Then a high pitched scream, 'Good God, they've cut off the sergeant's eyelids.'

'Look at the Russian dead,' shouted another voice. 'They're all bloody Siberians. Primitive bastards. Well we've got Siberian prisoners. Let's do the same to them.'

'Stand still, all of you,' Peiper's voice rang out. 'Officers, get your men in hand. Get them to their posts. That Ivan infantry attack is not crushed yet. Concentrate on that. That's our first priority. Then we'll settle with the swine that did these mutilations. Right lads. Back to your posts. Runner, please have our Siberian prisoners and the interpreter sent to me.

'Lieutenant Schlank, you look ghastly. You're not used to Socialist humanity in this form are you?'

Schlank fought to control his twitching body and his shattered nerves.

'I'm looking for somebody. Someone whom I know - knew - in the rearguard.'

'Sturmbannführer,' a voice broke in, a voice filled with disbelief at the shocking things that it was witnessing. 'Sturmbannführer, come quickly. We've found the officers. The Red bastards have...' the voices tailed off.

'Stay here if you wish, Schlank, but I must go and see.'

'No,' the Luftwaffe lieutenant insisted. 'Perhaps the man whom I am seeking is among the group you are going to look at.'

The two men turned a corner to find neatly laid on the ground the pegged out, castrated bodies of the unit officers. Schlank looked uncomprehendingly. Then he screamed in horror and stumbling over some of the dead bodies flung himself across the corpse of a blond-haired young man. His arms embraced the frozen torso and he kissed the dead face. Peiper was shocked with embarrassment. This sort of girlish behaviour did not become a German officer; Schlank was breaking down in the presence of his subordinates.

'Back to your posts,' he ordered the nearest men. The Sturmbannführer stood over the Luftwaffe officer and ordered him to stand up. When Schlank did not respond Peiper grasped him by the shoulder and pulled with all his strength.

'Get up Schlank, we have work to do. Come on.' The young Luftwaffe officer was dragged forcibly from the dead body.

'What's the matter with you?' Peiper asked. 'You are behaving as if he and you had been...' A sudden light illuminated his mind. 'You're not a...?'

122

'Yes, I am a homosexual. Hansl here was my lover. I loved him.' Schlank's body shook with convulsive sobbing. 'Now even he has been taken from me. I'm completely alone. I have no one.'

'Schlank, I don't understand you. You have decorations for bravery. How can you be a queer?'

'Do you really think that homosexuals can't be brave, Sturmbannführer? Did you stop and wonder, ever, why I was so little upset when my brother and my fiancée were both killed in that plane crash. Well, did you?'

'Yes, Schlank, I did. I thought you were a cold, callous sod. I didn't know about this homo business.'

'Well, now you do know. My brother despised me, did you know that? Despised me for my weakness - well that's what he called it. It was he who told my parents that I was homosexual. It was they who chose a fiancée for me in the hope of bringing me back to the straight and narrow.

'It didn't work, of course. They even had me posted from one unit to another in order to part me from those other men whom I have loved. They needn't have bothered. The demands of war - crashes mostly - took care of those other friends of mine. Then I met Hansl. He and I have been together for only a few weeks. They, my parents and the others, didn't know about Hansl and I. You didn't guess either, did you? You didn't know that I volunteered to join this operation just to be with him. It wasn't bravery and it certainly wasn't a desire to help the war effort that inspired me. Just a desire to be with Hansl. Just one poor little poof waiting to be with another little poof. Shocking, isn't it?'

'Stop it, Schlank. This is nonsense. It's a court martial charge, you know that? What's the matter with you? What's wrong with girls anyway? I can't understand you lot. Stop your snivelling. We're going into action in a couple of minutes. Don't do anything stupid now, will you, like rushing out to take on all the Ivans single-handed. I've seen it happen to men who have lost good mates. Remember, you are not David and they're not Goliath.

'And don't do anything silly with your pistol, either. This operation has cost us enough men and I don't want to bury you, understand? So let's not have any dramatic suicide scenes. I'm trusting you now not to bugger things up with your pistol. OK? Now on to other things. Where the hell are those bloody Siberian prisoners?'

123

'They're coming, Sturmbannführer.' And indeed they were, driven forward crouching and flinching under a rain of blows from rifle butts and kicks from the SS guards. The prisoners were forced to group themselves round the German dead to view the mutilated corpses.

'Who's the senior man?'

'This officer - Captain Barik.'

'Interpreter!' Peiper's anger was frightening.

'Herr Sturmbannführer?' Lewinski, an Army man, did not use the Leibstandarte's mode of address when talking to a superior. '

'Ask that murdering bastard why his comrades should want to do this to a medical unit?'

There was a rapid exchange of words between Lewinski and Barik. The interpreter turned back to Peiper.

'He says that this is not the work of soldiers. It is the work of politicals. He says that the NKVD are responsible.'

'Of course he does,' Peiper interjected impatiently. 'Anything to evade the blame. Anyway, we can't think of this now. The sods in the wood who I think did this are making a fresh assault. Guard the prisoners. Keep them here. We'll drive off this lot attacking us and then we can channel the 320th across. Then we'll deal with these Siberian butchers.'

In an agony of hate and with black murder in their hearts, the soldiers of Peiper's Kampfgruppe settled down to fight off the new Siberian assault. It was a half-hearted affair. There was no fire in the attack. The lines advanced hesitatingly. There was doubt in every footstep. The iron resolve of the stalwart Riflemen was beginning to break. They had been shot at by Lipski and crushed by Peiper's armour. Now they were going in to face God alone knew what hurricane of fire. They had had enough.

The first line was halfway to the German positions. Not a shot had been fired but then, as if with a single accord, the assault wave fragmented. Men ran back towards the woods, knocking down those who strove to hold them to the assault. Let the officers go forward to find out what is happening, was the opinion of the men. We're tired of being targets in a shooting gallery. The Siberians knew that the Germans now held Krasnaya Polyana, and that theoretically the Nemetski should have welcomed them with open arms. Yet they had been fired on. It was a dodgy situation and the Riflemen were not prepared to offer their defenceless bodies as targets until the officers had established whether the surrender which the Regiment wished to make would be accepted or whether the Riflemen would have to fight on.

'Runner!'

'Sturmbannführer?'

'My compliments to General Postel. The 320th can now begin to pass behind us and over the bridge to our 1st Battalion's sector.'

The runner drove away. The slow convoy of lorries inched forward, their wheels following the path in the snow made for them by the tracks of the heavy panzer. The trucks groaned and grunted their way into and then through the narrow streets of hovels that made up the dismal village of Krasnaya Polyana. General Postel arrived in his staff car.

'I understood from you that there would be a main medical team here ready to attend my wounded. Where the hell is the main medical team? Are those quacks of yours perhaps more figments of the SS imagination? Are they? And by the way, I do not receive reports from other ranks - I expect messages to be brought to me via your aide-de-camp, but we'll let that pass. Where the hell are you taking me?'

Silently Peiper led the fur-coated General to the mutilated bodies of the officers of the medical team.

'Merciful God in Heaven.' Postel fumbled for words, his facility for the *bon mot* for once leaving him. He struggled to express himself - and failed. Stumbling and faltering, finally he grasped the shoulder of the young SS commander.

'My dear Peiper -' he began, but halted and turned away to return to his own headquarters, there to check on the passage of the lorries carrying the wounded of his Division across the little river.

Chapter 17

Lipski's NKVD group was settled in a small wood some way removed from Krasnaya Polyana, and as this was on higher ground there was a distant view of the wooden bridge over whose shuddering timbers the first lorries of wounded were crossing.

'Send a tank commander to me.'

'Certainly, Comrade Major.'

'Tell me,' Lipski asked when a young lieutenant had reported to him. 'Tell me. Do you think that you could smash that bridge? Stop the fascists from crossing?'

'Well,' began the young officer hesitatingly. 'It is a very small target. The light is poor and the range is well over two kilometres,' but then seeing the impatience in the Major's eyes, he went on, 'but I shall certainly do my very best; you can be sure of that, Comrade Major.'

'Right then. Don't sit about here chatting. Get out and begin the bombarding. Those swine are getting their lorries across in a steady stream and I want them stopped.

And it was true. There was an easy flow of vehicles. Road discipline, reinforced by the Divisional Traffic Police detachment accompanying the Battle Group, ensured a smooth flow. One vehicle only at a time was allowed on the rickety structure and while that lorry crossed at a slow and steady speed, another was already on the first timbers, its weight preventing an excessive vibration. The system was working well. Then the first shots from the NKVD tank began to fall. The tank gun was bracketing; ranging just over and just short of the target. One direct hit would smash the bridge completely. The sudden explosions brought Peiper from a morbid contemplation of his murdered comrades. The firing increased, coming closer to the target. If the bridge were to be destroyed then the crossing by the lorries would be made horribly difficult. He listened. Those were tank guns. He had to silence them.

'Signaller! Can you raise Division? Yes? Then tell them we want a Stuka strike on the tanks in the wood to the east of Krasnaya Polyana. Lieutenant Schlank will give you the co-ordinates. If you meet with any obstruction from anybody get the Lieutenant to deal with it. Right, Schlank. Get working on the map references. I want those so-called Black Hussars of the skies to pour down enough shit to smother the tanks in the woods, and I want it done before the

Ivans hit the bridge. So the Stukas won't have much time. It's after 13.00 hours already, so chop chop. Got it?'

The lorry column inched its way forward, each driver hoping to pass through the village and onto the bridge before Ivan hit it. . Despite the gloom and the poor visibility the vehicles were without lights. Military Policemen at the approaches to the bridge held blue shaded torches to guide the drivers through the murk. On the far side of the rickety structure men of the SS unit holding the line were hard at work feeding the rescued. Medical teams from the whole SS Panzer Corps were moving down to a hastily organised reception area. Behind a small hill and screened by trees, an emergency landing strip was being cleared and flare paths laid out. Luftwaffe transport squadrons were already being briefed on the evacuation of the casualties of 320th. The services were swinging into action.

'Sturmbannführer?'

'Yes, Schlank?'

'There is a little difficulty with the Stukas. I'm on to the Squadron now. The unit is preparing to leave the Eastern Front and a lot of the personnel have already been sent away. There are no mechanics or ground staff to load the bombs or to service the machines.' Peiper exploded with frustrated rage.

'Give me that bloody hand set. Hello. To whom am I talking? Captain Rauch. Well, Rauch, you just listen to me. I want your machines airborne and bombarding those bloody tanks in fifteen minutes. No ifs or buts. I am giving you a *"dienstliche Befehl"*. You know what that means? If you've forgotten I'll refresh your memory. A *"dienstliche Befehl"* means that if you do not carry out the instructions to the letter - to the letter mark you- then the officer, that's me, giving the order is legally empowered to shoot you. And I tell you this, too, Rauch. I won't stop at you. I'll shoot the whole bloody Squadron if I have to. You can load your own bombs, can't you? Aren't you trained? Well then, get out there.

'Get your boozy chums off their fat arses and flying. You've got fifteen minutes and I want to see you knock seven colours of shit out of those bloody tanks. Get it? Fifteen minutes from now.

'Don't give me bloody arguments about how long it takes. Sod the necessary checks. Load your bombs. Get enough petrol into the fuel tanks and fly here. smash Ivan's armour and then you can bugger off where you like; but I want you here, bombing that wood in fifteen minutes - understand? Right, then listen, once again. I am giving you a *"dienstliche Befehl"*. If you don't carry it out you and your whole Squadron are dead men - Out.'

For the moment the situation was in hand. The half-hearted Siberian attack had petered out, the evacuation of 320th was flowing although under shell fire, and the Stukas would soon be out to deal with the tank guns. Now for the Siberian prisoners.

'Bring Captain Barik of the Siberians and what's-his-name, the interpreter- Now,' he began when the two men had come forward, 'about the mutilated men of my unit.'

'With your permission - ' the interpreter broke in. 'I have interrogated some of the officers of the Siberian regiment. They all say the same things. Firstly, they don't mutilate and kill prisoners, secondly the SS dead were killed over a day ago. The Siberian dead, here in Krasnaya Polyana, are freshly killed. Not more than six hours dead. They ask for a German doctor to examine the fallen and to prove their story. He will confirm that what they say is the truth.'

Peiper was unconvinced.

'The bastards are in collusion. Of course they'll invent stories that fit the circumstances. I'd do the same. Still, we'll give them the doctor. Runner, my compliments to Dr Stranjc and ask him to report to me.' There was a silent five minutes wait and then, 'Ah Stranjc, thank you for coming so quickly. The interpreter will explain the Siberian viewpoint. I want your professional opinion.'

Quickly Lewinski gave a résumé of the Siberian statements. The SS doctor turned to Peiper. 'Sturmbannführer. What they say is very possibly true. I'm not professionally qualified to judge, but the prisoners claim that certain changes occur in frozen, dead meat - forgive the term. The prisoners ask you to select any of our mutilated comrades, any one you like, and they will tell you how long he has been dead. Their tests cover a body dead up to three days. After that no further changes occur. If you would like to select a body - not one of those in the ice coffins, of course...'

Peiper moved across to one of the blinded drivers. 'This one,' he indicated. A Siberian Rifleman knelt beside the body, opened the shirt to expose the belly, pressed down with both hands, rolled the corpse onto its face and then pressed again above the pelvic bone. Tenderly, he readjusted the clothing, stood up and reported to the interpreter.

'He says,' began Lewinski, 'that this man has been dead for over one day and a night - '

'Let him try Hansl,' Schlank burst in, his voice shaking with emotion. 'Let him try Hansl. I want to know.'

The Siberian knelt to the task. 'He was killed a few hours after this man. Not more than two hours later.'

The Russian then went to one of the dead of his own regiment who was lying nearby. The same procedure. 'He says that this man has not been dead for more than a few hours. Probably he was killed this morning.'

Stranjc was interested - professionally interested. 'How does he know that?' There was an exchange of words. Lewinski turned back.

'He says that if you have a probe he will show you.' Stranjc searched in his medical chest and produced a gleaming instrument. 'The Russian says,' continued the interpreter, 'that food in the stomach is the last thing to freeze. There's a sort of fermentation, an alcohol present. At this time of the year it takes a normal stomach at least one day and a night to freeze solid. If the officer probes the stomach of this man,' Lewinski indicated the body of the blinded NCO, 'he will find the food in the intestines is frozen solid. In this man's case- ' he pointed to Schlank's lover, 'the food will not be quite as solidly frozen. And in this man's body,' a wave indicated the dead Siberian, 'the food will be moist and there may even be liquid blood on the probe. He knows without using a probe that these things are so. He knows by finger-tip feel, but you will need a probe to show you.'

'It seems sensible to me, Sturmbannführer. Shall I try?' Receiving Peiper's nodded consent, Stranjc worked quickly. 'His assertions are correct. This Russian corpse has blood that is still in liquid state. The SS NCO has solid frozen food and the officer almost completely frozen. Logically therefore, they died at different intervals of time, but more than that I cannot say. I am no pathologist. If you accept the finding, Sturmbannführer, then the Siberians who lie dead here could not have been from the unit that desecrated our comrades.'

Peiper remained angry. 'Well, we'll never resolve who did it until we get our hands on those Siberians who attacked us just a while ago. Tell the Captain - what's his name - Barik. Tell him to parley with the Siberians out here and find out if they want to surrender as I've heard that they do. If they want to jag it in then they should send one of their senior officers up here to talk to us.

Now, Schlank, those bloody tank guns are finding the range. Where are your sodding Stukas? Christ, what's that?'

A sheet of flame illuminated the bridge. A shell fragment had struck the fuel tank of a lorry. The heavy truck was quickly enveloped in flame. The driver accelerated, hoping to clear the bridge and to bring his load of wounded men quickly to safety. In his haste the truck fouled the bridge end and the vehicle swung sideways on, to block the exit. Flames from the truck ignited the rotting timbers. Above the noise of the flames there were the sounds of screaming as the wounded, unable to escape, perished in the flames. Soon the whole structure of the bridge was burning. Concurrently, the Stukas arrived and mistaking the bridge for the target swept down and released their bombs.

'Do something, Schlank. What's the recognition signal for "cease fire"? Shoot off half a dozen of them quickly. Those stupid sods are killing my men.'

A cluster of violet flares soon hung in the sky. One JU 87 seemed to skid sideways as the pilot strove to abort the drop. The machine swayed, recovered and began to climb again. Schlank loaded the pistol with white flares and fired them so that they burst over the area from which Lipski's group had been bombarding the bridge.

The noise of the exploding bombs drowned all other sounds but a shower of sparks rising high into the sky showed that the bridge had collapsed. The escape route was smashed. Now it would be a matter of channelling the 320th down the banks of the river, across its frozen surface, and up the far bank and the safety of the German lines.

'Please tell unit commanders O Group in five minutes,' Peiper ordered and then turned to upbraid Schlank for the failure of the Luftwaffe to identify a target. Their mistaken dives had destroyed several trucks; the one on the bridge and two others which had been hit by bombs, Dead soldiers of the 320th were scattered wide and were lying in grotesque attitudes on the snow. Whether the dive bombers had hit Lipski's tank concentration none knew, but there was now no fire coming from the wood.

'Comrades,' began Peiper, when his commanders were gathered round his tank. 'From reports, only a quarter of the 320th crossed the bridge before it was destroyed. This means that we have to construct shallow ramps for the lorries to drive down and up the far bank. It would be easiest if we blew away sections of the bank to loosen the earth and then flattened the banks down with tank tracks.

The 1st Battalion will be asked to do the same thing on their side of the river.' Turning to Thiele, his adjutant, he ordered, 'Please liaise with 1st Battalion about that. Now.' Once again he addressed the whole group. 'There is a Red tank formation on our eastern flank so we must be prepared for an attack from that quarter. It's a sensitive sector. The Siberian prisoners are seeking to establish whether that infantry mob which we duffed up this morning are the same group as mutilated our comrades. That sector, where the Russian infantry are - the southern sector- can be considered as only marginally less dangerous than the eastern flank.

Our 1st Battalion holds the ground to our north, so that sector may be considered totally safe. The western flank is wide open and God alone knows who is out there. You will appreciate that we must hold our bridgehead here until all the 320th has passed over. Only then is our task completed. Even if this bridgehead is quiet now, there is no guarantee that it will remain so. Vigilance is the watchword. Now,' turning to the Pioneer Officer, 'place charges in the river banks to blow them up so as to loosen the soil. You tank commanders then flatten the earth to make a series of shallow ramps down to the ice. Any questions? No? Thank you gentlemen.'

A small party of men marched out from the positions which Peiper's group held at Krasnaya Polyana. The group, made up of Captain Barik, another Siberian, Lewinski and four SS guards, trudged through the snow past the bodies of the Riflemen who had fallen in the several attacks and then down the shallow incline towards the woods in which the Siberian Regiment lay.

At intervals of two hundred metres the group halted and Barik shouted through cupped hands the cry, 'We come in peace. Send your senior commander forward.' During those halts the rest of the parley party stood silent, their breath crisping in the cold air of the February afternoon. There was an almost total silence. No sound came from the Riflemen in the woods. No sound from the Battle Group holding the line in the village, except just the faintest murmur of lorry engines as the vehicle motors were kept warm.

The group had now made three such halts and were a long way in front of the SS outpost line. 'Bugger this for a game of soldiers,' Bauer, one of the guards, complained in a low voice. 'Those whore's sons can see in the dark and they've probably got us in their sights. If aught goes wrong, we're dead men.'

131

'Don't fret. I know these people,' Lewinski consoled him. 'I was a POW in Siberia for most of the Great War - the Kaiser's war, you know. That's where I first learned the lingo. I can even speak the local dialect of these blokes- it's Baikal. I tell you we're all right. If they had wanted to kill us they'd have done it back there, when we set out.'

'Thanks for nothing- '.

Captain Barik called softly, 'Tishe.'

'He's telling us to keep quiet,' Lewinski muttered and then out of the darkening day came a bellowed 'hallooooo' and then the words, 'Brothers in peace, we have been waiting for you.'

The parties - the German group and that of the Siberian Regiment - came slowly towards each other. Barik saw the leading figure of the Russian group.

Comrade Colonel,' he began, 'why have you come here on this parley?'

'Can you think of why I should not, Barik? I could not ask a subordinate to do anything that I myself would not do. So here I am. Tell me, Barik, how goes it with you - in German hands, I mean?'

Lewinski broke in. 'Ask him about the mutilations.' Then to himself he said, 'If those sods did do those brutal things then, in truth we are dead men.'

The Russian talked and then suddenly Lewinski turned to Bauer. 'I know that I can't order you to go, but this is vital and your Major should know it quickly. Will you take a message back? It is this. The Siberians were not responsible for the massacre. This was done by a Major Lipski and the men of an NKVD group. Lipski and his NKVD have been pursuing these Siberians for days. Apparently the Siberians had mutinied and shot some of the NKVD officers. Somehow, they don't know how, Lipski got here before them and shot down the riflemen as they tried to surrender to what they thought was a German defence position here at Krasnaya Polyana. These men want to surrender. They're all that's left of a three battalion regiment. Have you got the message? Good. Away you go.'

Ten minutes later Grenadier Bauer was delivering the message to Peiper. The commander went into a deep reverie which lasted for long minutes. Suddenly he snapped out of it.

'Right lad, back you go. Accept the surrender. I'll make sure the outposts are warned. It will probably be half an hour or more before the Russian battalions start coming through. Hands in the air, of course. No weapons, not even pistols for the officers. Now repeat the message.'

Bauer repeated the instructions he had been given. 'Good,' Peiper remarked when the Grenadier had finished speaking. 'Return to Lewinski and the Siberians, please. Thiele,' he called to his adjutant. 'Get some runners. Tell everybody, not just commanders, that a body of Ivans, a large body, is surrendering. There will be no firing and no display of ill will, but, on the other hand, no fraternising with them.'

Seated in the dismal room which he had selected for his HQ, the SS commander waited. Two lamps powered by a generator cast a dull, yellowish light. Thoughts tumbled through Peiper's mind. The mission was nearly over. Thank God. Soon he would be rid of Postel and his whining. The Pioneers should be about ready to blow the river banks and once the ramps had been made he could continue to pass the 320th across the river. The one worrying detail was that NKVD group. What was its strength? Was it preparing for a fresh attack? If the mutilating whore's sons did come back he'd teach them a lesson. No mercy for that lot of shit. He felt bile rise in his throat. He tasted the bitterness and coughed in disgust. Soldiers entered the room.

'Herr Sturmbannführer, permit me to present,' began Lewinski's formal introduction, 'Colonel Marenko of the Baikal Regiment of Siberian Riflemen. He has come to offer his surrender.'

'Oh, has he? Bring that sod in here. I want to talk to him about my comrades who were murdered by his men. And I've got some other bones to pick with him. Wheel him in.'

Marenko entered the room and saw Peiper standing in the light of the bulbs. The two men looked silently at each other for a few moments. Each saw the strain etched in the face of the other. Marenko saluted. His hand remained at the front edge of his fur cap waiting until the greeting was acknowledged. The SS officer was grateful that the Russian had made no attempt to shake hands. He returned the salute with every fibre of his body taut with hate, for he was still unconvinced that the NKVD had carried out the massacre. Those bloody Siberians would spin some yarn about dead bodies. Without a proper autopsy he could not prove their assertion that they were innocent. Their statements could not be checked. He was determined to get the answer from this furtive-looking sod who stood before him. Peiper gestured, without speaking, towards a chair. Marenko sat down, his face a sickly yellow in the glare of the unshaded bulbs. He nursed his right arm which had been struck by a bullet during the battle against the NKVD.

Peiper saw that the Siberian was wounded but the discomfort of a single man was of less importance than to gain the truth about his dead comrades.

'You know about the way in which we found our rearguard?' Peiper put the question bluntly and without preamble. Then turning to Lewinski he said, 'Ask the Colonel why his men mutilated our comrades.'

There was a long and earnest conversation from the start of which the Siberian showed anger. Finally his feelings could no longer be contained. In a dramatic gesture he stood up, tore open his greatcoat and tunic so that his breast was bared.

'We do not mutilate our country's fallen enemies,' he declaimed. 'I am a soldier. We are all soldiers. We honour those who deal honourably with us. If you doubt me, then kill me. See, I open my coat willingly to die at your hands if we are guilty.'

Tears flowed down his cheeks. These accusations against his regiment struck at his personal honour. If he would not allow Lipski to doubt the bravery of the Riflemen then equally he would not permit this German to question his men's honour. Peiper impressed by the passion of the outburst, waited until Lewinski had translated the tenor of the Siberian's protestation.

'Tell the Colonel that I accept his word, that the NKVD killed my men and I want the bastards who did it.' Sibilant sentences passed between interpreter and the Siberian officer.

'The Colonel offers the help of his men to track down and to find the political criminals. He also offers any help that you may require.'

'Well, yes. There is something in which his men could assist,' replied Peiper. 'We have to bring the 320th into the German lines. If the Colonel's men would help in this task, then once it is completed we can concentrate on tracking down the murdering swine. Thank the Colonel, please; explain to him that I am grateful.'

Some time later the freezing, dozing passengers in the long column of soft-skin vehicles were suddenly alarmed by the appearance all round the trucks of tall fur-hatted Red Army men. Voices raised in alarm. There were shouts and cries from the wounded Germans who saw themselves as mutilated victims of a fresh Soviet outrage. Peiper sent out Grenadiers to every truck to calm the fears of the men of the 320th and soon Siberian Riflemen and German Grenadiers alike were struggling to bring the lorries across the frozen river. The pace at which the Siberians worked was a killing one and the Germans and the Grenadiers saw how quick the Russian soldiers were to use natural materials to help in the task. The Siberians worked almost by instinct. A natural discipline exerted itself and while the lightly wounded of both sides walked across into the sector held by 1st Battalion of the SS Leibstandarte, the empty lorries were winched by muscle power across the Udy and up its northern bank.

Marenko and Peiper were absorbed in conversation, during the course of which the tall Siberian turned to the interpreter and said, 'I have no wish to alarm the Major but the ice is dangerously thin. If he listens he can hear the river beginning to flow quite fast. This means that the frozen crust is no longer thick enough to bear the weight of his armoured vehicles. We cannot build a bridge that could carry such a heavy weight, but a lighter one could be quickly constructed. It is for him an alarming situation.'

Lewinski interpreted the Colonel's words. Peiper called for his maps and studied them intently.

'I had already appreciated the possibility that the ice would not take tank weight, but the alternative to destroying all our vehicles and leaving them on the Red side of the river is to drive the Kampfgruppe through the Ivans' area until we find a bridge that we can use. Signaller!'

'Sturmbannführer?'

'I want a message - top priority - to Corps HQ repeated to Div. I need an accurate map of the Leibstandarte's positions in this area and to the west of here. Also ask for a fuel and ammunition column to be sent to us, plus hot food and cigarettes.'

The transmission time was only minutes and then the signaller turned to Peiper.

'Div instruct you to send a runner to 1st Battalion HQ where a map will be waiting for him. The other things will come forward soon.'

'Thank you. Runner! Please present my compliments to the CO of 1st Battalion and receive from him the map on which our positions are marked.' The runner dismissed, turned and dropped down the river bank, on to the ice, raced across this and scrambled up the far bank and into SS Battalion's positions. Peiper had now about half an hour to wait before his runner's return. The night air was chill although it was only seven in the evening, and the young commander decided on a quick tour of the defensive positions Everywhere his Grenadiers were alert but showing the strain of lack of sleep and the need for maximum effort. 'Not long now, lads,' he encouraged them and they smiled wearily, their eyes filmed with tiredness, sunken in their pallid faces.

Some distance away from the houses of Krasnaya Polyana a group of Siberians was breaking the large clods of earth which controlled explosions had torn from the frozen ground. They were digging mass graves; one for their own dead and one for the fallen of the German Kampfgruppe. At a depth of one-metre-twenty the ground was no longer bound hard with frost so that digging with a pick and shovel was possible. Peiper saw through brooding eyes the progress on the graves and heard, as if in a dream, not only the dull sound of spade against earth but the crisp, hard knocking of a hammer against wood. His adjutant came up, a smile lighting his face.

'Excellent news, Sturmbannführer. The Russians have rebuilt the bridge. Yes,' in answer to Peiper's unframed question, 'yes, even in the dark. The rebuilt bridge can now take lorries, so long as these are driven slowly. Christ, how those blokes work. Their pace is quite astonishing. They've already begun passing trucks across and if they've got a sort of ferry system going with sledges to transport the wounded. They've also laid a wooden foot bridge on the ice for the rest of the walking wounded and for the fighting echelons of 320th. Isn't it splendid?'

The young commander, although deeply aware of the importance of passing the Infantry Division quickly across the river, had his mind fixed on the next phase of the operation: The fight back to the lines of his own Division. The runner came in gasping with the strain of the journey.

'Sturmbannführer. Here is your map. I am to tell you that officers of our 1st Battalion are en route to liaise with you. The wounded are being dealt with. The supplies which you asked for are coming forward together with a hot meal.'

'Thank you. You've done well. Send me another runner. What?' Peiper asked as the Grenadier shook his head. 'Are you still prepared to run on? Very well. To all unit commanders; an O Group here it ten minutes and now,' turning to Thiele, 'let us say our goodbyes to General Postel.'

The fur-coated Divisional Commander was seated in his staff car when Peiper and Thiele walked briskly across to him. The two officers saluted.

'Respectfully beg to report, General,' began Peiper, 'that the main of your Division has crossed the river. The wounded are being treated. Those requiring immediate surgery are being operated on. Those who can be flown out are being air lifted now. There is hot food for the fighting groups on the other side of the river. I respectfully request permission to dismiss in order to prepare a route for the return of my own Kampfgruppe.'

'Why can't you cross the bridge? Don't tell me; it is structurally unsound.'

'Not only that, General, but the ice is weak. It will be breaking up soon. Even though at night the cold thickens the ice again, it cannot make it sufficiently strong to bear the panzer. Therefore, I am stranded on this side of the river and cannot move northwards in the direction of Kharkov. If I move my Kampfgruppe eastwards I should run into the great mass of the Red Army's offensive. I can thus only move westwards and pass through those areas which are held, lightly, I hope, by Soviet spearheads. My Kampfgruppe must carve its way across those spearheads and back to our lines. Ammunition and fuel are coming across to me, but as you know we are few in number. Thank God, we have had few casualties, but even so the loss of any one man places a heavier burden on those who survive- '

The General interrupted Peiper. 'Forgive me, Peiper, just for a moment.'

'Riedl,' the General called to his adjutant. Ask Captain Stumke to report to me,' and turning back to the SS officer he explained:

'What I intend to do is to ask for volunteers from Stumke's battalion to serve with you. I tell you frankly that much of the Division is clapped out. Only Stumke's unit is still a fighting formation in being, the others are fighting units in name only.'

There was a long silence between the two men which was broken only by Stumke's arrival.

'Ah Stumke,' the General began. 'I have been telling Major Peiper of the first class fighting capabilities of your men.' Postel went on to explain what he had in mind. When he had finished he looked through his monocle at Stumke. 'Well?' he barked.

137

'Speaking for myself, General, I am ready to fight on. Give me a hot meal and a warm billet for an hour or two and I'm ready for action. All my men would be keen. Whether they would actually volunteer once they know the Div is leaving the Line I don't know, but I can make up a Kampfgruppe from my battalion with fifty good men who would be ready in a couple of hours.'

'Bravo Stumke, spoken like a Prussian. Well, what do you say to that, Peiper?'

'I accept with gratitude the Captain's expression of comradeship and willingness to help. Can I ask you a favour, Stumke? I have a Luftwaffe Oberleutnant with me. Schlank is his name. He is pretty cut up. He lost a brother and a fiancée in an air crash the other day and then he found his best friend among the men of my group who had been massacred by the Reds. I can't look after him. Will you do it, please?'

'Of course, Herr Sturmbannführer.'

'In which case may we dismiss, General? I have my men to bury and a hot meal to arrange before planning my anabasis.'

'Anabasis! What a lovely word to use,' Postel chortled happily. 'A lovely word. Gentlemen, of course you may dismiss. Good luck go with you on your anabasis, Peiper. Lovely! Lovely! Drive on, Hummel.' And the driver let out the clutch of the Horch staff car. The vehicle crunched through the snow. Postel was soon back across the bridge and into the SS sector. Both young men, Peiper and Stumke, heaved sighs of relief. The General had been hard going.

'I've called an O Group,' Peiper said. 'Good God, it's only a couple of hours short of midnight. The officers will be waiting. '

Peiper was correct; his brother officers had been waiting with some impatience in the little shabby room in which he had set up the headquarters.

'Comrades.' Peiper was still unsure of himself when making a speech. 'Comrades, we have carried out that part of our orders rescue the 320th. But it has left us with a problem. The bridge which the Siberians have built cannot carry the weight of our panzer and the ice on the river is too thin. There is a choice open to us Somewhere to the west, better still to the north-west, lies our Division. My plan is to strike westwards with our left wing resting on the river Mush. This will stop Ivan from taking us in flank. The map which Division supplied this evening shows that at 18.00 hour this evening elements of the Divisional Pioneer Battalion are holding

Mirgorod. It is my intention to aim for that place moving via Budovky, Sidki, Artyushchevka and then on to Mirgorod.'

His fingers traced the route.

'I am happy to tell you that Captain Stumke and volunteers from his battalion will fight alongside us. He will have about fifty men each of whom will be a weapons tactics expert from the 320th's battle school.

'According to Corps Intelligence at least five of Ivan's infantry divisions, elements of 5th Guards Tank Corps and a hell of a lot of cavalry are between us and Mirgorod. Let's hope we don't meet all of them at one and the same time.

'Schlank, I've posted you to Captain Stumke's battalion. You will be his liaison with me. Right, that's all, I think, on future moves. Now, get the men under cover for the night. God grant us a good night's rest. Just after first light tomorrow we shall bury our comrades. A hot meal just after the funeral and move out two hours after that. The time is now 22.30 hours. First light is 08.30. Good night, gentlemen.'

Kampfgruppe Peiper settled down to watch and ward through the long hours of darkness. There were no attacks during the night and stand-to at dawn brought no alarm. The group seemed to be living in a military limbo. There was no sound of any description as the light slowly improved. By full light it was clear that there would be no attack against Krasnaya Polyana. Leaving only an outpost line of sentries, Peiper ordered the men of the Kampfgruppe to parade for the burial of their comrades.

At the site of the mass graves a tense situation had developed. The German and the Siberian soldiers were both on parade and the SS resented the presence of men from an Army that had carried out atrocities upon the living and who had desecrated the dead. Insults were being flung as the SS officers appeared on parade. Peiper's temper flare immediately.

'Sergeant Majors at the double,' he bellowed. The senior NCOs halted in front of him and reported. Peiper's anger boiled over.

'What the hell is going on here? This is a funeral - a military parade - not a bloody parliament. I want the names of those men who were shouting when I came onto the square. Got it? We'll have no repetition of this loutish behaviour. Got it? I don't care a bugger what the men think, I will not have such shocking behaviour. Now return to your units. Officers, I will talk to you later on the state of unit discipline. Interpreter, get the Russian Colonel here - now.'

139

Marenko held himself erect despite the ache of his undressed wound. He marched, ramrod straight, through the snow; then halted and saluted. Peiper acknowledged the greeting. The SS officer addressed Lewinski.

'Ask the Colonel why he is so tactless as to bring his men on parade at the same time as mine? Does the Colonel- not know how bitter my men are towards all things Russian?'

The interpreter talked and then listened as the Colonel of the Riflemen began to speak. Finally, he turned back to Peiper.

'Herr Sturmbannführer. The Colonel says that this is the first occasion on which he has been able to bury his dead with decency, in a Christian fashion. He says that his men and yours are soldiers. Both sides are Christians. You wear crosses on your tunics. The Red Army does not give its soldiers spiritual comfort like priests The Colonel asks for your unit chaplain to bless the fallen of both sides. Yours and his.'

The point about a military chaplain was embarrassing. There was no such person in the German SS Divisions. It had not been thought necessary for such a post on the unit War Establishment. Lewinski coughed delicately. He knew that the SS was not a Christian organisation and he had seen Peiper's embarrassed reaction to the Russian request.

'Permit me to suggest, Herr Sturmbannführer. I was a Baptist lay preacher until I was called up. I still have my Bible and prayer book. Not only can I pray for our men but I also know some Russian prayers that might be appropriate.'

Of course, Lewinski. Thank you for the offer. Please tell Colonel Marenko that you will be performing the ceremony and explain him how we bury our dead.'

Lewinski went across to the Siberian officer. Marenko nodded, saluted and then rejoined his regiment. Peiper and his officer moved to the edge of the German communal grave on the lip of which a birch-wood memorial shaped into a runic cross had already been erected.

'Comrades,' began Peiper, 'we are met today to bury our own dead and,' with a salute to the Siberians, 'those of our comrades of the Russian Army, who were once our enemies but who fell in battle and who are as much to be honoured as our own soldiers. Our men fell in the fight so that Germany should live and theirs so that Russia might be freed of the plague of Bolshevism. Chaplain,' he turned to Lewinski, 'we shall now begin to inter the dead. You may read your prayers. Parade, parade 'shun. Adjutant, call the roll of our fallen comrades.'

Thiele's voice began to intone the alphabetical list. 'Grenadier Albers,' and at the name four men raised the shelter half on which the body lay. They carried the full-dressed corpse into the shallow grave, gently laid a rifle alongside the body, turned the pallid face towards the east, folded the shelter half protectively round the dead comrade and stepped back out of the trench. The next name was called; then the next. The roll call was a long one.

The Russian dead had already been laid in their grave; a much deeper one than that of the Germans. In accordance with Red Army regulations the Siberians were laid head to foot, dressed, but without weapons. Having blessed the German dead, Lewinski moved across and began to speak in Russian the 'Litany of the Fallen'. The Siberians stiffened in surprise. A gentle sigh ran along the ranks. It swelled into a moan. For the first time in their military lives the Riflemen were hearing prayers being said for their dead comrades. From a sigh to a moan, then to a louder moan, out of which a deep bass voice began to sing. A single staccato word, repeated and sung so that it echoed like a tolling bell. Four tenors took up the melody of the ancient chant 'Today the Master of Creation is crucified,' and at the end of the first phrase the remnants of the Siberian regiment, as if upon a word of command, knelt on the ground. From the kneeling ranks a fervour of religious emotion poured as the blending voices rose into the lightening sky.

Marenko rose to stand in front of his officers and moved to the edge of the mass grave. He crossed himself, bent down and picked up a handful of soil. With the spreading movement of a sower scattering corn he flung the crumbled earth across the bodies of his dead men. The other officers followed and then, at a sign, four Pioneers began to cover the bodies of the Riflemen with earth.

The Russian voices stopped. The silence could be felt and then in that deafening silence Lewinski's voice proclaimed the Easter message; the certainty of Resurrection. *'Kristos voskreziye'*, "Christ is risen", burst from his lips and the joyful expression was taken up by the choir, exultant, singing the conviction of victory over death.

During the singing Peiper noticed Schlank turn pale and sway. Grenadiers were carrying the Luftwaffe officer's lover to his resting place. Schlank took a short pace towards the burial party.

'Stand still.' Peiper's voice was unnaturally harsh. Schlank stiffened to attention at the iron in the SS officer's command. At last the interment was over. Earth was shovelled over the single long layer of SS dead.

'Comrades,' Peiper began the valediction to his dead soldiers.

Surprising himself, he felt inspired to oratory.

'Comrades, here in the East we have buried so many of our comrades. For we Teutons the East is that cardinal point out of which barbaric hordes have poured, in ages past, to invade our German Fatherland. The history of Germany is filled with accounts of how we, the Teutons, saved Europe by our warrior spirit. We are saving Europe today in our crusade against Bolshevism. It is, therefore, fitting that these our honoured dead lie with their faces towards the East. That they, even in death, face as if on guard and ever vigilant that territory out of which repression, hate and destruction are storming to destroy our country.

'But out of the East, as our Teuton forefathers taught us, rises the dawn. The start of a new day, the symbol of rebirth. The blackness of Bolshevism is symbolised by the night that comes first to the East, obscuring everything in dark and gloom. But the dawn in the East is the start of Germany's day, of a Reich that will last a thousand years.

'Our dead who lie in a shallow, provisional grave will, when we have won this war in the East, be gathered together to rest in a vast field of heroes on the banks of the Volga. That hallowed field and the giant memorial which will overshadow it will be a symbol for as long as Germany lives of the war which we are fighting and winning in a heathen land.

'The war goes on. Today, in a few hours, we march again to fight for Europe's freedom, for Germany's existence. Comrades, to our honoured dead - *Sieg Heil* - hail victory.'

When the salute had been given Peiper gave the order, 'Firing Party ready.' Realising no similar honour guard existed for the Siberians he ordered a second group to the Russian grave. The gesture was appreciated. 'Firing parties; aim. Fire.' Three times over each grave the salvoes crashed out in salute.

'Parade, the SS anthem,' and in the biting east wind the young German voices rose in song. 'Parade, dismiss. A hot meal is ready.'

The ceremony was over. Yesterday's dead had returned to the earth. Who would fall in today's battles? There was a sound of feet crunching through snow. Peiper turned. Marenko and the interpreter were hurrying to catch up with him.

'Herr Sturmbannführer. The Colonel requests that he may go with you on your drive back to the German lines.'

'How the hell does he know what we intend to do?' Peiper's temper began to flare again. What bloody blabbermouth had told the Siberians what the plans were for the Kampfgruppe?

'The Colonel says it is obvious. You cannot cross the river. Either you abandon your vehicles on this side and walk across to your parent unit's lines or else you must look for another crossing place. He knows that you will not abandon your equipment, so you must be preparing to find a way back. He requests permission to accompany us.'

It was not an easy request to grant. It was an officer's duty to stay with his men. Peiper's automatic response, had he been taken prisoner, would have been to stay with his soldiers. He also knew that this was a naive view and that officers and men were soon separated and placed in different prison camps.

'Does he want to come alone?' Peiper asked. A whispered talk.

'He has a small group, about ten in number, who wish to fight alongside us. They're nearly all survivors from Soviet camps, or the children of survivors. They don't want to waste time in a prisoner of war camp but want to bear arms against the Reds.'

Well, why not? thought Peiper. It had been accepted that German units have 'Hiwis'; former Red Army soldiers who had volunteered to serve in non-combatant roles within German units. He would merely extend the principle so as to include combat roles.

'Right,' Peiper decided. 'Let them join. Assign them to Captain Stumke's group. Now let's have a meal and get ready to march.'

Marenko's ten man squad stood outside TAC HQ in Krasnaya Polyana, watching stolidly and without emotion as their comrades of the Rifle Regiment marched away, over the wooden bridge and into captivity. Then they, the ten men and their commander, together with the SS officer went to eat. It was midday.

'Good food,' Marenko told the interpreter. 'Red Army rations have not been so good in the last weeks. Shells and bullets are considered to be more important than food, so the shells come forward and we go hungry. This is quite good food. What do you call it? Gulasch? Is it horse meat? No? Anyway, it's good stuff.'

During the meal the interpreter appeared again in front of the Kampfgruppe commander.

'Not you again,' chided Peiper. 'What does your tame Rifleman want now? To lead the Kampfgruppe, perhaps?'

'No, Herr Sturmbannführer. But he saw signs of us preparing to leave and suggested that we can trap the NKVD unit.'

'How?'

'Well, it is embarrassing to put into words, but simply said, the German Army makes a lot of noise and betrays its intentions with unnecessary movement; so the Colonel says. He suggests that the mass of our Kampfgruppe leaves at last light, making the usual noise but with the vehicles half empty. We make it look as if the whole group is pulling out, but we leave behind a heavily-armed ambush detachment. The NKVD must come down to Krasnaya Polyana. They will have to pass through this place to shadow our vehicle column. Colonel Marenko says we should hide in the houses and trap them.'

'Yeeees,' said the SS officer. 'It has all the classical elements. Let's try it. We'll wait here until dark and then put the Colonel's plan into operation. Perhaps the Colonel will be good enough to tell me in more detail what he thinks should be done. Runner! Please tell units to get ready to drive off. They must be ready in ten minutes, before last light. Officers to me beforehand. Please ask Colonel Marenko to join O Group and, of course, the officers of Captain Stumke's battalion.'

Already Peiper's mind relished the pictures of the destruction of the political swine who had mutilated his men. If he could get them in his gun sights, the bastards would pay for their crime.

At the briefing, the Russian Colonel was asked to explain his very simple plan. Two panzer would stay behind inside two houses, one at the entrance to and one at the exit from the village in which they were already positioned. When the politicals came into Krasnaya Polyana - the main armoured strength would be at the head of column, Marenko explained- they would halt. The German guns would destroy the first and the last Red tanks. This would bottle up the rest. The killing could then begin. How, Marenko was asked, could the NKVD observers be convinced that the correct number of tanks had left Krasnaya Polyana? Simple. There would be two mock-up tanks; lorries made to look like tanks. The observers would look for the gun because in the dark they would not be able to identify vehicles accurately. The lorries, mocked up as tanks, would be sandwiched between two real vehicles. The Kampfgruppe's half-tracks would each hold only half the number of Grenadiers. These men would be encouraged to light cigarettes at irregular intervals, to indicate that the vehicles were occupied.

In the short street of houses which made up the village of Krasnaya Polyana the ambush group would be concealed. The men were warned by Marenko that total quiet was demanded; if necessary, total quiet throughout the night. There would be no movement, no talk, no smoking. No activity to make the NKVD suspicious. Marenko rejected the offer for his men to be taught how to use German anti-tank grenades. It was unnecessary, he said, for the Germans to bother. It was superfluous. Red Army infantry training had already taught Russian soldiers how to use all enemy material.

Peiper's final words set the tone for the operation.

'We have the chance of catching those swine who killed our comrades. I don't want the trap to be sprung prematurely by any idiot smoking, snoring, farting, talking or coughing. We can catch those sods and kill them, but only if we keep absolutely quiet. So watch it.'

Just after last light the vehicles of the Kampfgruppe - panzer, SPs, lorries and half-tracks - roared away, making a lot of noise; the sort of noise that Marenko accused the Germans of always making.

Behind, in the silent village, the Grenadiers, Stumke's men and the Siberians, lay wrapped in shelter halves and blankets. The cold was bitter; the dark an almost tangible thing. There was no movement from the waiting soldiers. Not even to change position, not even to scratch at the vermin which irritated the unwashed bodies. There was no sound, no smell, no hint that in Krasnaya Polyana half of Peiper's Kampfgruppe lay ready in ambush position.

Towards 20.00 hours, with the intense cold seeming to freeze the soldiers' very minds, there was a sudden sound. A hissing, swishing sound which moved quickly from left to right. Then another and another. Marenko pressed Peiper back to the floor from which he had begun to raise himself. He laid a finger on the German's lips. 'Insolent bastard,' thought the Sturmbannführer. The swishing sound was repeated this time from right to left. Marenko whispered in the interpreter's ear. Lewinski cupped his hands round Peiper's ear as the Siberian had cupped his.

'A ski patrol checking that we've left.'

For another long hour the group inside the hovels waited and then, in the far distance, there was the rumbling noise of tank engines. The sound grew louder; nearer. The ground began to shake and the first T34 swung hard on its left track and entered the village street. It stood, menacing, like a wild beast snuffing the air for a scent of the enemy. Satisfied that there was no danger the T34 rumbled slowly down through the row of houses.

'Oh Christ,' thought Peiper as the tank did not halt but drove out of Krasnaya Polyana and into the open snowy countryside beyond the village. 'Bugger it. Now we won't be able to trap the sods.'

The rumbling continued. The whole of the armoured advance guard of the political group was passing through the village without halting. Peiper realised that any attempt to intercept the follow-up column of NKVD infantry would result in his being trapped by the armour which had just passed through. Now there was a higher sound. Lorries bearing infantry were passing by. Then the sound of motor cycles, a few more tanks of the rearguard and silence. The politicals had avoided the trap.

'Well, that was a right balls up,' Peiper snarled at the interpreter.

'The Colonel says that success is not guaranteed. He suggests that we sleep until we are ready to move out tomorrow morning.'

Peiper's brain rejected sleep and turned to tactics. His mind appreciated the tactical possibilities as quickly as a shot through the brain. Of course. Why had he been so stupid? He turned to Lewinski.

'How many tanks were there in the column?' Faint whispering came to him.

'The Colonel says eight in the advanced guard, two in the rear, ten trucks and four motor cycles. Infantry about two hundred and fifty.'

'I have a plan. Does the Colonel think it safe for a single man to pass between the houses to carry a message? I also want to send several wireless messages. What about the noise of the transmission?'

Whispers; more whispers and then, 'The Colonel says one skilful man could carry a message but only once or twice during the night. Not more often. On wireless signals, short and muffled should be all right.'

Peiper's plan was a simple one. Ahead of him was part of his Kampfgruppe under the command of Obersturmführer Hennecke. Lipski's NKVD formation was following it, shadowing the column.

He himself and his group in the houses of Krasnaya Polyana were at Lipski's back. The communist pervert and murderer could be trapped like the meat in a sandwich - but only if Hennecke's group could be told of the plan. It was, therefore, vital to talk to him by radio. '

'Signaller, raise Obersturmführer Hennecke, please.' A long, long pause and then the familiar voice.

'Rudi here.'

'Rudi, I shall speak quickly and in dialect so that Ivan's lot listening to us won't understand,' and Peiper began to gabble a flow of broad-vowelled words. He was gambling that though the message would be picked up, by the time that the Reds had reacted to it the moves that he now proposed to make would have been completed. It was a mountain man's dialect that he spoke; guttural, harsh, low-pitched and with the words only half enunciated.

The gist of the message was to order Hennecke's group to return to Krasnaya Polyana, but before it did so it was to make a Chinese demonstration. When the SS group began to move back on Krasnaya Polyana it would meet the NKVD. The politicals would certainly not offer resistance but would withdraw to Krasnaya Polyana hoping to make a stand in the houses.

When the Red group neared the village it would come under the fire of Peiper's ambushes. The order for Hennecke to return to the village would be given later during the night and the group was ordered to fire white signal flares at regular intervals to indicate its progress as it returned to Krasnaya Polyana.

'Runner. Take this message to every house which we are holding. They are on this side of the street only. The senior officer or NCO in the house is to initial it. Bring the messages, properly initialled back to me here.

'I have selected you because you are our best scout. You can move silently and almost invisibly. Tonight you have got to prove the confidence that I have in you. Ivan must not see you. Understand? Right, away you go and good luck.

'Lewinski, please tell Colonel Marenko our plan. What? Oh, you didn't understand my dialect. Well, tell the Colonel that part of our group, that part which went out with Major Hennecke, is being recalled and that we shall crush the politicals between his and our groups.'

Out on the steppes Hennecke had a battlefield discussion with his Section Leaders. He knew what Peiper meant by a Chinese demonstration. Individual vehicles were to be sent out over a wide arc. At a given time they would return again to his group and en route they would fire off fixed patterns of signal flares. Observers on Ivan's side would see this activity as evidence of a link up of forces with a strong main force and would report it. Lipski would react accordingly; he would feel himself to be facing a much stronger enemy and would prepare to fall back upon Krasnaya Polyana.

And thus it proved. Just after 01.30 hours, Lipski was told that across a small arc of ground recognition flares had gone up and had been replied to by the fascist armoured group which they were following.

'How many flares?'

'Six separate, single red flares, answered by the Kampfgruppe with a double red flare.'

Lipski considered. It could mean that the fascist group had linked up with a rescue team, or that the group had received reinforcements. The reinforced group, and Lipski did not doubt that these had been reinforcements, might even be preparing to strike at his NKVD group. He made plans for a speedy withdrawal to the village of Krasnaya Polyana.

He checked his watch. It was just short of 02.00 hours. Well, until the fascists did make a move he would maintain his watching position some way behind them, but he would send an outpost detachment forward which would warn him of any move that the fascists might make. The remainder of his Battle Group would get their heads down.

Chapter 18

'What the hell is it?'

Colonel Satrushkin of 6th Army Intelligence reacted violently to the shaking which his aide-de-camp was giving him.

'What bloody time is it? What is happening, you dolt?'

'Comrade Colonel, a message from units to the south and west of Krasnaya Polyana. Recognition flares have been seen. German recognition flares. It would seem that a German unit in that area has linked up with or been reinforced by other units.'

'Armoured?'

'So far as can be determined, yes, Colonel. Reports speak of tank noises. One puzzling thing. Some reports indicate the presence of a second group of armoured vehicles halted some way behind the main body of German AFVs. This other group fired no flares. It might be some sort of back up or specialist unit. Do you think that this is some new sort of German armoured tactic?'

'I'm buggered if I know.' The Colonel was an honest man.

'Likewise I'm buggered if I know why Krasnaya Polyana should suddenly achieve this prominence. There's nothing there, yet the Nemetski are gathering round it. I thought it odd some days ago when they first started acting up in the area.

'I think they're preparing an offensive and that the point of maximum effort will be around Krasnaya Polyana. Incidentally, anything significant about the flares?'

'No, Colonel. One red challenge followed by two red flares in reply.'

'Make a note of that. Put it in the Intelligence Summaries as a new German recognition signal pattern. Anything else? No? You know I think it might be advisable to move up some armour and some cavalry into the area around Krasnaya Polyana, just in case. Find out available units and allocate areas to them. There's sod all in that bloody bleak area - just that stinking little village. No proper roads, nothing. I feel sorry for our poor blokes who are going to have to sit out there waiting for the enemy; there's bugger all shelter they can get. Right, carry on.' Satrushkin rolled over to fall instantly into a deep sleep.

In a small and grubby anteroom the aide-de-camp checked a battle map of the area to the south and south-west of Kharkov. Like his Colonel the aide was baffled. Krasnaya Polyana really was the arsehole of the world. It was a nothing place. Of absolutely no strategic or tactical importance. Still, Satrushkin had ordered a covering force so a covering force there would be. Now, who was available? Ah, there was a group of units, resting now, but which would be put back into a blocking operation.

'Orderly. Send the following messages. To commanders and commissars of 343rd Infantry Division, 28th Cavalry Division and 133rd Armoured Division. Action: immediate. Vacate present areas forthwith and concentrate in the area around Krasnaya Polyana; specifically Vodnayoya, Shmarovka. Task: to be a blocking force against a possible penetration by the SS Panzer Corps.'

The aide saw the tidy chinagraph circles which he had drawn around the places he had named. He felt a sense of power. At his word the units would move and his clever grouping allowed the force to be deployed to meet a threat coming from any direction between the south and the south-west. Yes, he felt a distinct pleasure from a job well done. I should reward myself, he thought; some vodka and a sandwich, to acknowledge the achievement.

At 02.30 hours, in huddles of tents, in hovels, huts and houses around the little towns of Losovaya and Mikhailovskaya, sergeants were rousing their men from sleep. The Divisions had been alerted. The wildest rumours circulated among the half-wakened men. We're going back up the Line to stop a German breakthrough, was the most popular belief, and the simple soldiers grumbled as they worked - but only to themselves. In the Red Army expressions of discontent voiced aloud were followed by extra guard duties, by dangerous patrols or months in a penal battalion. It did not pay to complain too loudly, because there was always some tell-tale bastard who would report you to the Communist Party men. There were some good rewards for informers.

Red Army infantry and cavalrymen needed little time to pack. From the rude reveille just after 02.30 to being fully dressed and ready to march took the fighting echelons, the rifle companies and the sabre squadrons less than half an hour. They marched out. The other echelons and the armour could take a little longer, but those who might be committed to battle that day needed to be quickly under way.

The infantry columns were silent as they marched. The only sounds were the crunching of boots through the unbroken mantle of knee-deep snow, the rasping of breath in the cold night air and the occasional clink as one piece of equipment struck another. There was no talking. Early morning reveille and no breakfast are not inspirations to sparkling chat or to lively debate. So the infantry columns, twelve ranks abreast, tramped their way through the snow-bound countryside.

At half hourly intervals the leading Company halted and its men moved to the side of the track. The column passed and the halted men at the side of the road took their position at its rear. stamping out a track through the virgin snow was a task that tired even the hardiest. The Red Army infantry method of making a road through the deep snow was the simple, effective but exhausting one of a whole Company of men stamping down the snow into a hard-packed layer of ice. It was, of course, an infantry task. Only they could achieve it.

Later, along that track the cavalry horses would march. They, too, would tire easily in such a depth of snow. Also along that track would pass the soft skin vehicles which, being wheeled, would not cope as well as tanks. Three Divisions were on the march, moving to positions to the south and the west of Krasnaya Polyana and it was the infantry - the patient, burdened infantry - which stamped out the road so that the Cavalry and the lorries could pass in comfort.

Chapter 19

'Signaller, get me Obersturmführer Hennecke.'

A longish pause followed and then, 'Rudi, on the set.'

'Rudi, come home. I repeat, come home. Out.'

Peiper's cryptic orders were for Hennecke's little group to return to Krasnaya Polyana. Twenty minutes later, far away on the distant horizon, a single white light blazed in the night sky. The sentry who saw it reported it to the Sturmbannführer. He issued orders.

'Runner. To all officers. Alert the men in fifteen minutes and make sure that everybody has a hot drink. '

It was a little early, perhaps, to get the men ready for action. Hennecke was still about an hour's drive away. But a hot drink would do a lot to restore spirits which would be flagging after hours of cold and fruitless vigil. Peiper accepted a cup of coffee and felt the blessed warmth spread through a body that ached with cold. The coffee was bitter. It was ersatz, a substitute, and not for the first time the young commander wondered why it had tasted so foul. Surely German scientists could invent a more palatable brew? Rustling in the room sounded where men searched through pockets and haversacks for crusts of bread or for pieces of biscuit. The Siberian soldiers in Peiper's house drank just hot water flavoured with what looked like fluff from their pockets, but which they claimed were tea leaves. Everybody drank appreciatively. Faces were partly visible in the flickering flames of the little cookers fuelled by solidified methylated spirit.

'Sturmbannführer,' the sentry reported. 'There is another white flare.'

From its position Peiper estimated that Hennecke was now about six kilometres distant. This meant that Lipski's group, withdrawing in front of Rudi, would be about four kilometres away. The time for battle was approaching.

'Warm the tank motors and once they are running at full power swing the vehicles so that they face westwards. The remainder of the Group will stand to, now.'

The wooden houses of Krasnaya Polyana vibrated as the tank's Maybach engines roared and then the two vehicles, the one in the first house of the village at its northern end, and the second in the last house on the southern end, rolled backwards out of hiding, swung on their tracks and halted facing towards that area out of which Lipski and his murder group would come.

Another white flare hung bright in the sky. This one was very close. Time to take post. The SS commander walked over to his own panzer; that one at the northern entrance to the village.

'Good morning, crew. Is everything in full combat readiness? Good.' On the Command frequency he ordered the other tank commander, 'Number Two, you will stop Ivan from getting round our southern flank. I'll be responsible for stopping them infiltrating on the northern. The Grenadiers will hold the houses. Fire HE into Ivan's half-tracks and lorries. They are carrying his infantry. Let's concentrate on killing them.'

He yawned. It was pre-combat tiredness, a symptom which he knew was experienced by all fighting soldiers. No matter how often a warrior went into battle, every one began with this terrible tiredness. He yawned and stopped in half-yawn. He could see pin-pricks of light; the side lamps on Lipski's vehicles. Action was imminent now and immediately Peiper felt all tiredness vanish. With the prospect of sudden battle, adrenalin had begun to pump through his body until he felt that he had the power to conquer continents.

The little lights were now about the size of fire flies. About a kilometre distant, thought the commander, and they were closing quickly. The signal pistol jumped in Peiper's hand as he pressed the trigger. Seconds later a brilliant white magnesium flare burst in the sky. In its harsh light the vehicles of the NKVD column lay naked and exposed. Got them - the SS officer rejoiced. The Red swine were neatly sandwiched between the two SS groups - his and Hennecke's. The politicals were silhouetted against the white glare while he and his Command lay invisible in the shadows of the houses. More white flares burst in the sky. Hennecke was helping to illuminate the area. Peiper relayed fire orders to his panzer crew almost by instinct.

'Gunner. Enemy T-34. Seven hundred and fifty metres.' And almost immediately, so great was his faith in the skill of his veteran detachment, he gave the order to fire and saw in the light which bathed the battle area how the T-34 swayed on its right track under the impact of the solid shot. As the Russian tank came back onto both tracks it shuddered violently and blew up. In the few seconds that had elapsed since the first shot was fired the 7.5 cm gun of Peiper's tank had already begun traversing onto another target which had been indicated. Before it could fire again a T-34 at the end of the NKVD line swung away to the right and came to rest broadside on with its turret tipped at an impossible angle. Peiper's No 2 had got in his first shot. The German tank gunners fired off a third and a fourth round before the Red tank commanders reacted. There were still ten Soviet machines in action. Their inexperienced commanders did not concentrate fire upon the two German vehicles and this poor tactical handling negated the Soviet numerical advantage. The Red machines swerved and careered aimlessly about the area, crossing and re-crossing the lines of fire of their own comrades. From that confusion the German panzer crews profited. Peiper, upright in his turret, assessed the situation. He would draw the fire of the Ivans and while they were busy his No 2 could get in among the soft skins like a fox in a hen house.

'Number Two, move out and take out the Ivan infantry.'

Peiper sensed rather than saw the other machine drive towards the mass of vehicles huddled behind the T-34s. He sensed again the sudden explosion on his left. For a brief second his attention was drawn from the battle which he was fighting and he saw the No 2 machine halted and almost overturned by the impact of a Soviet tank that had rammed it - determined to stop the breakthrough. Both tanks were halted and damaged. There was no sign of the sergeant commanding the German vehicle.

'Report Number Two. What is the situation? Are you badly hurt?'

'A bit dazed, Sturmbannführer. The driver's concussed, I think, and the gunner's bleeding. I'll check and report back.'

There was movement on the Russian machine. Peiper shouted in alarm, 'Watch your enemy; watch your enemy.'

He had seen the NKVD tank commander reach down inside his machine and re-emerge holding something that he lobbed easily at the panzer's turret. The grenade hit the rim of the turret cupola. A river of flame flowed down as the phosphorous bomb burst. A second incendiary fell on the hatch, below which were the drivers and co-driver's compartments. A third grenade slipped from the Russian commander's hand onto the front deck of his own vehicle. Flames leaped up. The young Soviet officer made no effort to move, to escape from the flames that threatened him and Peiper knew why. The T-34 had a defect. Ramming another vehicle caused the breech of the gun to be forced back, crushing the legs of the commander standing in the turret. The NKVD officer was trapped in his tank and Peiper saw, as if in some terrible slow-motion nightmare, the Russian place a pistol in his mouth and slump forward dead in the turret.

Another T-34 began to burn - Hennecke's group was in action. The Soviet tanks, caught between two fires, twisted and turned desperately, firing their guns, putting down smoke and laying swathes of machine-gun fire. Red infantry poured from the trucks and carriers in well-controlled rushes, towards the wooden houses at the southern end of the village.

Lipski realised that he was now trapped between two groups of German armour. He needed help, but if he asked for it then he could no longer keep the vendetta secret. But it was a risk that he had to take to save his men and himself. Messages went out quickly for aid. Swiftly the replies came. A ski battalion of infantry was moving down in support immediately and three separate Divisions - an infantry, a Cavalry and an armoured Division - would also in the area before dawn. Lipski knew, if he could hold until first light, he would be in the clear.

In the village the determined assault by Red Army infantry had begun to turn the German left flank, the one which had been covered by Peiper's No 2. It was now wide open. The NKVD infantry burst at last into the first house of the village, bludgeoning and stabbing the German garrison. Two wounded Siberians who fell into their hands were tied, face to face, by leather belts . A grenade was placed between them at chest level and the pin deftly removed. There was a short, dull explosion and they fell dead. German wounded who tried to surrender were shot where they lay. This was not the time to shout 'Kamerad'. Prisoners were lumber and were 'dealt with.'

Blinded by Russian smoke shells, fires and explosions, Peiper did not see the ski troops arrive until the wind dispersed the acrid curtain for a brief moment and he saw through the wisps the speeding shapes. Before the smoke hid them again he could see that they were grouping on a slight rise to the south of Krasnaya Polyana.

'Driver - lock the left track. Spin the cow! Spin her! Bow gunner- spray the first house in the village. Ivan has got into it and he's being reinforced. Main gunner - enemy ski troop infantry four hundred metres, with HE load. Left a bit, a bit more. On. Fire.'

Turning to his control switch Peiper called up Hennecke.

'Rudi, we are under pressure here. Drive forward with two tanks and a half-track to evacuate the Grenadiers in the house. Out. '

Hennecke's voice came back to him. 'The Ivans in front of me are fragmenting. We are forcing his armoured fighting vehicles

155

southwards. If we drive them far enough away we can trap his infantry in the houses and destroy them at our leisure. I suggest that I continue to split Ivan's armour from his infantry.'

'Agreed. Rudi. You do that, but send the vehicles I need, now.'

The light of the signal flares in the sky was beginning to dim. Peiper could not recall that he had fired any during the battle and a parachute flare burned for well over five minutes. He checked his watch. Good God, the whole action had lasted less than four minutes and yet, in that short time, one of his panzer was dead; there were four Red vehicles burning and lots of the politicals and the ski infantry must have been shot down. All this in four minutes.

He fired fresh rockets into the night. Brilliantly lit, once again, by the magnesium flares, Peiper could see through the thinning smoke that the ski battalion was moving into the attack. The first men had already begun to propel themselves across the snow, striding in *Langlauf* taking advantage of every decline to gain speed. There could be no cohesion in such an assault. The skiers would have to move independently of each other and Peiper watched as the extended line of figures closed towards the centre and then formed itself into a single long column which swept down towards the village. The NKVD soldiers holding the house which had been lost by the Germans built up a storm of fire to cover the attack - firing through windows and cracks in the walls at the fascists in the nearby houses. Peiper watched the advance of the skiers with despair in his heart. It was such a senseless assault. Lightly-armed infantry should not attack enemy troops backed by armour, even though there was only his one tank to hold them off.

The column of flying, white figures, almost undetectable against the white snow, swished downhill. Peiper needed to silhouette them against a light and he fired signal flares which curved in flight and hung in the air behind the skiers. They were covering the ground in great strides or little runs, moving swiftly until the head of the column began to pass the village houses. The concentrated fire of German Spandaus from the garrison in Krasnaya Polyana and of Peiper's panzer struck the first skiing group and tore it to pieces.

Twenty men were tumbled in the first salvoes. Those behind skilfully slalomed through their fallen comrades, glided past the house in which the Grenadiers lay, and sprayed them with machine pistol fire. Hand grenades, flung by the Reds as they whooshed past the houses, burst inside rooms. Chattering machine-gun fire swept away sections of the silent ski-soldiers. It had become an infantry fire fight. The Ivans were now so close to the houses that Peiper could no longer fire his guns for fear of hitting his own men.

Suddenly, a file of skiers turned away from the houses and swooped towards Peiper's panzer, standing isolated in open ground to the west of the village. A hand grenade burst on the tank turret and the Commander ducked as the bullets of a Shpagin machine pistol rattled on the panzer's hull. He saw neither the two-man team fling a satchel charge of explosive beneath his tank's right track, nor the single skier whose incendiary grenade burst in a sheet of sudden flame on the panzer's skirting.

Peiper leaned right out of his turret. There was, he saw to his relief, no danger that his machine would catch fire. Just as well, for it was required urgently. The Grenadiers in the houses were under severe pressure and Hennecke's group had not yet come up. It was upon the Sturmbannführer's single vehicle that the defence of the village depended. He moved the panzer to a point from which he could directly assault the Reds in the first house.

'Driver, advance.'

The vehicle rolled a few metres and then the right track ran onto the satchel charge. There was a bright flash and a loud explosion. The Ivans in the house raised a cheer; two of the fascist panzer's were out of action. The joy of the politicals was short lived. Even if Peiper's tank could not manoeuvre, it still remained a steel fortress with a heavy gun and two fast-firing machine guns.

'Everybody OK?' The crew acknowledged. 'Keep the sods in the house under control while I check on the track.'

Schmeisser in hand, Peiper leapt from the rear deck onto the muddied snow and crouched in the dark lee of the damaged panzer. White skiers were still criss-crossing the area like tall and slender moths. One short chain of them swooped dangerously near the halted machine. They might try to rush the tank and destroy it with the grenades, thought Peiper. Still kneeling in the shadows, he held the machine pistol with its magazine on his knee and fired a long burst. The chain of men died without even seeing him.

Other white figures glided away into the darkness back towards the tank battle which Hennecke's group was still fighting to the sound of the village. Peiper ran his hand round the wheels of his tank. They were all south. The track lay stretched out behind he machine. The commander found the links which had been broken by

157

the blast of the explosion. Quickly he scrambled back inside the hull of the machine and radioed Hennecke.

'Rudi. Send a wagon over with spares and ammo. I've lost two track links.'

Out of the night loomed a half-track. Grenadiers debussed to take up all round protection and fitters began to wrestle with the heavy cold metal.

'Sturmbannführer, roll her back gently.'

Slowly the huge Panzer IV was inched back along the flat, laid out track. There was a continual hissing and buzzing in the air as Red snipers and machine gunners tried to halt the repair work. Mortars began to crump, crump. Within a minute they'll have the range and then, thought Peiper, we've had it.

'Gunner sweep the area to our right. See if you can see any mortar batteries. The bastards are getting persistent. Right lads,' this to the fitters, 'how are we now?'

The commander stood on the rear deck watching his men at work. While they were out in the open in the noise and the firing he could not take cover. There was a shuddering crash as the 7.5 fired and a voice in his earphones cried triumphantly, 'I think I got a mortar then, Sturmbannführer.'

A fitter sergeant looked up. 'We've replaced the broken links. The track should now be sufficiently long. Back a bit, Sturmbannführer. A bit more. Stop. You, Friedl, give us a hand to bring the track over the riding wheels.' The two ends of the track were joined. A quick hammering concluded with the words, 'Try her now, Sturmbannführer.'

The driver jerked the machine about in order to test the remade track. It held. Peiper's command vehicle was in action again and not before time. The commander of the Red ski battalion, convinced that both the German tanks guarding Krasnaya Polyana were out of action, had decided the time had come to launch a conventional infantry attack upon the stranded vehicles and the trapped Grenadiers in the houses. Discarding their skis, the men of the Soviet battalion moved forward in the classic Red Army pattern of attack - lines of men tramping forward.

'Good God,' Peiper breathed in surprise. 'Surely their officers cannot be so stupid. They can't be launching this type of attack against us.' A chilling thought struck him and he concluded more soberly, 'Unless the orders are to sacrifice the battalion. But I'm damned if I can see what they will gain by that. Sergeant.'

'Sturmbannführer. '

'Set up a line of machine guns between this vehicle and the houses. Quickly now. Ivan's preparing to attack us. We can kill them all inside a killing ground if we're quick. Get your men in position, but wait until I give the order to fire.'

There was no time for machine-gun posts to be dug out and set up. No time to put up tripods and to mount the guns. Speed was vital. A pair of guns formed a team. Each supported the other. The No 3 Grenadier on each gun stood with the barrel of the MG 42 on his right shoulder and each of them stood with his back to the enemy. The No 2s threaded the metal links of the ammunition belts through the breeches. The No 1s on the guns stood, fingers on triggers, eyes squinting at the short lines of silhouetted men wading towards them. The NCOs reported the guns ready to fire and the eyes of the corporals and sergeants in charge of the Spandaus were fixed on the advancing enemy infantry.

Light was needed, light and yet more light. Then, as the first lines of Soviet soldiers passed the wooden houses fresh flares exploded, throwing each detail into stark and clear relief. From the Reds in the first house came loud and hoarse cheering as the leading ranks of the ski battalion passed them. It was one of the few loud sounds that could be heard; cheering and the crunch of boots on snow. Otherwise the night was as silent as the grave.

Peiper watched. The lines of the Soviet battalion were now contained in the killing area. He dropped his raised arm and barked a single command into the microphone. From along the German machine-gun line the MG 42s poured tracer - like lines of lava. The Sturmbannführer's bow gunner sang softly to himself as he traversed his machine gun along the lines of Soviet troops now at very close range. Soon the first two ranks had been wiped away. The tired line marched, without flinching, over the bodies lying on the trampled snow, only to melt and die in the German fire. Then the fourth and fifth ranks died. The whole ground was covered with the dead of the ski battalion. The butcher's bill had been a very heavy one but not one soldier had turned back; they had all marched unhesitatingly into the German fire. 'Why?' the question nagged at Peiper. 'Why? What was the point of such a sacrifice?' And then, if in answer to his unspoken question, he saw in the night sky the answer.

About four kilometres distant - that's where Hennecke is, he thought to himself - a curtain of violet-coloured flares was rising to light the southern horizon. Violet flares - Oh God - they meant that

159

Hennecke's Kampfgruppe was under attack by a superior force of Soviet armour. The Sturmbannführer thought about the Red ski battalion; wiped out to a man. 'Poor sods. It was their task to hold us here until those tank reinforcements came up. And they did too.

'Rudi report please.'

Hennecke's voice came tumbling in excited words through the earphones.

'There is a whole bloody army out here and it's marching to Krasnaya Polyana. I fired a couple of white flares to keep the NKVD lot in our sight and then, bugger me, the flares showed a mob marching in as easy as you like, as if they were on manoeuvre. There's a whole mass of tanks out there; five hundred plus. Somewhere there is cavalry - the snow was black with them. There is infantry too. The whole lot are moving towards us - in the direction of Krasnaya Polyana. I shall have to pull back. I can't hold this present position against such odds. There's one fly lot of Ivan armour trying to get round my western flank.'

'Rudi. I shall come forward once I have put the garrison in the houses in the picture.

'Stumke, can you hear me? Yes? Right. There's a major grouping of Red armour just south of here. I shall go forward and resume command of the whole Kampfgruppe. Together Hennecke and I shall engage the Reds in battle and destroy them.

'This means that you will be on your own for the next few hours. It may be all day. I would suggest that you pull all the men back into the first house in the village; the one where I was last night. With the Red armour out of the way I can destroy the Reds in the house that they have captured and then the Grenadiers will burn down all the other houses in the village. That will give you a clear field of fire.

'It is about 06.00 hours now. Dawn is about eight. Get Schlank to bring in the Stukas if things get too hairy. I shall radio at midday and again at midnight. If any emergency arises, radio me. Good luck. Out.'

Peiper's machine stood off some hundred metres from the wooden house which held the Red garrison and then he opened fire. Soon the dry old wood was alight. Figures scrambled out of doors and windows and ran into the concealing darkness beyond the circle of flames. Bursts of Spandau fire encouraged the laggards and soon each of the few houses in the hamlet were ablaze. In the light of the fires Peiper could see the faces of his men at the windows of the house. They would be fine. Isolated yes, but only for a short time. A quick battle with the Reds and then he would come back and pick them up. Then the whole group would head for Mirgorod and the Leibstandarte's outpost position there.

He could rely upon his men. The garrison was determined. There were men of his own SS unit, some of Stumke's Prussians and some of Marenko's little group - and, of course, Schlank. The garrison had supplies and ammunition enough. He would be back in about four hours. Silhouetted against the flames of the burning houses of Krasnaya Polyana, Peiper raised his arm in salute. 'Panzer - *marsch*' and his tank, accompanied by the half-track, headed south to meet Hennecke and the other vehicles of the Kampfgruppe, which were withdrawing slowly and in good order, before the pressure of the three Divisions of the Red Army.

Chapter 20

Lipski and the commander of 133 Tank Division were in conference, crouched knee to knee in a command vehicle. The Comrade Major was in a happy frame of mind, now that the three Divisions which had been promised him were in strength on the battlefield.

'Colonel Satrushkin, the intelligence officer of 6th Army, tells me that the fascists intend to drive southwards from here in a new offensive,' said Kalchov, the Tank Division commander. 'Frankly I think this is a false assessment of the situation. What the hell could they hope to achieve? I don't see the sense of it. In the north they are being pushed back into Kharkov. They are under pressure all along the line and yet 6th Army Intelligence believes that they are preparing to mount an offensive here - here of all places.

'That German mob in front of us is quite small, isn't it? From your account and from other sightings - even allowing for exaggerations- present Company always excepted, of course, the Nemetski in front of us are about the strength of half a Panzer Division. No more. I don't think this is the sign of an offensive coming in. I think it's a Kampfgruppe returning home. That is my assessment of the situation.

'Let me speak frankly. I outrank you and have more experience than you. You, on the other hand, represent the all-powerful Party. But you know nothing about armoured warfare. Right so far? I am also the senior officer in the three Divisions that have been brought together for this mission. So I take command. Agreed? Right. I'll fight the battle, advising you of what is happening from a military standpoint. There is no question of politics here, I think.' Kalchov looked across at Lipski, saw the slight shake of the head and continued.

'We both want to kill the Nemetski bastards, don't we? I know how to do it swiftly and efficiently. Leave that part to me. Agreed ? Now, the first thing we do is regroup our forces. It's 06.00 hour now. Let my tank crews, the infantry and the cavalry rest for the next few hours. Sun up will be in about two hours. Full light will be half an hours after that. By that time our three Divisions will have fed, rearmed, and rested. Just after 10.00 hours we move off. Visibility is good. We can observe the fascists. It hasn't snowed for the past couple of days. I doubt it will snow today, so the Nemetski will be visible all day.

'They hold Krasnaya Polyana and it is some sort of pivot for their movements. We shall prise them loose from that village. Now, look at the map. See anything significant? No? Right, then I'll show you. The Fascist Kampfgruppe is on *our* side of the river Udy and they can't get back over it...Not unless they abandon their vehicles and they won't do that. There are no bridges - can't you see? - and the ice is too thin for their tanks. They must rejoin their own Army whose nearest outpost is here at Mirgorod.'

'You are assuming that the Fascists are only a small group and not the spearhead of a new offensive,' Lipski broke in. 'What happens if they are the advanced guard of a major counter-attack?'

'Don't be naive,' Kalchov barked at him. 'Are there any reports of the Nemetski building bridges? No? Well then. If that group ahead of us can't *go back* across the river because there are no bridges, then nothing can *come forward* either without bridges. There is nothing in the Intelligence Summaries about any enemy preparations for an offensive. Except here at Krasnaya Polyana and those reports are a load of balls. Some frightened sod at Army HQ is seeing more in the German moves than is intended.

'Right, you acknowledge that what we have to do is to get the Fascists away from Krasnaya Polyana? Agreed? I'll send in infantry to take the houses. I'll send in one strong tank group to come up alongside the village and squeeze the Fascist Kampfgruppe westward towards Mirgorod. In the meantime our Cavalry and one of our tank regiments makes a forced march. They will lay an ambush to intercept the Nemetski when they come up fleeing ahead of our strong armoured pincer. Got it, so far? Good. The rest of the infantry Division can be left to hold the front between Krasnaya Polyana and the river Mush.

'As I said, our right armoured pincer forces the Fascists westwards. They can't move eastwards here, across the Udy river, because of the ice.' Kalchov's stubby fingers swung from point to point across the map. 'The Fascists can't come south against the infantry- where would they be heading? - into the unknown. So they must move westwards...No; they can't move northwards, the river Udy still runs there. No, they must move westwards, and there we shall have prepared a trap for them.

'In this area between Krasnaya Polyana and Mirgorod is the ground on which we shall destroy that Nemetski Kampfgruppe.

That's my battle plan. Shall we get the other commanders together and tell them?'

Chapter 21

Dawn brought in a bright, clear day, cloudless and cold. As day lightened the Germans could see that the whole of the area south of Krasnaya Polyana was covered by masses of Soviet troops and vehicles. There were queues of men standing in lines at steaming field kitchens; others were tending horses and carts. Others were busy servicing vehicles. In the bright light the Germans could see the whole array of the enemy. The Soviet commanders had dispensed with the standard routines of camouflaging and digging as laid down in Field Service Regulations. Kalchov had decided to overawe the Germans with a display of force. Psychology was a battlefield tactic.

The conference of divisional and regimental commanders was quickly opened and closed. Lipski won over the divisional politicals and Kalchov was a decisive chairman. Like a good professional soldier talking to other good professional soldiers, he had no need to give rigid and formal plans committed to reams of paper. The thorny problems of liaison between the guns and the other arms, particularly the infantry, was dealt with by the acceptance on both sides that there were certain to be casualties.

It really was a glorious day. The sun, shining warm on Peiper's left shoulder, brought with it the realisation that the worst of the winter was past. For today, however, the first priority was to see off this lot, who were forming up so blatantly, so that his Kampfgruppe could turn westwards to gain touch with the Leibstandarte outpost at Mirgorod.

Surveying the enemy through binoculars, the SS commander could see a great mass of infantry - it looked like a whole regiment - busily engaged in digging in. Prime movers and tractors were bringing up anti-tank guns to lard the infantry line just as pieces of fat lard a tough piece of beef. Another group of Red infantry, a couple of battalions strong, some sort of Reserve he supposed, lay half left of him. Their heavy overcoats were distinctive against the white snow on which they were resting. There should be a third regiment, thought Peiper, and worried because he could not locate it. Nor could he see any cavalry, apart from a few squadrons wheeling about in the snow. Yet Hennecke had reported a mass of horsemen. Where had those Cossack sods gone? That was another worry.

The biggest worry of all was, however, the great mass of armour that was missing. Rudi had reported about five hundred vehicles. Well, there weren't that many, but there were certainly three hundred. But if Rudi had estimated five hundred then there was a whole regiment of tanks missing. The armoured group before him was drawn up in ranks and squadrons and this surprised him, for even this late in the War some Red Army commanders still paraded their tank units closely packed and in straight lines. Peacetime habits die hard.

Whoever commanded this lot wasn't a parade ground soldier. The squadrons were disposed tactically and were well positioned. The commander who led them must be a bloody good tank man, thought Peiper, but his eyes still looked for flaws in the Soviet dispositions. He could see none. A niggling thought crept into Peiper's mind and would not go away. He knew with absolute conviction that this was one fight which would end with his Kampfgruppe running for its life to reach Mirgorod.

Movement on his left attracted him. Russian SP artillery was moving. So that was the thrust point; the point of maximum effort, there on his left wing- their right wing. Thoughts about the Soviet units missing from the battlefield were not of immediate importance - the enemy was moving to the attack, or would be soon, just as soon as the right wing had been built up. The intentions of the Soviet commander were very clear - he intended to force the Kampfgruppe away from Krasnaya Polyana. The Russian intended to seek a decision on the open steppe. Against the three hundred plus Soviet armoured fighting vehicles, there were only the clapped out machines of his Kampfgruppe - fewer than twenty panzer and ten SPs. Thank God there was sufficient ammunition. But ammunition alone, nor even the veteran crews he commanded, could hope to meet and prevail against the crushing Soviet superiority. This would have to be reduced. Stukas were the immediate weapon.

'Signaller. Get me Captain Stumke, please.'

There was a whistling of static interference and then faintly the voice of the infantry commander came to him.

'Stumke, can you hear me? Yes? Good. Get Schlank to lay on a Stuka strike. We are in position four kilometres south of Krasnaya Polyana. The Reds are about two kilometres farther south. Tell him we want no balls-up this time. Bomb the Ivans; not us. We will lay out swastika flags and direction arrows. Even the bloody blind bastards of the Luftwaffe can't mistake them. I want those Air Force

166

layabouts over here, at the double, before the Reds start their attack. Tell their commander he is still bound by the *dienstliche Befehl* I gave him. He'll answer to the SS if he fails us. What? All right, I'll wait.'

Through the static interference Peiper heard whispering in the background. Then Schlank reported.

'Sturmbannführer. You are in luck. I've just spoken with the Luftwaffe. The Squadron has just had a mission aborted, so they are ready fuelled and bombed up. They will be over you in ten minutes. I must say that you are not very popular with them The move out of the Line that they were supposed to do has been cancelled, indefinitely. They've been ordered instead to support our Kampfgruppe until the end of the mission. Believe me, you are not the most popular man in the Army Group. Good luck.'

Flying low and out of the sun the JU 87s swept in single file over the short line of German armour, each vehicle of which was draped with the Nazi party flag. The squadron leader waggled his wings and the flights of aircraft, engines roaring, climbed high into the sky. At operational height the squadron banked and each plane swooped in an almost vertical dive. The cannon guns under the V-shaped wings puffed and puffed, pouring streams of large-calibre projectiles at the Reds. Showers of light bombs cascaded from containers held beneath the fuselage. The bombs were fitted with graze fuses which even the slightest brushing motion would detonate. Some of the Soviet tanks were soon concealed in flames and smoke as the bombs found targets.

One flight of Stukas, armed with small anti-personnel bombs, screamed down upon the Red infantry, showering upon the running men lightweight, butterfly-shaped messengers of death. Across the whole white steppe there was noise, confusion and fire. A Stuka, its tail section blown off by light anti-aircraft fire, somersaulted out of control and was hit by the plane diving behind it. The German machines, locked together, fell and exploded near a group of Russian petrol and ammunition trucks. The soft skins blew up.

Peiper sensed that the moment was right to exploit the confusion among the Soviets.

'Rudi, I intend to make a couple of raids. In and out quickly - a couple of times only. I'll take the centre. You take the SP's and dominate the left where his SPs are. There, do you see them? Use smoke to blind the buggers- there's very little wind. Right, move out now.'

Peiper's raid began. Echeloned in arrow-head formation on either side of his panzer were the machines of his Command. The panzer line streamed like ships at sea leaving a wake of snow crystals. Behind the fighting vehicles came the half-tracks of Grenadiers. the SS machine gunners alert but with eyes streaming with tears in the cold air. The Grenadiers made the last minute adjustments of soldiers committed to battle. Chin straps were tightened. Grenades were brought from haversacks and laid on ledges. Their little tin bases were unscrewed laying clear the ripcord and bead. Ahead of the bucketing steel colossi, only a few kilometres ahead, the Luftwaffe's Black Hussars of the air were making their last attacks, diving and rising again before heading north-eastwards to their front-line airfield.

Peiper's Kampfgruppe roared on and on towards the shaken Russians. Plumes of snow rose from behind each vehicle to hang in the air rainbow coloured where the sun caught the frozen white atoms.

'Range five hundred,' Peiper's voice came through the intercom, 'Soviet Command Vehicle. AP. Right, right, on; on. Fire.'

The commander knew that only a shit-hot crew could fire while the vehicle was on the move and be sure of hitting the target. He also knew that his crew were red hot. The Panzer IV shuddered momentarily as the gun fired and then a Soviet regimental command tank, struck just below the turret, swung broadside on and slowly began to burn. The red and vivid flames, almost invisible in the bright sunlight, lapped gently along the hull and dropped blazing gobbets of flaming oil onto the snow.

The Sturmbannführer turned in the turret to check the position of three vehicles on his left. He was shocked. One second they were there, maintaining distance and speed, roaring along in formation, guns trained and ready. Then they had vanished in three huge, dense clouds of black smoke. The vehicle nearest to Peiper burst suddenly through the explosion running easily, but trailing a plume of greasy, heavy and dense sable smoke. The noise of the violent explosion which then tore it apart was audible to Peiper even above the roar of his own tank's engine. Fragments were falling from the black cloud which hung over the place where the panzer had blown up. Debris, fragments of his comrades, perhaps, rained down; burning petrol flooded across the snow. Through the SS officer's thoughts ran the words of the German Army tank song '...then our panzer will be a bronze grave...

Peiper checked on the other two machines. Both were halted and were burning. How could they have been knocked out so suddenly? No Russian tank had yet fired a gun. They were too far away still to have achieved such destruction so quickly. If it was not the T-34s or the Russian SPs, then what the hell caused it? The Sturmbannführer turned to face the battle and saw to his horror, only a handful of metres away, a square block of snow fall from a snow wall. 'A block of snow from a snow wall?' thought Peiper uncomprehendingly and then realised, with sudden and stomach-churning fear, that he was within metres of a cunningly built and camouflaged ice wall.

Through the hole from which the snow block had fallen the Sturmbannführer saw the round, black bore of an anti-tank gun. And it pointed directly at him.

He reacted immediately. 'All guns fire forward; fire, fire, fire.'

The tank cannon boomed and simultaneously a yellow flame burst from the muzzle of the Russian gun. The flame filled Peiper's vision from horizon to horizon and from its height to its depth. He saw no other sight than the yellow flower of flame. The heat of the explosion struck him like a Khamsin wind. His panzer rocked as the high velocity shell, striking the turret a glancing blow, ricocheted and produced a coruscation of sparks that flickered in the sun.

The panzer reared up onto the wall and rolled badly as it ran over the anti-tank gun. The crew were running wildly across the snow, their hands covering their heads. Peiper's tank hit level ground, rocked, steadied and then drove on. The SS officer saw to his right front a deep pit excavated from the snow - a command post. On his present course the panzer would miss it. He looked with blank eyes at the Russian soldiers scrabbling in the trampled snow at the bottom of the pit. Them or me - the Eastern Front's deadly alternative. It was a primitive choice, but in this war there was neither mercy for an enemy nor compassion for the foe.

The Reds floundering in the snow looked up at the German commander, their eyes pleading to be allowed to live. The frightened expressions did not move him. Kill them or die yourself - it was the jungle law.

'Driver, right track lock.' The vehicle skidded to a halt as the brake was applied to the right track. The momentum turned the steel giant quickly so that the track was pressing down upon the command post and its screaming occupants.

'Driver, spin her on the right.' The panzer tilted slightly as the track screwed itself into the yielding snow. Peiper did not look to see the snow stained with blood and flesh. There were other priorities. He had lost part of his attack force and he was still not close enough to kill the enemy.

The clever bastard on the Russian side, he thought, had put out a gun line - a well-concealed gun line - and had caught the Kampfgruppe napping. The Sturmbannführer knew that if there was one Russian gun line there was bound to be a second. It was suicide to stay; it was suicide to carry on with the attack. There could be no question of carrying out a couple of raids against the enemy. It was pull-out time.

'All runners. All runners. Pull back. Rendezvous in the field west of Krasnaya Polyana. Rudi. Pull back.'

Peiper's machine had been the first to reach the wall and there was danger still to the other vehicles of the battle line. God alone knew how many anti-tank guns were still in action ready to shoot his Kampfgruppe up the arse as it high-tailed it for the rallying place. A quick look showed him. There were Russian gun positions almost parallel to him. He would turn right and run them down, enfilading them with fire.

'Driver, bring her round. Straighten her up. Forward.'

The great armoured machine bumped and bounced its way across gun positions, machine-gun posts and command points, all abandoned as the Ivans- commanders and the commanded, gunners and infantry alike - ran like hares through the snow.

'Jochen,' Hennecke's voice came urgently on the radio. 'I've lost an SP. I am coming back under smoke. We've been bamboozled, I think. There are already a couple of T-34s on our rallying ground outside Krasnaya Polyana. The bastards must have come up past my flank. They've cut off the garrison there. '

'Thank you, Rudi. I'll go back and sort the buggers out. I have briefed Stumke to hold out until we come to pick them up. In view of your news I'll drive the T-34s off and pick up the garrison in the house. All runners, all runners. The RV area is occupied by Ivans. My Company is going to sort them out. One half-track to accompany. Rally on Obersturmführer Hennecke. When I rejoin you the intention is to head towards Mirgorod.'

Peiper and three panzers, together with a half-track, turned quickly away from the battle and roared down upon the only house that was left in the village of Krasnaya Polyana. The two Russian machines stood squat, facing the house held by Stumke and his garrison. The Russians had their backs to the onrushing panzer. Peiper gave one short order.

'We'll take out the left hand T-34 and then the right one. All guns fire at five hundred metres. Fire when ready.'

Two shells struck the designated target; a third ricocheted screaming into the sky. The first T-34's gun drooped in its turret. It was a 'kill'. Immediately, the sweating gunners swung their turrets, laid on, watched as the target came on, and fired. Nothing happened. The turret of the Red machine suddenly swung, the gun elevated and moved as if to cover the Germans now only four hundred metres distant. Another salvo crashed in unison from the German tank guns. The second T-34 was dead. Then from the cupola a figure climbed, fell to the ground and slowly picked itself up. Drunkenly, the Red Army man staggered towards the panzer on Peiper's right as if to surrender himself. He leaned on the chassis and then with a sudden movement flung a phosphorous grenade onto the glacis plate. Before the astonished Germans could react, the Ivan had drawn a pistol and had begun to fire shots at the panzer commander standing upright in the cupola. Then, very slowly and wearily, as if overtaken by narcolepsy, the Russian crumpled and died.

'Christ Almighty, they never give up.' Peiper was aware, once again, of the determination with which the Russians fought. He had seen wounded and unconscious Red Army men whose first action on regaining consciousness was to reach for their firearm to take up the battle. In 1941 he had seen a Russian tank believed to be knocked out days before, suddenly become dangerous as the wounded gunner, the crew's only survivor, had revived and had brought the gun into action.

The demonstration by the Russian, now lying dead alongside the German panzer, was a reminder of the calibre of his enemy. Peiper reproached himself. The mission had not been as difficult as he had expected and he had allowed his guard to relax. The memory of the anti-tank wall came back to him. He was taking too much for granted. That way was the shortest road to the grave. He must tighten up his reactions.

There were faces at the window of the house. Then figures appeared at the door. Peiper jumped from his panzer.

171

'Captain Stumke?'

'Herr Sturmbannführer.'

'Evacuate immediately. We've got about five minutes. No more.'

He waved his arm to bring forward the half-track. The two remaining Panzer IVs stood guarding the evacuation.

'We have wounded,' announced Stumke.

'Serious cases?'

'Gunshot wounds. Light. They are all walking wounded. Two of them are serious, though.'

'Excuse me, Stumke. Sergeant.'

'Sturmbannführer?'

'Evacuate. Everybody out now. Set fire to the place. Oh, hallo Schlank. Enjoying it?'

'This is a picnic compared to real fighting.' Schlank was horrified at the bitterness of the warfare but he would not admit it 'You should see what we of the Luftwaffe have to endure.'

'Lying sod. Right Stumke. Everything go well?'

'We thought that we would be attacked by those T-34s. I think they were just about to open fire when you came along.'

'Lucky they had their backs to us. Everybody on board, Sergeant?'

'Yes, Sturmbannführer.'

'Panzer, marsch,' and Peiper's little group rejoined the main body.

The two groups met and the whole formation swept off. Snow swished high in the air as the panzers swerved and slewed to take up position. The formation was changed in shape from that of an arrow head to that of a bell. Behind the panzer shell came the SPs, ready to move from one crisis point to another. In their wake were the soft skin columns, the petrol, food and ammunition trucks. In the rear, forming a shield across the mouth of the bell, roared half-tracks bearing the SS Grenadiers.

Maintaining distance a few kilometres behind Peiper's retreating Kampfgruppe rolled the Soviet armoured regiments formed up into wide and solid blocks of steel. They advanced deliberately and menacingly over the steppe following the German Kampfgruppe which moved westward at a controlled and careful speed, en route to Mirgorod.

'We've got them,' Kalchov exulted. 'They can't force their way back to Krasnaya Polyana and now we're going to drive them away from the river.'

'Why do we need to do that?' Lipski could not follow the General's tactical reasoning.

'At the moment their left flank rests on the river. They think that this protects them on that flank. What they don't know is that we've got a line of anti-tank guns at this point here.' The finger pointed to a slight bend. 'Know anything about rivers?'

Lipski shook his head.

'No?' asked Kalchov. 'Well, the river's width narrows here and widens just past the bend. So I've set up our anti-tank guns just before the bend, where the river is narrowest and, therefore, where the range is shortest. The anti-tank gun fire will unsettle them and force them to move away from the river bank. To lead them on we send our cavalry over the river...'

'Horses against tanks?' Lipski asked incredulously. 'Horses against tanks?'

'Patience, Comrade Major.' Kalchov explained as carefully as if Lipski were an idiot boy. 'Patience. We send in the cavalry. They make a feint attack. Some of them will undoubtedly get killed, but you can't fight a war without losses.

'The horsemen rush away northwards as if in a panic, drawing the Nemetski from the river towards this balka here.' The finger indicated a long, deep, natural split in the ground running from west to east. Balkas, steep and narrow valleys, are a feature of the terrain in southern Russia and some were deep enough to conceal whole regiments. Others were significant enough to change the thrust line of a tank attack. They had tactical possibilities.

'In that big balka there,' Kalchov explained, 'we have part of our tank regiment - the one that marched away during the night.

Remember?' The tone was still that of a patient man explaining things to a slow learner.

'Our tanks are in the balka. Do you understand? They will stop the fascists from going too far north and if they retreat towards the river, then our anti-tank guns are still in position.'

'And if they turn eastwards,' Lipski was asking for confirmation, 'then this group with us is ready to meet them. And if they continue to withdraw westward then what is to stop them getting back to Mirgorod?'

173

'Can't you read a map?' the General chided gently. 'See the balka there? It runs north to south into the river. There - see it? It will force the Germans to move into this area here.' The spatulate hand swept over the outspread map. 'The balka peters out there. see it? It peters out and there is a little gap about four kilometres there between the end of that balka in the west and this balka in the north. The fascists will have to pass through that narrow gap in order to reach Mirgorod. That gap is lined with snow walls, behind which we have anti-tank guns. That little gap there on the map, between the two balkas, is the gateway to the killing ground. We may knock out one or two of their vehicles before we get them to the killing ground, but it is in that area there,' again the sweeping hand movement across the map. 'that we shall wipe out that gang of fascists. Understand?'

'Meanwhile?' Now that the end was so close Lipski wanted nothing to stop the realisation of his plan. He was convinced that the Siberians were still with the German Kampfgruppe and he wanted the whole lot - traitors and Fascists alike - dead; stone dead; killed to a man.

'Meanwhile? Meanwhile,' Kalchov assured him, 'we roll slowly along. In a minute there will be a signal. Ah, there it is,' he said as a semi-circle of emerald-green flares burst the sky. 'Those flares are from our ambush groups. That lot there are the tanks in the north - south balka. Ah, there are the flares from the gun line at the bend of the river. Those there are the signals from the group in the balka to the north of the river. Only one more group, that one in the killing ground. They're late. No, no they're not. That's the signal. All groups are in position now. Now we can stop pursuing the Nemetski and await developments.'

The Russian armoured regiments halted at Kalchov's order. Crews jumped from the vehicles and began to cook, to repair small defects. Petrol lorries came forward immediately. Kalchov was a strict commander. Every tank had to be a runner or the crew was sentenced and condemned as saboteurs. Penal battalion was the lightest sentence that the General ever imposed. War was not a game for dilettantes; it was a question of survival and that could not be prejudiced by the stupidity of a crew over the maintenance its vehicle. So his men worked and worked hard.

Chapter 22

'Sturmbannführer, the Ivan tanks have halted,' a sergeant in a half-track reported.

'Is nobody following us?'

'No, nobody.'

Why, Peiper wondered? Why had the Reds given up so quickly? The Red Commander was an experienced tank man; his dispositions in the battlefield south of Krasnaya Polyana had shown that. He had superiority and yet he had made no serious attempt to engage the Kampfgruppe in battle. Instead, the Ivan General had been content to shepherd the German group - to what? Peiper questioned. The memory of the snow wall came back. Peiper was certain now that the Kampfgruppe was being urged towards some new trap.

From which direction would the enemy blow come? Logically he thought, the trap would be placed in the north, that is, on his right flank. A line of guns in the north would pin the group against the river. But something was not right. There was something some instinct that was warning him. He would take stock and work out the next move that the Kampfgruppe would make.

'All runners, all runners. O group in five minutes. Half-track will guard the flanks and rear. Three SPs to maintain watch. All other commanders to me...'

'Fascist swine, we kill you.' The Red Army's listening service had broken in again. 'We know you. We know where you go. We kill you all. No more runners soon. All kaput soon.'

Peiper mustered his total command of the Russian language a said in broken phrases and in ungrammatical sentences 'You go away. You bad. You kaput. All Reds kaput. Death to all Communists.'

'Nazi pig, we rip your tongue out for that,' the voice laughed at his efforts to speak Russian. 'You wait. We kill you slow. Fascist pig.'

The battlefield O Group was dominated by the thought of the Russian armoured Division that lay just over the horizon. A collapsible table held the maps. Peiper gave his commanders ideas for the last stages of the journey to Mirgorod. The nagging doubt still troubled him.

'Does anybody know this area at all?'

'Sturmbannführer, I did a tactical training course here last autumn.'

'In this area?'

'Exactly here, where we are now.'

'That's excellent. Look at the map. Study it closely. Are there any features, anything which might give the enemy an advantage? Alternatively, is there anything that would help us?'

The young officer cadet studied the map, going slowly across the ground between the two rivers - Mush and Udy. Then he concentrated upon the sector between Mirgorod and Krasnaya Polyana.

The NCO straightened up.

'Sturmbannführer, our maps do not show the balkas. You know what balkas are; dried up watercourses, narrow valleys. They criss-cross this terrain. The Soviet maps do show them. I have a Soviet map of this area. May I get it?'

Five minutes later he was back with the brown ink Russian chart in his hand.

'There are certain differences between the two maps. Theirs tend to be very accurate about some things - balkas for instance- but wildly inaccurate about other things like the location of roads and railways.'

'Let us not worry about roads and railways,' Peiper insisted urgently. 'What about the ground?'

'You will note that there is a bend in the river here. The river Mush flows east - west until this point and then turns north-west. The point before it turns is solid rock for about one hundred metres. Then, past the rock, the stream broadens out because the ground there is sand. There is good cover among the rocks, sufficient to hide two Companies. I ambushed a panzer Company during an exercise last autumn. We were up against the Army. One of our SS junior officers placed a panzer Company in a balka just along from that bend. See, here it is marked on the Russian map, but not on ours. The balka runs up from the river. It is quite deep where it runs into the river but it gets shallower as it runs northwards. Here.' His finger indicated a point about four kilometres from the river. 'It is only half a metre deep. To the north here,' he indicated the place on the Russian map, 'there is another very long balka with enough room to hide a whole regiment. '

Peiper saw the situation immediately. 'This area here.' He indicated a gap, open ground between the two balkas. 'Anything there?'

'Nothing, Sturmbannführer. No balkas anyway.'

Peiper's eyes measured the distance from the gap between the two balkas to Mirgorod. Twenty kilometres. Half the difficulty of command was trying to think oneself into the mind of the enemy commander. What would he do if he were a Russian General with almost unlimited resources at his disposal. Obviously he would hide forces in both balkas and make the area between them the killing ground. The SS officer considered the situation. Every move made by the Red General had been designed to shepherd the Kampfgruppe to that place; the gap between the two balkas. No wonder there had been no serious attempt by Red armour to fight an engagement. It wasn't necessary; the battle would be an ambush and end with the German armour shot to death. The Sturmbannführer saw it all as if in a picture. He considered and pondered, his dark face drawn with fatigue and responsibility, his brown eyes sad and introspective. His left hand rasped over a chin not yet shaven that day.

'Right.' He had decided upon a course of action. 'Now this is what I think Ivan has in mind.' He pointed to the ambush points at the river and in the balkas.

'They will try to bounce us between the river and the east - west balka here, and as we stagger from those blows there will be an ambush here in this river balka, this one running north-south. If we get past that then we have a clear run home through the open country here. We are few in number but we do have certain advantages. We can guess at their plan of action. We know that their reactions are slow because in the Red units only the command tank has a transmitter. The others have only receivers, so if they run into trouble they can't let anyone know.

'We do not know for certain what they will do so we must be alert to exploit them. We shall fight them the Leibstandarte way. Accuracy in firing, fast firing, quick manoeuvre. We must expect to lose men and machines. So what I shall say now applies to us all. If anybody's knocked out we'll pick them up if we can, but no unnecessary risks will be taken. If there is no chance of tank crews or Grenadiers being picked up, then they will fight where they are with what they have. You do not need reminding of what the Red swine will do to us if we are caught. So we will fight to the bitter end. Save the last bullet for ourselves. Don't give the NKVD the pleasure

177

of torturing us. It is a gloomy prospect for those of us who will fall out. But we in the SS know that for the greater good of all the sacrifice of one or two is a small price to pay. Now fuel up. Load with ammunition. SP commanders! You can put layers of rounds on the floor. That way you can carry more ammo. Grenadier officers, you may think your units have little to do, but I am convinced that somewhere out there are Ivan infantry and cavalry. The chance will come for your men to take part in the fight. Does everybody understand? Thank you, Cadet Officer, for explaining the ground. Well, gentlemen, a midday meal, I think, and then let us see what the afternoon holds.'

The sun was only just past meridian when the men of Peiper's Kampfgruppe mounted their vehicles and set off. Eyes ranged across the open terrain. Eyes accustomed by years of hard combat quartered the ground, looking for traps. The pace of the advance was slower now, controlled and watchful. Tank guns travelled through short arcs, ready at any moment to swing and aim at a target.

'Cossacks on the left, Sturmbannführer.'

'Thank you, I had seen them.'

Regiments of horsemen were riding out of the south towards the river. The first Sotnias had already reached the southern bank of the Mush and were moving along this to the west. Each enemy studied the other through binoculars - the riders of the old style and the riders of the new. Peiper saw something odd about the way in which the leading horses in the column were picking their way delicately along. One of them slipped and fell. The threshing hooves dislodged some snow; a man-made wall and behind it Peiper could see the wheel of an anti-tank gun.

'All runners. Right wheel. Move northwards.'

The bell of vehicles swung away from the river heading north-east. Peiper recalled the lie of the land from the Russian map. He would close up and make a tight formation. In that way he could be out of effective range of the guns on the river bank as well as those on the tanks which he believed to be hidden in the northern balka. There was about three kilometres to drive to the gap between the two balkas. The panzer vehicles rolled over the snow - sharply outlined in the early afternoon sun.

'All runners fire smoke.' From each machine canisters were projected to burst ahead as well as on either flank of the group.

Canister after canister was fired until the whole area was covered with a dense curtain.

Peiper was taking a calculated risk. In the smoke the Reds could not see his vehicles but neither could the Germans see what the Russians were doing. The Ivans, if they had tanks in the balkas, would now move them into the open to pick off any German vehicles seen dimly through the smoke.

'All runners, increase speed.'

With luck the Kampfgruppe would be in and through the gap in five minutes. Three hundred seconds - that's all I ask, the SS officer prayed fervently. One hundred, two hundred, and still no enemy fire. Two hundred and fifty and then the German machines broke through the thinning wisps of smoke. Not a sight, not a sound of Russian armour. Had it all been a false alarm? The armoured fighting vehicles bunched as they passed through the narrow gap between the two balkas. They were through! They had escaped! Peiper raised his hand and the vehicle speed dropped. The whole group now cruised gently along, relaxing in the bright sunlight.

At point blank range Russian 7.62 anti-tank guns hidden behind snow walls opened up. The attack was totally unexpected and Peiper cursed his stupidity in not having anticipated how the Russian commander would deploy his forces - his almost unlimited forces thought Peiper, bitterly.

Three Panzer IVs were hit and crippled by the first salvo. Others were hit less severely They could still run and fire their armament. From his position on the right flank, Hennecke turned to the sound of the guns, swung his machine in a half circle, roared forward in the charge and then swung the panzer back again to face the west. The tank straddled the wall and aided by the momentum of the charge lurched along crushing the enemy gun crews and spraying them with machine-gun fire. The 7.5 cm cannon boomed repeatedly as shell after shell was fired at point-blank range. To aid the destruction Hennecke, leaning out of the command cupola - fired magazine after magazine from his Schmeisser.

Reacting to Peiper's hand signals, three SPs pulled back from their close support role of the panzer screen and swung into action.

The German gunners slipped and slithered on the heavy, shiny shells which layered the floor of the platform as they loaded, aimed and fired an intense bombardment at guns in the southern wall.

The Kampfgruppe, by some accident, had halted between two parallel lines of Soviet anti-tank guns. With the opening of the Russian fire the battle tested tactics of the SS panzer crews swung into action. The northern line was the target of Hennecke and a second Panzer IV which had moved forward in his support. A half-track halted behind Hennecke's panzer.

'Grenadiers out,' and at the command SS infantry, some of Stumke's men and the survivors of the Marenko group leaped from the carriers and rushed forward in the attack. Hennecke had already rolled over four of the deadly 7.62s before the first Grenadiers reached him. The infantry advanced firing their automatic weapons from the hip. From east to west they fought their way along the snow wall with machine pistol, grenade and entrenching tool, crushing the fierce but short-lived resistance of the gun teams.

Kalchov had made one error. In his confidence he had overlooked the need to give close infantry support to the anti-tank gunners.

The gun crews paid with their lives for his oversight.

The assault group kept pace with Hennecke's panzer; two Grenadiers were balanced on the rear deck of the hull firing bursts at the Ivans. Here and there along the wall of death Soviet gunners tried to hold back the storming advance with Shpagin machine pistols and with hand grenades. They were outfought by men who were determined to battle their way through to Mirgorod.

For the Germans near the southern wall the situation was critical. The first two anti-tank guns maintained the speed and accuracy of their opening shots. Two soft skins - one ration truck and the second loaded with infantry ammunition - were burning quickly. A Panzer IV, its tracks blown off, was still standing, crippled but defiant, a steel fortress, exchanging shot for shot with the 7.62s. The Russian guns concentrated on it. Two shots struck and penetrated the hull. The turret swung aimlessly as the dying gunner's hands dropped from the grips. The SS sergeant commander, erect in the turret, felt a terrible burning pain, looked down to see its cause and shouted in horror. His legs ended just below the knees. A solid shot from the Russian pak whizzing round inside the hull of the panzer, buzzing like a hornet, was smashing and destroying everything in its mad career.

The 7.62s fired again. An armour-piercing shell hit the reinforced mantlet on the panzer turret, and fragmented. Glistening, whirling splinters burst like shooting stars; visible even in the bright sunlit afternoon. One large piece struck and cut away the sergeant's face. A second solid shot struck through the glacis plate into the hull and in its dervish progress fractured a fuel pipe. Fire whoofed up inside the fighting compartment, incinerating the crew and bursting through the open cupola partly blocked by the body of the dead NCO.

'SPs form a screen around the soft skins.' Peiper knew that the fuel and ammunition trucks had to be protected. A quick, all-encompassing glance took in Rudi and the Grenadiers beating down the Reds along the northern wall. That flank was secure. The southern wall was still a problem.

'Grenadiers to the south wall. All runners concentrate on the south wall. Aim carefully.'

The flow of battle favoured the mobile panzers over the fixed and unprotected anti-tank gunners. Within a few minutes Peiper felt easier as the tactical situation changed very slightly in favour of the Kampfgruppe. He checked the map. According to the German chart there was no other likely ambush place. Once out of the present trap and it was a clear run home.

Shots from the Russian guns were single and isolated now, separated by long pauses. The storming Grenadiers were rolling up the gun line and killing the crews. To artillerymen, guns had the sanctity of Regimental Colours. The guns could not be abandoned and yet Death was coming closer with every step that the fascists made. The Russians worked their guns frenziedly, hoping through familiar and repeated drills to subdue the fear that infected them.

They died at their posts, still feeding the hungry breeches, still squinting through gun sights and still obedient to the artillery code that so long as one man lives the gun will be served.

Ten minutes elapsed. The battle was dying. The sounds of firing died away. Groups of Grenadiers, agonisingly tired, emotionally drained, stood puffing cigarettes, sweating with post battle nerves. It had been a dodgy do, this time.

'Right. Grenadiers rest for a short time. NCOs and officers will stand guard. Sergeant Major Auer, send a party to see what can be collected from the burning trucks. You three,' Peiper indicated a trio of SP commanders, 'Go and keep watch. Rudi, go with them please. They might need panzer support.' The vehicle group drove to the flat and open ground between the two balkas. There was not a single Red tank to be seen. Both balkas were empty.

The Grenadiers rested, sitting in the snow, laying down in the carriers, smoking and talking. Minutes passed. Nerves were less taut now. Even though the veteran SS were accustomed to battle they were still affected with post-combat exhaustion, a terrible lethargy that flooded in once an immediate crisis was past. There was little sound but the noise of the vehicle engines and the crackling of the burning trucks. A sad and sombre silence hung over the Kampfgruppe survivors.

'Sergeant Majors to me!' The senior NCOs lined up in front of their young commander.

'The men are getting careless,' Peiper accused them. 'I know the reason. They've been under intense strain with little sleep and poor rations. I know that I myself am feeling half daft with tiredness But we are the SS. We keep going when the rest stop and then, when the other SS regiments stop, we of the Leibstandarte still fight on; because we are the best there is. So I don't want them sitting about like broody hens. Once they've rested awhile get them working. Picking up equipment, helping with the casualties, bringing in our dead. Anything, but keep them occupied. Dismiss.'

'Sturmbannführer. A message from Obersturmführer Hennecke He says that there are no Red tanks in either balka. It was a false alarm.'

'Thank God for that,' replied Peiper. 'Right. Please ask Obersturmführer Hennecke and his group to return to me. We shall start for home in about half an hour.'

Chapter 23

'What did you say?' Lipski thought he must be going mad. The earphones crackled as an officer reported to him the happenings of the past half hour.

'You saw all this?' he bellowed. 'Where were you?'

'My job was to keep watch on the fascists. I am alone here in an observation post. General Kalchov gave me direct orders to watch. May I speak with him please?'

'No you cannot,' Lipski shouted. 'General Kalchov is talking to 6th Army. Talk to me. I am Major Lipski of the NKVD on this Front. Now tell me again what you said.'

As he listened his face paled with disbelief and then coloured as if he were in the grip of apoplexy.

'Wait out,' he barked and beckoned to Kalchov. 'You'll never believe this. Those German bastards have broken through. The idiot I am talking to says that the fascists put out a smoke screen under cover of which they broke into your killing ground. When the gun lines opened up, the fascists merely ran them down. it's unbelievable. And this oaf here was sitting in a hole in the ground watching it all without telling us.' Lipski eyed the General. He was calm and impassive. 'You seem to be singularly unmoved by the escape of the Nazi swine.'

'Forgive me, Comrade Major, but it is a tactic. I told you to leave the battle to me. Psychology is a battlefield tactic. I wished to mislead the fascists. Put yourself in their position. Think like a Nemetski commander. You know there is a killing ground somewhere. There must be, the Soviets always set up a killing ground. But you, as the fascist commander, don't know exactly where. Then you notice a pair of balkas with a gap between them. You reason, as a trained Nemetski officer, that the balkas are where the Soviet tanks will hide. So you blind them with smoke and belt through the gap. Once through that you are safe, aren't you? But, oh dear, no. You reason that there will be a third Soviet trap, an anti-tank gun line. Remember you are thinking like a Nemetski, you guess that the gun line will be blocking the gap between the two balkas. But it isn't. So, once through the gap you halt.

'We had two lines of guns there. If we had killed them all then I should have been pleased. As it was, they fought better than I had expected and they beat down two gun walls.

'Now, put your self back into the mind of the fascist commander. You have blinded the idiots in the two balkas and you've smashed the Red tank walls. How do you feel? Elated. There's a Knights Cross in this for you.

'You have killed the two anti-tank gun lines and buggered up the armour. What do you do now? Why, you regroup and rest your men, refuel the vehicles and prepare for the last stage of the journey to Mirgorod. You feel marvellous. It's a straight drive now into safety. You are confident - very, very confident. You've beaten the stupid Slavs. You've anticipated their every move - and you have won. You start getting careless. You have taken, without realising it, the Soviet baited hook. You have become criminally careless. And you remain so as your Kampfgruppe rolls on towards Mirgorod. You are not concentrating so deeply. Careless!! And then you run into a Pak front. Do you know what a Pak front is? Do you know what gun density is? No? I'll explain.

'A tank front is a German idea. Brought out when their puny anti-tank guns couldn't smash our T-34s. So they set up first of all groups of guns, but without success. Then gun lines; finally, Pak fronts. Pak, as you know, is their word for anti-gun. A Front is a whole square of guns. It can be battalion strength; more usually in brigade. That's a Pak front. A whole mass of guns aiming at one target. That target in this case is the Nemetski Battle Group. '

'Now gun density means that if you are working in an anti-tank gun role you must have more guns than the enemy has tanks. If you are a tank man, then you must have more tanks than the enemy has guns. Savvy? If you are an enemy tank commander attacking an enemy gun line and you are weaker, the enemy will knock out all your proud panzer.

'Now; that fascist sitting up there in the killing ground and priding himself on having outwitted us all, will shortly come up against our Pak front. He won't have the advantage of gun density. We shall. We outnumber him and his little group by about four to one. Believe me, the fascists are dead men. They don't realise it yet because they're still breathing. But believe me; they're dead.'

'Why didn't you tell me?' Lipski asked petulantly.

'Insurance. This is part of a fail-safe tactic,' replied Kalchov. 'We might have killed most of the Nemetski between the snow walls. But we didn't. We want to kill them all. The Pak front is set up and when it goes into action, we shall kill the lot. War and fighting, Comrade Major,' Kalchov went on in his I-am-talking-to-an-idiot

184

voice, 'is a matter of luck and planning. We have done our planning. Now we get the luck. The fascists are at this moment supremely confident. I shall forecast their next moves. They will have a meal. It is still early afternoon. Knowing those sods they will probably start tidying themselves up ready for a triumphal entry into Mirgorod. What is going to happen is that the Nemetski will be driving to their deaths with shaven chins and freshly-washed faces.'

Chapter 24

'Comrades.' Peiper was addressing the officers of the
Kampfgruppe gathered around him. 'Comrades - Lewinski, translate
my words for the Siberian officers, please - we are on the last lap of
our mission. Just over a couple of hours steady driving will bring us
to Mirgorod. There we shall rest overnight and tomorrow we shall
return to our own units. I shall ask whether Colonel Marenko and
his men may be attached to one of our units. They have proved
themselves to be true comrades.

'In order to ensure a safe passage to Mirgorod and a friendly
reception, I have asked Lieutenant Schlank to organise air cover by
the Luftwaffe. They will also recce the ground ahead. I have also
wirelessed to the Leibstandarte outpost at Mirgorod organising the
last details.

'Before we set off it only remains for me to thank you for
your loyal comradely support. I am deeply grateful to you all. Yes,
Schlank?' he asked, as the young Luftwaffe officer marched up and
reported in true Prussian style.

'Sturmbannführer, the Reds are jamming all frequencies. I
cannot contact any Luftwaffe unit.'

'Try the Command set which is contacting the SS outpost.'

'I have done that. They cannot contact anyone either, not
even the post at Mirgorod. All we get are static and those bloody
gloating Red bastards laughing at us. We cannot pass messages to
any unit.'

Peiper considered - decided - and then spoke.

'You will have heard Schlank's report. We cannot gain
wireless touch with any German unit. So we are still on our own.
We'll get home without the Luftwaffe. Transport officer. Fuel state?
QM ammo state?'

The officers checked in their note books, calculated and then
reported.

'It seems said Peiper, 'that we have fuel enough in each
vehicle for eighty kilometres. The most recent tanking has exhausted
all our supplies. Right?' The Transport Officer nodded in assent.
'Then burn the fuel truck but drain the tank first. We don't need the
truck. There is no more ammunition other than what we now have?'
The QM shook his head. 'Well then,' continued Peiper, 'there should
be enough fuel for the journey so long as we are not involved in lots

186

of manoeuvre, and enough ammunition for normal consumption, but not for a protracted battle. Burn the ammo trucks. Now we are the armoured shell. We have no more soft skins. We are all fighting vehicles now, panzer, SP and carriers. In our drive home, should we meet opposition, we advance in solid wedge breakthrough and run for home. Move out in ten minutes. Comrades, once more, thank you.'

The panzer wedge moved off into the sun now well past its highest point in the sky. The tight bunch of armour thrust on, each commander checking the ground ahead and on the open flank, searching for signs of the enemy. Fifteen minutes, thirty minutes, an hour. The sun was slanting obliquely now, shining directly into the eyes of the men standing erect in the cupolas. The Kampfgruppe roared across country, up slight rises, down gentle slopes. Then the ground began to fall away. The group was entering a wide and shallow valley. As the vehicles crossed the balka floor, Peiper noted a change in the speed and engine noise. The panzer was slipping and sticking! Sticking? How could it stick?. The ground was still frozen. But he was wrong. Beneath the snow lay a marsh and the few days of sunny weather had been enough to strike through the snow and to thaw the swamp a little. Not much, but just enough to slow the vehicles, to affect their speed and to cause their motors to burn more fuel as they strained to pull the heavy-armoured chassis through the sticky morass.

'All runners. The ground is sticky where I am.'

'And here, too.'

'Shit! That's all we need,' Peiper thought. 'That's all we need, to be bogged down here.'

There was a sudden flash of light on the low ridge which rose before him. Using a folded map to shade his eyes, the Sturmbannführer looked carefully at the place where the flash had shone so briefly.

'What the hell was it?' It worried him. He knew that whatever it was on top of the ridge it was not a natural phenomenon.

'Driver, right lock.' The vehicle swung through a ninety-degree turn. As it churned its way along the valley bottom, the blinding sun was obscured for just a few seconds by a higher piece of ground. Without the dazzling light shining in his eyes Peiper could see clearly. His heart dropped.

'All runners. There is a Pak wall ahead on the top of that ridge. Is anybody on firm ground? There is none where I am.'

There was no firm surface. The Kampfgruppe was in boggy ground.

'All runners. Rev up. Get a good turn of speed and follow me. We will smash through their line.'

'What's behind it?' a voice asked.

'I am not clairvoyant. I don't know what is behind it. I should think probably a second line of guns. But I do know that half an hour's drive behind that line of guns is safety. Kampfgruppe Peiper - *marsch*.'

The thundering reverberations of the tank engines and the heavy motors of the carriers thundered in the shallow valley, filled the air and vibrated through the earth. Standing in the panzer turret Peiper waved his arm forward and then balled his fist. He jerked it in a pumping motion and at the signal each vehicle of the Kampfgruppe thrust forward keenly. The ride was on.

The group made up a narrow, shallow block. The Panzer IVs formed the first two lines, spaced so that each gun could be brought to bear upon a target without obstruction. Forming a short, single, solid wall, screening the half-tracks, roared the vehicles of the self propelled artillery. The last of the four lines was that of the armoured personnel carriers with their Grenadier passengers.

Up the slight slope and the blinding glare of the sun made it impossible for the Germans to judge how great was the distance between their armour and the Russian guns. For nearly half a kilometre the uphill charge continued and with every turn of the trucks the men of the Kampfgruppe dwelt upon the storm that the Russian Pak would soon unleash upon them. Nearer and nearer the armoured wedge rose up the rise towards the guns. A kilometre and still no fire from the Russians. They seemed to be so close now. Then, as the panzer breasted the rise, the commanders saw that it had been a false crest. Behind it lay a flat and open steppe. As far as the eye could see, or so it seemed to the shocked eyes of the panzer men, there were guns. They seemed to cover the whole ground.

'Good God,' Peiper sighed. A Pak front. Oh God.' He took a deep breath.

'All runners. Ahead of us is a Pak front. Increase speed. As fast as we can go. We'll break through them.'

The huge square of artillery pieces was not concealed. No attempt had been made to camouflage them. The batteries stood almost wheel to wheel, a low and spiky growth, black against the glistening white snow. The sun, no longer shining directly into the eyes of the panzer commanders, illuminated the whole group, clearly bathing the vehicles in a golden glow.

'All runners. Load with HE.' Peiper intended to knock out the gun crews with high velocity shells.

'Range five hundred metres. We are aiming for the centre. That's the point from which their fire will be directed. Smash the control point and the buggers are hopeless. Keep going at all costs. We have a chance only as a single solid block. Good luck.'

'Do you think there's any point in laying smoke?' Hennecke asked, his voice unnaturally calm.

'No point at all. The wind is too strong. Anyway it's blowing away from us and we could never fire enough shells to lay any sort of cover. I think fast firing and momentum is all that we can rely on. Don't forget the Moujiks are probably just as frightened as we are. Right, Comrades. *Hals und Beinbruch'*. It was the traditional greeting to a skier - 'May you break your neck and legs.' It was a good luck wish.

The very air above the panzer block throbbed and vibrated, not merely from the thundering noise of the heavy engines but from their heat. The air over the armoured machines shimmered with heat waves. Sergeant Major Auer looked at the Grenadiers in his carrier. It was an unnerving experience for them, this drive towards death in a machine whose only armament was machine guns. Veterans though they might be, they were young veterans. Not like him with war service going back to Poland in '39.

'Krauss!' A young face, sombre under the rim of the heavy steel helmet looked towards him. 'Krauss, you sing well. Let's have a song to pass away the time. We'll have a song you all know from Hitler Youth days.

'"Onward, onward. " Ready Krauss? Sing.'

Faintly heard above the roar of the engines came fragments of the verse of the song, 'Onward, onward the heroic fanfares sound. Youth recognises no danger...no aim that youth cannot achieve...' and then fragments of the verse being sung by men of another carrier, 'We shall march through until everything is laid to waste, for today Germany hears us, but tomorrow the whole wide world.' The crash of guns drowned out the last words of the chorus. The fighting vehicles had opened fire. In the Pak front Red Gunners fell as shrapnel struck out of the skies. The black whipcrack explosions of the 7.5s smothered the gun lines with lethal, red-hot fragments. As men fell, others rushed forward to replace them. But still the Soviet guns had fired no shot. The range was shortening. Kill them all with the first salvo, thought Kornulov, the Colonel commanding 6th Army's Pak front. Judging his time nicely he gave the single order 'aim'.

The panzer commanders looked towards the Pak front now only a hundred or so metres distant. Their stomachs contracted as they saw those guns to their immediate front - those guns towards which they were racing - depress their barrels. The layers were aiming direct at them. They saw the guns on the flank, row after row of them, hundreds of barrels all pointing towards their little group. Kornulov judged the time to be right. The armoured colossi were almost upon him.

'Fire,' and the edge of the Pak front was hidden in a smoke cloud. The shells of the first salvo screamed as they crossed the little gap that now separated the enemy teams. A panzer on the left', hit by six shells, blew up in a dramatic explosion which produced a blood-red fire ball. Another to the right of Peiper swung suddenly broadside on, swung again and swerved towards the thundering lines of SPs, and personnel carriers behind it. The machines of the self-propelled artillery turned on their tracks to pass on either side of the careering, dying monster. This movement opened a gap and exposed the lightly-armoured carriers. Three vehicles of No 1 Platoon were driving almost wheel to wheel. A solid shot crashed through the windscreen of the centre half-track and cut its way through the bodies of the men crammed into the hull. The driver still had his foot pressed hard on the accelerator, still held the steering wheel, but the effort was too much for his dying grasp. The half-track lurched out of control and its load of dead, mutilated and shocked Grenadiers crashed violently with the machine on its right. That vehicle, struck at full speed, turned over and spilled its Grenadier group onto the snow.

The left-hand carrier, disobeying orders, halted to pick up the men of the platoons. The senior NCO gave the order, 'Grenadiers out. Pick up wounded.' Thirty men, crammed into a space intended for twelve, erupted over the vehicle walls in a flowing human wave. Some took up positions near the machine gun from which they opened a withering fire upon the Russian gun line. Others ran to carry off their comrades. A thundering explosion rocked the area. A salvo of Russian shells had hit the standing carrier. It had blown up. The Grenadiers were alone now.

Sixty metres away the remaining half-tracks, the SPs and the panzer were crashing towards the Pak front now firing at point-blank range. The armour vanished in a cloud of smoke and snow powder.

In the lee of the two knocked out carriers a small O Group was in progress. Stumke as senior officer led it with Schlank as his second in command. Of the Siberian volunteers only Marenko and two men had survived. Ten men remained from Stumke's 1st Battalion. The other soldiers from the carriers were all SS Grenadiers.

The wounded were grouped behind the armour of the carriers so that they were protected at least from small arms fire. Most of the wounded were from the first vehicle. An NCO with no legs lay alongside Grenadier Bauer who had lost his right hip and part of his stomach. The solid shot that had destroyed the vehicle had torn through the soft human flesh of the packed soldiers. Those whom it had killed were lucky. The smashed bodies of the others lay on the snow, dying men gasping out their lives on the cold steppe.

'Sergeant Major Auer. I know that you in the SS relieve your men of pain. You know what I mean. I also know that it is an officer's duty. I must organise the next move and it is I think unfair to ask Lieutenant Schlank to assume the burden. You know what you have to do? Will you do it? Thank you. Carry on Sergeant Major, please.' Then in a commanding voice, 'Everybody except Sergeant Major Auer and another NCO will leave this area and move behind the second carrier.'

All thoughts were on the terrible duty that the Sergeant Major had shouldered. Soon, to their listening ears, and sounding unnaturally clear even above the noise of explosions and the tank engines, came the crack of individual pistol shots. The SS NCOs were ending their comrades' sufferings.

Chapter 25

'Christ,' Obersturmführer Hennecke cursed. 'As if it's not bad enough that Ivan is flinging shit like this at us, he's got snipers out there too.'

Hennecke, young in years, old at war, had known what the sharp crack above his head meant. That sound, clearly audible above the background noise of battle, had been a bullet passing only an inch or two away.

Hello, here we go,' and into the intercom, 'hold tight. Weare running over their Pak line.'

The heavy machine lurched and staggered as its thirty-six ton weight rose upon and then crashed down upon the Russian 7.62. To the left of Hennecke the other machines of the two panzer lines were storming across the artillery. As the tracks of Peiper's tank smashed back onto the snow he felt rather than saw a solid shot, a brilliant silver flash, scream past his head. Behind the second line of tanks came the SPs. Crunching across that part of the shattered gun line through which the panzers had driven a gap.

Ahead of the German group lay the second line whose gunners were already sweating with excitement or fear or the zest for battle. An SP was hit and halted. Its crew worked like demons to maintain the rate of fire. They were as good as dead already, but before the shells that would destroy them crashed down, their bounden duty was to load and fire, clearing the way even in the very last seconds of their lives, so that the advance could swing forward.

Over the second line of guns - there was death before, behind and on either flank now, but the cry was 'press on' and the Kampfgruppe survivors forced their way forward. Each panzer commander stood erect and upright in his turret; the code would not allow him to hide himself inside the hull and to batten down the hatches. In any case with the hatch closed how could the commander contribute to the battle? So each stood, spraying the peasant Moujiks over whom they were riding with machine pistol bullets.

Hennecke leaned out of his turret as the panzer thundered across the second gun line and fired at the Ivans running through the snow. Some looking back at him in fear did not see the next tank in the line until they were under its tracks. One man with his overcoat caught in the tracks was knocked down by the roaring panzer, dragged along and then flung clear with a shattered leg.

Away to Hennecke's right a Russian gun team was trying desperately to bring their gun round. It was thirty metres but by leaning back in the cupola Hennecke thought he might reach them with a hand grenade. There would be no time to check the result of his throw, things were happening too fast. He lay back to gain impetus for the throw and a bullet tore across his chest gouging out a shallow trench of skin. The pain burnt. Well, it can't be all that serious, he thought. Severe wounds don't hurt; flesh wounds hurt like hell. Still, he consoled himself, if he had been standing erect he would be dead now.

Warmth on Peiper's right drew his momentary attention. The vehicle next to him was alight. The Sergeant Commander waved to him, 'Carry on; good luck.' As the Sturmbannführer responded, the NCO's head vanished and from his shoulders a fountain of blood gushed. His headless body fell back inside the tank hull.

Ahead lay the third line, but now the Russian gunners were not aiming and firing with determination. To the third rank men it seemed that nothing could halt the fascist bastards and the frightened gun crews wavered indecisively as the panzer, bearing now the raw and shining fresh scars of this battle, rushed down upon them. Peiper's panzer roared over a third line - or was it the fourth line of guns? God, would there never be an end to the fury? Then, suddenly, miraculously, the first two ranks were through.

'All runners turn one hundred and eighty degrees and cover the escape of the SPs and the carriers.'

The eight remaining machines turned at Peiper's order and, facing eastward, began to blanket the sides of the escape corridor with high explosive shells. The self-propelled artillery came through, halted a hundred metres or so behind the tank lines and began their own bombardment. The gunners worked like madmen, firing a barrage of air bursts into the Red gunners. The half-tracks roared up over the broken guns, crashed down onto level ground and battled through. Some had been hit. Blood flowed from side vents in the walls of one whose interior was like a knacker's yard.

Urged on by their commanders the Soviet crews swung their gun trails ready to open a new and destructive barrage at the vehicles roaring westwards, but only the rear line of guns could bear. Demoralised by the drive and thrust of the German assault, the shaken crews could not load with speed, lay with accuracy nor fire with precision. The steppe was covered by a criss-crossing pattern of whizzing, shining projectiles and, although some struck, none destroyed any more of the Kampfgruppe's machines.

'Retire by bounds. Carriers move off. Don't halt. Bash on for Mirgorod.'

Peiper was gambling now that the Pak front had in truth been the final obstacle. Putting himself into the mind of the Red commander he could imagine that the Kampfgruppe should have been wiped out by the Pak front. Logically, militarily the German vehicles should now be dead on the steppe; shot to pieces like rabbits in a ride. The gun density had been overwhelming. Yes, Peiper concluded, the Reds must have been so confident of victory that between the guns and Mirgorod they would have placed no other barrier.

'All runners. Panzer pull back a distance of two kilometres. SPs to cover. '

By fire and movement the battered vehicles of the Kampfgruppe withdrew out of range of the Russian guns. Then came the order, 'Take up wedge formation. The objective is Mirgorod.'

Twenty minutes later a two man post in the fire blackened ruins of what had once been the ambitiously-named rural hamlet of Mirgorod reported, 'Panzer approaching. They look German.' A white rocket fired from Peiper's vehicle burst in the darkening sky. The outpost fired an answering flare. A few minutes later a recce patrol was guiding the vehicles to Company TAC headquarters which was set up in the cellar of a house famous in the SS Engineer battalion, not merely for the fact that it was bomb proof, but that it harboured a variety of vermin of unusual size, colour and tenacity. Kampfgruppe Peiper was home. The Company Commander handed over a signal flimsy.

'Once you are reported in German lines,' read the message from Obergruppenführer Dietrich, 'I shall come down myself to see you. Wait for me. Rest as much as possible.'

The Sturmbannführer walked out to the men and vehicles of his Command.

'Dismount. ' When the unit was paraded he read the signal aloud. 'The General is coming forward to see us. We have a whole night in which to rest. Reveille will be before first light. I want everything ready for his inspection. Before we turn in for the night - it is not yet dark - I want preliminary maintenance of the vehicles. All ranks will clean and oil their personal arms. Right let's make a start.'

An hour later, contemplating a night without responsibility, Peiper gave himself up to his tiredness and, like his exhausted men, fell immediately into a deep and dreamless sleep.

Chapter 26

'Comrades.' Stumke was addressing the men lying around him in the snow. Five minutes had passed since the vehicles of the Kampfgruppe had driven away, pursued by Russian gun fire. Now only isolated shots sounded from the Pak front.

'Comrades, there is no point in deceiving ourselves. We are in front of a mass of Russian guns. Any minute now the Reds must come down to destroy us. We have all seen what they are capable of doing. We shall lie here in the shelter of these vehicles and when they attack we shall shoot them down. We shall die fighting. We shall...'

His final words were drowned in a thunder of fresh gunfire. Having failed in his attempt to destroy the whole Kampfgruppe, Korulov, the Pak front commander, had ordered the destruction of the wrecked carriers and of the infantry group. Soon the upper walls and sides of the machines were perforated like colanders. Then the gun barrels were depressed. Shots smashed through just above ground level, causing casualties to men kneeling or lying in the snow. Solid shot removes limbs as cleanly as a knife. The little group was forced away from the carriers and into the open. Immediately, a shower of rifle grenades fell around them. Casualties mounted. Then as suddenly as it had begun the grenade bombardment stopped. Leisurely, almost casually, a Russian infantry group stood up and moved across the open steppe towards the survivors. Weapons slung, laughing and joking, the Red infantry strolled along.

'Bastards, arrogant bastards,' shouted Stumke. 'Right lads, Let's get our own back.' Spandaus cut down the Red Army men.

Their destruction brought a fresh shower of grenades. Although the little bombs had no great blast power they were sufficient to shower lethal shrapnel. The number of wounded grew. Men looked at the sun. It was lowering in the western sky, going down in a glorious harmony of red and orange and gold. The survivors all knew that this was the last sunset they would ever see. There, over there, there where the sun was declining lay Germany. Goodbye Germany! For your sake we are here - but then the maudlin thoughts vanished as the evil scream of Katyusha rockets filled the air. The Cossack batteries had arrived too late to intercept the armour, but they could be used against this group of miserable fascists trapped in front of the guns.

For ten minutes the barrage of rockets continued. Black smoke trails hung in the air. The concussion of detonations still echoed.

When the barrage ended there were more dead and wounded than whole men.

'There is little point in lying here waiting to die,' said Stumke. 'I am going out into the attack. Will you follow me?'

'What about the wounded?' asked Schlank. 'Do you intend to leave them?'

'The walking wounded can come if they choose. Those too badly hurt we ease out of this life. It's up to us now, Schlank. You and I. The Sergeant Major is dead. Shall I, or will you?'

'You, please.' Schlank was afraid that his coup de grâce would fail to kill and that he would thereby inflict extra pain upon the wounded men.

'Right.' Stumke went about his grisly task. Presently he returned.

'Comrades,' he shouted. 'Let us arm ourselves and say our farewells. Thank you all. Schlank, do you have any Russian? I should like to say goodbye to Marenko and his men.'

'What do you want to say?' asked the Luftwaffe officer. 'It'll have to be simple. I know only a few words.'

'Can you say - "thank you, you have been good comrades"?'

'Yes,' said Schlank and in halting phrases gave the Siberians Stumke's message. Ignoring the flying bullets and shrapnel, Marenko stood up, saluted and then bent down to shake hands with the two German officers.

'We say goodbye,' said Schlank. 'We,' pointing to the ground around them, 'walk with our Brr, brr, brr,' he imitated the sound of the machine pistols.

'We also come,' declared Marenko. 'We all comrades.'

'Comrades.' Stumke shouted so that all the men could hear his voice. 'Thank you all. The officers will lead. Forward.' And holding his rifle and bayonet at the high port, the Prussian officer marched towards the Russian guns. Out of scrape holes in the snow men rose up and walked forward. Some moved quickly across so as to be directly with him. These were the men of his own battalion. The SS formed themselves into a single group under the command of a corporal. Schlank and the Siberians marched together.

The whip, whip, whip about their heads told them all that they were under fire and then came the crash of rifle grenades.

197

Heads bent as if walking in a rain storm the tiny group marched stolidly and unflinchingly into the fire. A Maxim machine gun set up near the command bunker tak-takked its slow way along the line. A group fell.

'Forward - forward - for Prussia- for Prussia.'

'For God and Russia, For God and Russia.'

'Mein Führer, mein Führer.'

Each group encouraged itself with its own battle cry. They were hoarse, for these cries from throats dried with the expectancy of death.

'Hurra, hurra.' Stumke waving his rifle above his head began to charge the Russian guns now only a handful of paces away. A ragged cheer went up as his men followed him. Stumke's rifle came down to the on guard position. The lust was upon him. Just to kill one more before I go - dear God - just to take one more with me. Something only feet away took his eye. It was sunlight. Flashing on the muzzle of the Shpagin whose bullets killed him as he covered the last paces. The same burst of bullets took Schlank in the belly. He sat down in the snow, hands pressed to his stomach. Suddenly he felt abnormally tired. His head drooped and he looked disbelievingly, uncomprehendingly, at the thick blood which was discolouring his overcoat and oozing between his clasped fingers. Gently, and without emotion he felt his life drift away. He died, sitting upright, on the trodden and dirty snow.

Marenko reached the guns and slashed at a cowering gunner with a long-bladed Siberian machete. The blow was misjudged. The blade shattered on a gun barrel. The Siberian was defenceless. Frenziedly, he looked about, picked up a grenade that lay on the ground and pulled the pin. He clasped the cowering gunner in his arms and waited for death to claim him. His two comrades were already dead; machine-gun fire at close range had cut them down. Some of the group died singly. Four SS men, the last of them, all stood back to back, fighting off with rifle and bayonet a circle of Russians. A barked command. The circle of Red infantry opened. An artillery corporal stepped through the gap and levelled a machine pistol. A long burst. It was all over.

Within an hour it was pitch dark. The Russian detachments stayed on the battlefield all night and at sun up marched away to that rest area out of which they had been brought for this 'tidying up' operation.

Chapter 27

Kalchov and Lipski were, to begin with, furious at the outcome of the battle. The tank General was angry and bitter that some of the Kampfgruppe had escaped. Lipski was angry because he could not positively identify one of the three Siberian corpses as Marenko. The Soviet gunners had been encouraged to show their contempt for traitors by kicking in the heads of the dead mutineers. Both commanders accused the other. Then embarrassment set in. Finally they decided to word the reports so as to gain the maximum benefit. It would never do to admit failure of any part of the plan. The events were shaped to fit the result. It was a SOP. General Kalchov and Comrade Major Lipski decided upon the wording of their reports, wrote them and then returned to 6th Army HQ to present them in person and to congratulate Colonel Satrushkin. They praised his brilliant planning which had met and defeated the German counter-offensive, of whose strength they had had personal, first-hand knowledge and experience.

In the post-battle report that Satrushkin wrote, the roles of the two commanders in thwarting the fascist attack were stressed. The operation had been a strategic success - a Colonel of Intelligence had claimed so. The GOC of a Tank Division confirmed it and a senior political officer had corroborated their statements. Of course it was true - the report can't lie, can it?

A personnel carrier escorted by a single panzer drove carefully through the grey dawn, taking advantage of every fold in the ground to conceal its approach. Mirgorod had the reputation of being a quiet sector and it was only just after first light, but still there was no need to bring down shit by drawing attention to one's presence in the area. And particularly not when the VIP in the half-track was Sepp Dietrich.

Both vehicles came to a halt on a slight reverse slope where Peiper's Kampfgruppe was already drawn up. The senior officers of the Division got out of the carrier to a flurry of salutes.

'Morning, Peiper.'

'*Melde gehorsamst*, Obergruppenführer.'

'What's left of your command?'

Peiper gestured towards the white tarpaulins draped over the vehicles and to the three lines of men drawn up in the snow. The

Obergruppenführer and his aides marched along the ranks. Dietrich noted the tiredness in their bodies but he also noted the cleaned and oiled weapons. These were good soldiers, reliable men.

'These men are from 1st Battalion, 585th Regiment, Obergruppenführer, under the command of Captain Stumke. They volunteered to fight with us and they have since volunteered for the Leibstandarte.'

The SS General was delighted. 'Capital, capital. Bloody good soldiers. Is Captain Stumke on parade?'

'No, Obergruppenführer. He was in one of the three carriers that were knocked out when we smashed through the Russian Pak front.'

'You did what?' As a tank veteran of the Great War, Dietrich was well aware of the risk of a frontal attack against prepared positions, and he had had no details of the battle.

'No, don't tell me now. Put it in the post-battle report. Your first one, the simple one, I expect tomorrow. The more elaborate version will have to go to those in Berlin. What you have done in this operation has set a precedent, I think. Now I will address the men.

'Comrades. I thank you on behalf of the Army Group Commander, on my own behalf and on that of all your comrades. I should like to have sent you back for a rest but the military situation here, around Kharkov, is critical.

'Every man is needed. For the rest of the day I can spare you. But tonight you will be going back up the Line. Your comrades of our Division and of the SS Panzer Corps have been holding fast against terrible odds. The arrival of you men in the battle line - you veterans - will tip the scale in our favour. I know you will not fail. Comrades, *Sieg Heil.*'

Just after full light on that morning the wind changed direction to due east. The temperature dropped. It began to snow. The first flakes were large and soft but as the precipitation increased these became small and icy. The bitter wind, the dreaded Buran, lashed the flakes into a horizontal curtain of ice. Out on the steppe where the Pak Front had been sited the bodies of the fallen were already partly covered. Back in Krasnaya Polyana a Red Army penal detachment worked in the snow storm digging up the cemetery in which the SS and the Siberian dead had been interred. The bodies were flung into a pit. The fascist scum and their lick-spittle traitor allies would not be allowed to rest in special ground. A common pit was good enough for shit like them.

In his headquarters west of Kharkov, General Postel was engaged in composing a beautifully worded account of his Division's recent action. His report was not complimentary to the SS. On the Alexeyeva Kolkhoz, Grenadier Bauer's big-breasted devochka walked into a cow stall, moved one of the beasts, pulled out some straw from the covering on the floor and took out a small wireless transmitter. She settled down to send off a routine signal report to local partisan headquarters.

Out on the steppe there was no trace now of the fallen. They had vanished under the blanket of cold white snow. Only where rusting vehicles showed black against the white was one aware that there a stand had been made, an attack undertaken and a short-lived defence established. Without those indications who would even know that there were dead men beneath the vast, white, smooth blanket, nor how many there were?

The snow fell and fell and fell.

It was winter on the Russian Front.